THE

wines

of

CHILE

TO BOB THOMPSON

With great respect and admiration
Un fuerte abrazo

Douglas Murray

Santiago, Chile, April 2010.

THE ★ wines ♪ CHILE

Hubrecht Duijker

The creation of this book was made possible thanks to the help and support of
Cristalerías de Chile; ProChile; Wines of Chile International and ACI Chile Corchos

CONT

The Wines of Chile
Copyright © Uitgeverij Het Spectrum B.V./
Segrave Foulkes Publishers 1999
Text copyright © Hubrecht Duijker 1999
Maps copyright © Uitgeverij Het Spectrum
B.V./Segrave Foulkes Publishers 1999

Created by Uitgeverij Het Spectrum B.V./
Segrave Foulkes Publishers

Published by Het Spectrum B.V., Postbus 2073,
3500 GB Utrecht, Netherlands

Printed in Spain by Book Print, S. L.
ISBN 90 274 6913 X
www.spectrum.nl

ENTS

Index of Wine Names

Many producers have several wines/ranges/brands, especially for exports. This list, alphabetized as you see the name on the label, cross-references wine names to the relevant producer.

FOREWORD

It is fair to say that this is a book the world is waiting for – something that was certainly not true of the Chilean Wine Book which
Jan Read and I launched on a world all unprepared in 1984. We had
found Chilean wine in a time-warp, still content with methods and
standards adopted early in the 20th century. In those first glory
days Chile was the only country immune from phylloxera; her winegrowers made fortunes. Exporting was easy, especially within South
America, the domestic market uncritical; and in their position of
isolation beyond the Andes the Chileans saw no reason to change.
Besides, they grew accustomed to wine aged in old, not very clean,
barrels. While the technocrats of Australia and California were re-
inventing the wine industry for an age of new consumers Chile hung
on to dusty tradition, repeating its mantra (which was never entirely
true) 'we have the world's only ungrafted vines'.

The time for change came in the late 1980s. With a dwindling
domestic market but a pro-business government, with a world
looking for the next source of modern inexpensive wine, with an
unprecedented number of whizzkid winemakers wandering the
world and banks bullish on wine investment, Chile had the look of
a balloon only held down by a fraying cord. When it went up everything was in place, from irrigation systems installed by the Incas to
marketing schemes hot from San Francisco.

Chile was even in place for a second boost from phylloxera as the
scourge struck again in California. Chile's grapes, of the fashion-
able varieties, from old vines growing in near-perfect conditions,
were everything the world was looking for.

Now, after 15 years or so of frenzied activity, we can take stock.
Promise is now reality. Chile has won world-wide acceptance for its
wines faster than any country in history. But what are they like?
How good are they? Who makes the best – and how much better are
they going to get?

Hubrecht Duijker is the best person to tell you. Since his first
books, it must be twenty-five years ago (among his first, charac-
teristically, was a previously unresearched subject: Bordeaux's
modest little châteaux), I have learned to trust and follow him
implicitly. He has been my valued collaborator over the years,

while producing a series of classics of penetrating insight and dogged research. Hubrecht has spent long enough in Chile to meet everybody and taste everything. You have the fruit of his labours in your hands: the key to hundreds of good and good-value newcomers to the world's wine-list.

Hugh Johnson
London. 1999

INTRODUCTION

During my travels in Chile I was often reminded of the words of the most famous poet the country has ever had, the Nobel prize-winner Pablo Neruda: 'Chile was discovered by a poet'. What I saw and tasted was often pure poetry. Snow-capped mountains, tawny hills, intensely green vineyards, dark-red wines, wine cellars full of atmosphere, courtyards full of flowers, gleaming fermentation tanks, cloudless blue skies, horsemen on dusty roads, shady squares, colourful markets and a rich palette of scents and tastes are among the many sensual and spiritual impressions made by this remarkable country. I have visited Chile four times now, beginning in 1989. My last trip, a few months before the 1999

vintage, took me to some 65 wine estates. At the end of three arduous weeks I was told that no one before had visited so many producers. Of course I tasted the wine at all of them – some 515 samples altogether. My aim was to discover the style of wine at each establishment, their best wines and their specialities. These tastings were almost always a great pleasure. Not only is the quality of the wines of Chile higher than ever before, but they are nearly always quite charming too. If they have acidity then it is very rarely aggressive, and if they have tannins these are usually smooth. Besides this, most Chilean wines have a very attractive, enticing fruitiness. My conclusions about the wines and the firms that make them are given in the descriptions of the producers: these form the nucleus of the book.

That my journeys around the Chilean wine estates proceeded with such flawless precision is due to perfect organization by Wines of Chile International, in which all the major exporting wine producers are involved. This association has also helped with the collecting of all kinds of material. A special word of thanks is due to the expert and indefatigable Deputy Director, Rodrigo Alvarado, and the ever-enthusiastic and helpful Board Director Douglas Murray, as well as to Elizabeth Díaz, Virginia Fuenzalida and Professor Alejandro Hernandez. And of course I am most grateful for the great hospitality that the producers bestowed on me.

Opposite: the wide skies of the Chilean winelands. Above: the enormous scale of many of the wine estates makes a horse a helpful companion. Left: Bernardo O'Higgins, liberator of Chile.

After visiting the country, the eminent British taster and author Michael Broadbent MW wrote that in Chile the wines are apt to be just as delightful as the people – and the reverse is also true.

Hubrecht Duijker
Abcoude,
Netherlands

Wineland Chile

Europe and the south-west edge of the Americas, now Chile, first came into contact in 1520 when the Portuguese navigator Fernão de Magalhães – Ferdinand Magellan – discovered the straits named after him and opened the gateway to the Pacific. However it was the Spanish, moving south from Peru, who were to conquer the country. After several failed attempts they invaded in 1541, led by the *conquistador* Pedro de Valdivia. He imported settlers to farm the land and founded towns, including Santiago, La Serena, Concepción and Valdivia – named after himself – before he was killed in a battle with the Mapucho Indians in 1553. Francisco de Aguirre is said to have planted the first vines, on an estate from which the north Chilean town of Copiapó later developed: the first vintage was 1551.

Originally the Spanish made wine purely for sacramental purposes, but soon this spread to daily consumption. The first vineyards around Santiago, in the middle of the country, were laid out in 1554 by the soldier Juan Jufré de Loaiza y Montesano. He had been given estates, including Macul, by de Valdivia in return for his military service. The grapes spread on southwards, beyond the Bío-Bío river. The most common variety was the País, a simple black grape that was also planted by Spanish priests in California (where it became known as Mission). Besides País, the colonists grew Muscatel and other Spanish varieties.

The war of independence

During the Spanish period, which lasted for nearly 270 years, Chile developed into a wine producer of importance – so much so that the colony eventually became a formidable competitor to the mother country. Royal decrees were repeatedly issued from Madrid to restrict winegrowing in Chile; the planting of new vineyards was forbidden, and taxes were imposed on existing ones. When these measures had little effect, the Spanish authorities took more drastic steps, such as totally banning exports, uprooting vines, and even stopping the growing of grapes. Other restrictions included a ban on any trade except with Spanish merchants. This, and similar interference with their colony's economy, helped to fuel the discontent and unrest that, combined with political events in Spain during the Napoleonic Wars, culminated in 1810 in a war of independence.

A leading role in this revolt was played by Bernardo O'Higgins, the illegitimate son of an Irishman, Ambrosio O'Higgins, who had risen to become governor of Chile – and Viceroy of Peru. After achieving some early successes along with another leader of Irish origin, John MacKenna, O'Higgins' force was eventually defeated at Rancagua in 1814.

The general fled with 120 soldiers, first to a wine estate which now belongs to Viña Santa Rita – whose best-known brand is the '120' – and then on to Argentina. Together with the Argentinian general José de San Martin, O'Higgins built up an army four to five thousand strong, crossed the Andes in 1817 and at last defeated the Spaniards. Although some Spanish strongholds still held out, independence was declared on 12th February 1818. Bernardo O'Higgins became *director supremo* at the head of the new republic.

French influences

In 1830, with the help of French scientist Claude Gay, the Chilean government set up an agricultural research station where experiments were conducted with every possible kind of plant. Here, at Quinto Normal, trials were conducted with French and Italian grape varieties – but it was primarily through the influence of wealthy individuals who owned land or mines that the whole aspect of the Chilean wine industry began to change radically. These people travelled to Europe, and especially France. They became familiar with French culture – including the great wines of Bordeaux. Fired with the hope of making such wines

themselves, these prosperous Chileans took grape-vines home with them. Most often these were the varieties then cultivated in Bordeaux – Cabernet Sauvignon, Carmenère, Malbec, Merlot, Sauvignon Blanc and Sémillon – with sometimes the German Riesling as well.

The pioneer of this new wave of planting was Silvestre Ochagavía, in 1851. His example was quickly followed by others – among them the founders of estates still in existence today, such as Viña Carmen, Viña Concha y Toro, Viña Cousiño-Macul, Viña Errázuriz, Viña San Pedro, Viña Santa Rita, Viña Santa Carolina and Viña Undurraga (these are all their present-day names). Frequently, the new wine producers hired French experts to lay out the vineyards, design the wineries and make the wine.

In a short time, Chilean winegrowing underwent a total metamorphosis. A few decades after the first French-style vineyard had been laid out, Chilean wines began to win prizes in Europe, and the first exports came in 1877.

Times of trouble

As Chile was the only important wine country to remain free of the phylloxera pest (see the  Winegrowing chapter), exports to Europe at the end of the 19th and in the early years of the 20th century expanded enormously. This halcyon period of prosperity came to an end, however, with the revival of European wine production, and with the introduction in 1902 of heavy taxes on wines and spirits. Later in the 20th century new planting was prohibited, and the government imposed an annual limit on the amount of wine made.

Then came the government of Salvador Allende (1970-73), whose radical land reforms resulted in the splitting up, and often the expropriation, of large estates, through which thousands of hectares of vineyards were lost. It was a long time before the Chilean wine industry recovered. From about the mid-1970s until around 1986 there was an almost permanent crisis. Wine consumption dropped, and political problems during General Pinochet's dictatorship, which begun in 1973, put a brake on exports. For years grapes sold at below cost price, causing the uprooting of tens of thousands of hectares. Of the 109,000 hectares growing wine grapes in Chile at the end of the 1970s, nearly half subsequently disappeared.

The revival of exports

Economic recovery began in the second half of the 1980s, and continued after a national referendum in 1988 heralded the return to democracy. The return of civilian government meant that Chilean wines were once more welcome the world over. In 1989 exports rose by around 66 per cent, with a further 50 per cent in each of the next two years – and that growth has continued. Two figures show how spectacular that increase has been. In 1988 the country exported 17.3 million litres of wine; ten years later it had risen to 230 million. This explosion was at least as impressive in money terms: from $35 million to $503 million.

To keep up with world demand vines have been planted on a large scale. By 1998 there were almost 75,000 hectares of vineyards (not including those for the distilled drink Pisco), and 90,000 hectares could be reached by 2005. As is described in the chapter on Winemaking, producers in the 1990s have invested in modern cellar equipment on an incredible scale – so much so that you could almost speak of a revolution. The advances in grape-growing in the 19th century have been followed by a revolution in technology in the 20th.

New wineries – but little wine tourism

A direct outcome of the explosion in exports was the creation of new wineries, and quite a few firms that had formerly only supplied wine in bulk now began to bottle and sell it on their own account. The number of exporting wine firms rose to nearly 70. Most had head offices

A timeless image: herdsman and his charges in the Rapel Valley.

in Santiago, with their centre (or centres) of production in the wine valleys. These wineries are often difficult to find. Signposts are scarce, and the roads leading to the wine estates are mostly unsurfaced and very dusty. Besides this, entry to an estate is nearly always blocked by a gate, barrier or chain, attended by a gatekeeper or security man in a hut. Just dropping in on a winery is not possible as a rule. An appointment has to be made through the head office – and it is a sound idea to ask for detailed directions at the same time.

In Chile, wine tourism for pleasure and relaxation, as in Beaujolais, Alsace, in Germany's Moselle or the Napa Valley, is as yet hardly possible. However, this situation is set to change. There are a couple of nascent wine routes, and many companies are now planning reception, tasting and

sales centres where casual visitors will be welcome. Among those that already have such facilities are Viña Balduzzi, Viña Concha y Toro, Viña Cousino-Macul, Viña San Pedro, Viña Santa Rita (which boasts its own restaurant), Viña Segú Ollé, the Sociedad Vinícola Miguel Torres, and Veramonte, with its château-style, California-scale building in the Valle de Casablanca.

A melting-pot

Chile is a melting-pot of peoples. A considerable number of the original inhabitants, the Indians, still live in the south: these belong to the Mapuches people. Aymaras, who are descendants of the Incas, still inhabit the far north-east. Living in Chile, along with the many who are descended from the Spanish colonists, there are descendents of Germans (especially in the south, where there are even German-language schools, newspapers and a television station) and Swiss, Italians, Arabs, Chinese (particularly in the north), Yugoslavs (in the far north and south), Israelis, British and French. About 85 per cent of the population lives in towns.

Other exports

Apart from wine the country's biggest foreign currency earners are copper, of which Chile has about a third of the world's reserves, wood products such as cellulose and paper, fresh fruit – more than 100 million boxes a year – and fish products: after Norway the country leads the world in salmon farming, and also catches large amounts of swordfish and other species, as well as shellfish. Tourism is now a growing source of income.

The shape of the country

The worldwide popularity that Chilean wines are coming to enjoy is not just due to the right grapes and the right techniques. Nature plays at least as important a role. The country is 4,274 kilometres long (more than the distance from New York to San Francisco, or from

Lisbon to Moscow), with a width that varies from about 90 to 380 kilometres. It is surrounded on all sides by natural boundaries: the high mountains of the Andes to the east, the vast Pacific Ocean to the west, a desert to the north and, to the south, Antarctica. This gives Chile a unique microclimate, as the Wine Valleys chapter shows.

The spine of Chile is the Ruta 5 highway – also known as the Pan-Americana – which runs from north to south over a distance of 3,455 kilometres. All through-traffic has to follow this road: there is no other route. Many side roads, both surfaced and unsurfaced, lead east towards the Andes and west to the coast. Large stretches of the Pan-Americana cross deserted landscapes but, especially south of Santiago, it goes by towns and villages, past stalls selling basket-work, furniture, pastries and fruit.

Getting around

Buses are everywhere in this country, transporting a large part of the population. The capital Santiago has a metro system, but nevertheless an estimated 14,000 buses run here, including those to and from the suburbs. Travelling by bus is very cheap. The bus from Curicó to Santiago, a distance of some 200 kilometres, costs only around 2,000 pesos – not much more than the toll charge on the Pan-Americana – and the fare is less at weekends.

Gastronomy

The success of Chilean wines abroad has had an impact on the home market, where a considerable number of quality wines have become available alongside the simple everyday ones.

At the same time the standard of the Chilean cuisine has also risen. In Santiago in particular, there are now a number of excellent restaurants. Many of them are mentioned in the *Guía Gourmand*, published annually in Spanish and English. The country has an abundance of fine ingredients

Below: local cheeses. Right: empanadas, filled with spicy meat.

bursting with flavour, including some excellent shellfish, fish such as congrio and swordfish, myriad vegetables and heaps of fruit. Among the fruit is the chirimoya: not really exportable, its taste is a sort of mixture of pear, kiwi and melon. The most famous Chilean snacks are the *empanadas*, a kind of dough casing usually filled with a spicy meat mixture.

Pisco

This colourless drink is the national distilled spirit in Chile, drunk either in combination with a cola, or as Pisco Sour, or neat. Little is exported – only 25,000 cases a year out of a total production of five million. The Pisco vineyards lie in the north, in the La Serena area, and cover some 10,000 hectares. Most of the vines are Muscatels of various types, supplemented mainly by Pedro Jiménez (the Ximénez of Spain). Pisco Sour is served as an apéritif everywhere in Chile. Capel, the biggest Pisco producer, offers a recipe for it: three parts Pisco, one part lemon juice, a teaspoonful of caster sugar and slivers of ice. All of this has then to be shaken in a cocktail mixer. Pisco Sour can also be bought ready-mixed.

Wines of Chile International

Wines of Chile International was established on January 1, 1998. In this, two pre-existing wine producers' organizations work together closely in their activities abroad. The older of the two is the Asociación de Exportadores y Embotelladores de Vino. Dating from 1949, it was originally intended as a pressure group to get the duties on wine lowered, and numbered about 20 members – among them many large, long-established firms. The association's members are not only active in the home market, but also attend to 80 per cent of total wine exports. Chilevid – the Asociación de Productores de Vinos Finos de Exportacion – was set up in 1993. This body is very export-oriented: at least 95 per cent of the wine its members produce crosses the frontiers. Many smaller wine estates are members, and quite a number of family firms. Membership is around 50 companies.

Wines of Chile International's address is: Luis Ojeda 0130, Of. 708, Providencia, Santiago; tel (56-2) 335 7250, fax (56-2) 335 7167.

The evolution of quality

In quality, the wines that Chile now exports have developed just as much as have the wineries where they are made. In comparison with the late 1980s they have gained in cleanness, depth and length, while their charming fruitiness, created by nature and made the most of by man, has remained. That they now have greater complexity is due to better control of both winegrowing and vinification techniques, as well as a greatly increased use of oak casks, chips and staves (see the Winemaking chapter). Competition at home and with other countries has pushed up the quality. It seems as if the Chilean producers are collectively busy making each new vintage surpass the standard of the one before. Typical of Chile's almost insatiable urge for quality is the creation not only of ever-better Reserves or Reservas, but also of ultra-premium wines, wines that are just as expensive as celebrated *grands crus* from Bordeaux – and basically just as fine. In fact, the kind of wines the founders of the first quality vineyards had in mind when they brought Bordeaux vines to Chile: a dream that after a century and a half is at last being realized.

The highest and coolest part of the Maipo Valley, with the Andes in the background.

The Wine Valleys

The narrowness of this elongated country means that both its topography and its climate are dominated by the towering mountain barrier of the Andes to the east, and the Pacific Ocean to the west. Measured from Santiago in the centre, the wine-belt stretches from about 400 kilometres to the north of the capital down to 650 kilometres away to its south, seamed by the lush green east-west valleys carved by the rivers as they wind from mountains to sea. The floors and slopes of these valleys provide the setting for Chile's vineyards: the name of each wine sub-region begins with the word 'Valle'.

These are grouped into five large *regións vitivinícolas* – from north to south, Atacama, Coquimbo, Anconcagua, Valle Central and Sur. Of these, the latter three are the most important for winegrowing (see map, over), with the greatest concentration in the Valle Central, which begins near Santiago and ends just below Cauquenes, 300 kilometres south.

Within the Valle Central area lie many other smaller valleys, with a great variety of soils and differing climates. To the east are the Andes and to the west a second, lower, mountain chain, the Coastal Range, sprawls over a great distance. You therefore see hills and mountains practically everywhere you look in the wine regions, from close at hand to the far distance.

In this central slice of Chile it normally rains only in the winter and early spring; the summer temperature averages 21°C, with a winter one of 12°. For

Map 1 Chile's wine belt

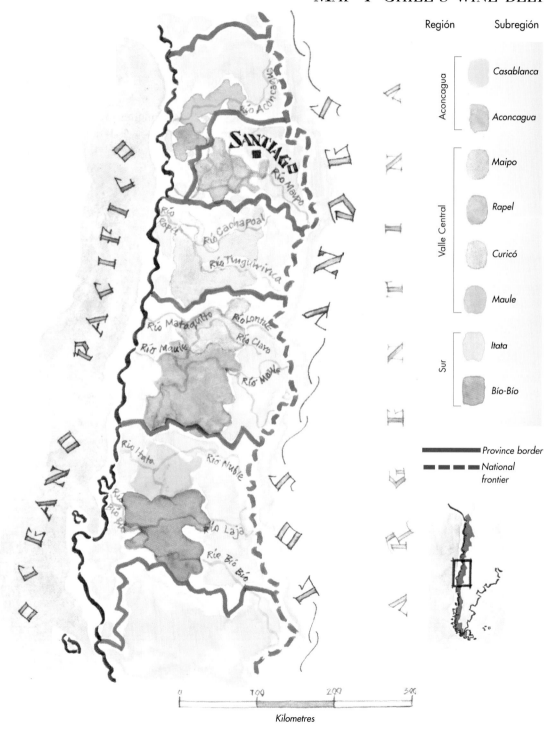

Región   Subregión

Aconcagua
- Casablanca
- Aconcagua

Valle Central
- Maipo
- Rapel
- Curicó
- Maule

Sur
- Itata
- Bío-Bío

——— Province border

- - - National frontier

Kilometres

the wine grape to thrive – and the other fruits which the country grows in abundance – irrigation is needed in summer. Meltwater from the Andes is used, with water from underground springs in areas too far from the mountains. The many place-names ending in –*agua* show just how important water is as a source of life.

Thirteen sub-regions are distinguished within the five large wine regions (*see* The Wine Law); it is the names of these sub-regions that appear most often on wine labels. As the following summary shows, each sub-region has its own characteristics. They are dealt with from north to south, under their main region.

REGIÓN DE ATACAMA
Valle de Copiano and Valle del Huasco
These are Chile's two northermost sub-regions, lying within the desert-like Región de Atacama. At present, wine-grape varieties, from some 800 hectares, are only used for the distilled drink Pisco. Table grapes grow in abundance, too.

REGIÓN DEL COQUIMBO
Valle del Elqui and Valle del Limarí
We are near La Serena here, and the harbour town of Coquimbo. Observatories set up on the mountaintops above the Elqui Valley bear witness to air that is among the clearest in the world. Wine grapes are grown in the Valle del Limarí in particular, for this again is Pisco country. About 10,000 hectares are covered in vines, mostly grown in pergola fashion, and these supply the fruit for Chile's national distilled drink. This is made mainly from various types of Muscatel grapes and Pedro Ximénez. In 1993, however, the first significant winery, Viña Francisco de Aguirre, was set up here. This belongs to the biggest Pisco producer

and yields good to very good wines. The area is proving to be highly suitable for growing grapes for table wines. The valley floor has a good deal of clay and stones, with a limestone sub-soil, but vines also do well on the slopes.

A surprisingly moderate climate for this northerly – i.e. hot – location prevails here, thanks to the influence of the sea close by. There is often a sea mist in the mornings, and temperatures in the afternoons seldom rise above 27°C. There is no frost in winter, when daytime temperatures may even reach 18°C. The drop in temperature at night – down to 9° or 10°C in summer, and to around 4°C in winter – is the same as in more southerly areas. The low rainfall makes irrigation necessary, for which reservoirs are used.

REGIÓN DE ACONCAGUA
Valle del Aconcagua
The Aconcagua Valley, 3–4 kilometres wide, lies some 100 kilometres north of Santiago.

Table below compiled by Alejandro Hernandez & Virginia Fuenzalida.

HECTARES OF VINEYARDS PER WINE VALLEY			
Valley/sub-region	1995	1996	1997
Elqui	0.00	0.00	1.00
Limarí	92.80	108.40	213.00
Choapa	0.00	1.50	2.00
Aconcagua	307.70	366.20	408.00
Casablanca	1,552.00	1,440.70	1,720.00
Maipo	4,853.90	5,904.20	6,499.00
Rapel	8,804.20	9,173.00	12,840.00
Curicó	10,042.40	10,197.60	11,871.00
Maule	15,725.30	15,812.30	16,997.00
Itata	11,344.10	11,329.60	11,330.00
Bío-Bío	1,669.90	1,669.90	1,669.00
Total	**54,392.30**	**56,003.40**	**63,550.00**

It was first developed for winegrowing by Maximiano Errázuriz in 1870, and the firm named after him is still the most important wine producer here – although Córpora (Viña Gracia, Viña Porta) has also invested a great deal in a vineyard.

Features of Aconcagua are an early spring and late autumn: this relatively long growing

Valley, some 80 kilometres to the west of Santiago. The land there lay mostly untilled, with cows grazing it.

The first grower to lay out a small vineyard – at his own expense and risk – was Pablo Morandé, then the winemaker at Viña Concha y Toro. He sold its first, mainly white, grapes to his employer. Later harvests went to

Fishing boats at Coquimbo

season helps the development of the grape aromas. Then, too, the Aconcagua climate is Mediterranean in character, with a cooling-off in the afternoon and annual temperatures that average 14°C. With 240–300 cloudless days a year there is great luminosity, and a rainfall average of 250 millimetres a year. There are alluvial soils here, as well as terrains that are rocky or pebble-covered. Together, all these natural conditions make the Aconcagua Valley especially suitable for growing black grapes.

Valle de Casablanca
Until 1982 not a single grapevine grew in the entire 16-kilometre length of the Casablanca

Viña Santa Rita, and then to Viña Carolina – which happened to have a brand called Viña Casablanca. Vintage after vintage the wines from Morandé's grapes made a great impression with their expressiveness and

KEY

Viña Erráruriz/Seña

Viña Casas del Bosque

Veramonte

Villard Fine Wines

MAP 2 REGIÓN DE ACONCAGUA

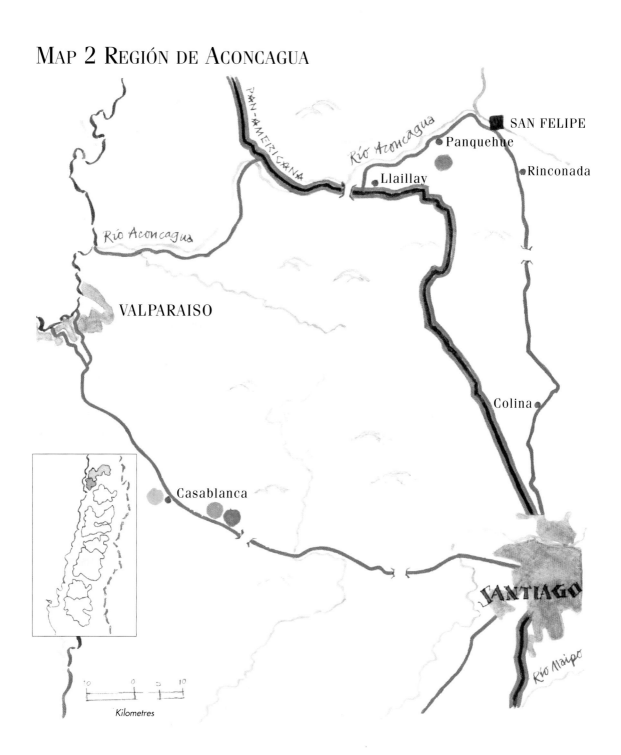

MAP 3 VALLE DEL MAIPO

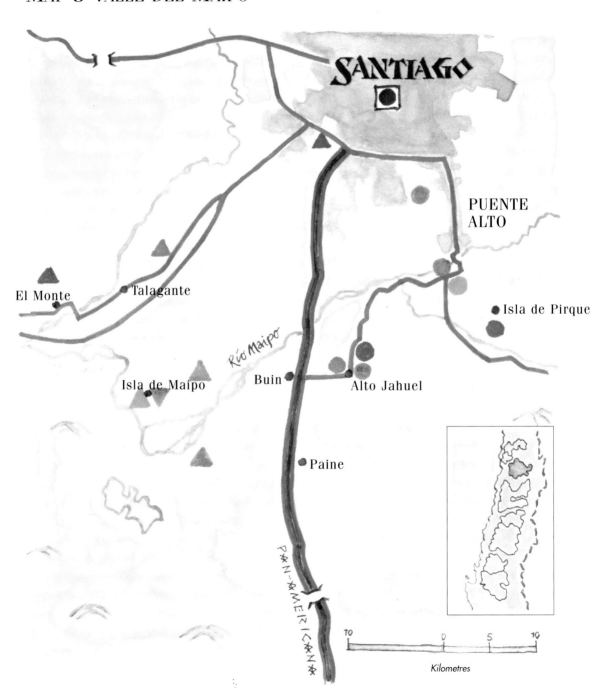

SANTIAGO

PUENTE
ALTO

Isla de Pirque

El Monte

Talagante

Río Maipo

Isla de Maipo

Buin

Alto Jahuel

Paine

PAN-AMERICANA

10   0   5   10

Kilometres

freshness. As a direct result, producers large and small followed Morandé's example by planting vines in the Valle de Casablanca. Concha y Toro, Errázuriz, Santa Carolina/Viña Casablanca, Santa Emiliana, Santa Rita and Veramonte all now have estates here of over 100 hectares. The biggest landowner is probably Augustín Huneeus of Veramonte. In 1991 he bought 3,000 hectares, not least because Casablanca reminded him so much of the cool Californian area of Carneros.

Casablanca delivers remarkable white wines, chiefly Chardonays and Sauvignon Blancs, but also good reds from Merlot and Pinot Noir – thanks in part to its special microclimate. Every sunny afternoon in summer and spring, a sea breeze gets up and lowers the temperature by 9 or 10°C. This moderating influence, which also results in cool nights and frequent morning fogs, gives the Valle de Casablanca a growing season that is often a month longer than in other wine valleys. This enriches the aroma of the grapes, while the evening cooling ensures that the fruit keeps its acidity and does not develop too much sugar. The yield here is relatively low: the soil is poor and the topsoil thin.

With an annual average temperature of 14°C and a rainfall of 450 millimetres a year, irrigation is necessary. Meltwater from the Andes is too far away to be used, and springs have to be found. Most producers have had difficulties locating these: most of them are 50–80 metres down. Night frost is another problem, which at times causes huge parts of a harvest to be lost – and explains why small stoves are sometimes stood among the vines, or hot-air fans driven through the plots. Considerable differences of temperature occur in the Valle de Casablanca – sometimes within short distances. There are only about two kilometres between the Villard Fine Wines vineyard and the one around the guesthouse at Viña Santa Emiliana, but it is so much warmer at the latter, more easterly property that not only do the grapes ripen quicker, but the plums are ready as much as ten days earlier, too.

If these factors make winegrowing in the Valle de Casablanca fairly expensive, the investment is rewarded with wines of world class. The district also has potential for development as a tourist area, since it is on the main route from Santiago down to Valparaiso and Viña del Mar on the coast.

REGIÓN DEL VALLE CENTRAL
Valle del Maipo

'The best wines in the world in our view are made in the warmer areas of cool climates, such as Bordeaux, or the cooler areas of warm climates, such as the Maipo Valley.' This philosophy was propounded by Bruno Prats of Viña Aquitania to the British wine writer Tim Atkin, for an article in the magazine *Wine*. The Frenchman (whose knowledge of Bordeaux stems from his years as proprietor of Cos

KEY

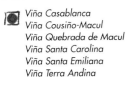

Viña Casablanca
Viña Cousiño-Macul
Viña Quebrada de Macul
Viña Santa Carolina
Viña Santa Emiliana
Viña Terra Andina

Viña Canepa
Viña Undurraga
Viña Dona Javiera
TerraMater
Viña Santa Ema

Viña Santa Ines
Viña Tarapacá Ex Zavala
Viña Almaviva
Viña Concha y Toro
Viña William Fèvre Chile
Viña Santa Alicia
Viña Carmen
Viña Santa Rita
Viña Portal del Alto

MAP 4 VALLE DEL RAPEL

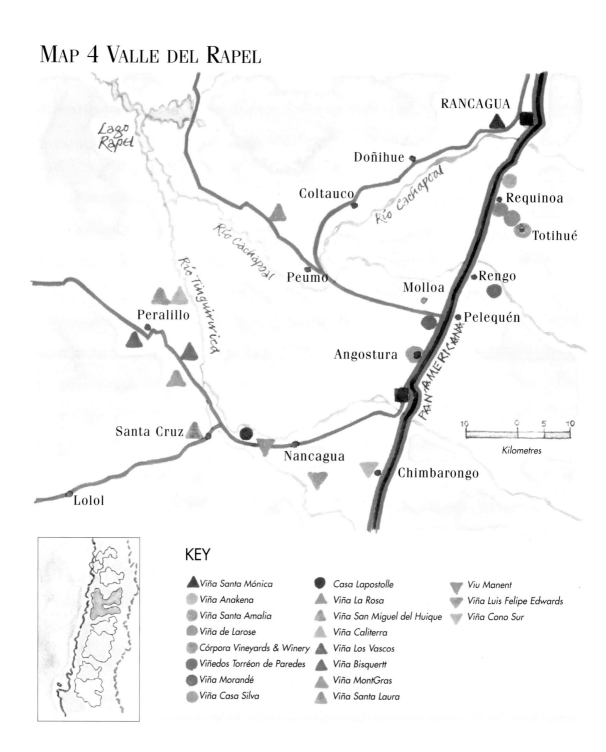

Lago Rapel

RANCAGUA

Doñihue

Coltauco

Río Cachapoal

Requinoa

Totihué

Río Cachapoal

Río Tinguiririca

Peumo

Molloa

Rengo

Peralillo

Pelequén

Angostura

PAN-AMERICANA

Santa Cruz

10   0   5   10

Kilometres

Nancagua

Chimbarongo

Lolol

KEY

▲ Viña Santa Mónica
⬤ Viña Anakena
⬤ Viña Santa Amalia
⬤ Viña de Larose
⬤ Córpora Vineyards & Winery
⬤ Viñedos Torréon de Paredes
⬤ Viña Morandé
⬤ Viña Casa Silva

⬤ Casa Lapostolle
▲ Viña La Rosa
▲ Viña San Miguel del Huique
▲ Viña Caliterra
▲ Viña Los Vascos
▲ Viña Bisquertt
▲ Viña MontGras
▲ Viña Santa Laura

▽ Viu Manent
▽ Viña Luis Felipe Edwards
▽ Viña Cono Sur

d'Estournel in St-Estèphe) and his partners had looked all over Chile before choosing the Valle del Maipo for their winery. Their choice was a confirmation of Maipo's long-standing position as a leading wine district. It was here that Chile's first quality vineyards were planted in the mid-19th century. This was in part thanks to the valley's position just south of Santiago, but its natural assets were a factor as well. Various aspiring winegrowers – all of them well-heeled – hired French experts to find the best possible sites for high-quality varieties such as Cabernet Sauvignon, Merlot and Carmenère. Maipo was their choice.

The present vineyards in the Valle del Maipo lie mainly between the Andes and the Coastal Range, where there are plateaux, rolling hills and more mountains, as around Viña Tarapacá. The highest parts are about 1,000 metres above sea level, the lowest around 480 metres. And the higher the location, the lower the temperature. In Pirque, at the foot of the Andes, grape-picking can take place two weeks later than in wine communities lower down. There are, too, wide differences in soil: sand, clay, lime, gravel, pebbles, loam, and various combinations of these are all to be found.

It is thus difficult to speak about the Maipo Valley in general terms, the natural environment can vary so considerably. The mean average annual temperature is around 14°C; the difference between the warmest daytime temperature and the coldest night is 15–18°C. The rainfall in the valley varies from 300 to 450 millimetres a year.

Suburbs have already spread out around the Río Maipo near Santiago, and this process is continuing. It has already caused the loss of vineyards, and others will undoubtedly follow.

In response to this new vineyards are usually laid out at a greater distance from the capital.

Black and white grapes both do perfectly well in the Valle del Maipo. A slight eucalyptus aroma – in other words a suggestion of menthol or mint – is typical of Cabernet Sauvignons from Chile's oldest district for quality wines.

Valle del Rapel

The Rapel sub-region is dominated by two rivers, Río Cachapoal and Río Tinguiririca. These, joined by a number of tributaries, carry water from the Andes to Lake Rapel, and from there the Río Rapel flows on to the sea.

The most northerly town in the Valle del Rapel is Rancagua with some 300,000 inhabitants, the most southerly the smaller Chimbarongo (the Chilean-Indian name means 'Place of Mist'), where a good deal of basket-work is produced. There are also two wine-growing *zonas* (see The Wine Law) in Valle del Rapel: in the north the Valle del Cachapoal, and in the south the Valle de Colchagua.

The Coastal Range in this part of the Valle Central is fairly low, so the climate in large parts of the Rapel Valley is subject to a moderating maritime influence. At 710 millimetres the annual rainfall is somewhat greater than in the more northerly valleys, while the average annual temperature is at the same level, around 14°C: during the hot summer, daytime winds from the south bring some cooling. The difference between day and night temperatures in spring and summer is around 20°C. There is a lot of quite fertile land in Rapel, with clay, loam, lime or sand – in some cases with a layer of well-draining gravels beneath. However, other, poorer soil types do occur.

In the 1990s, winegrowing in the Valle del

Rapel has experienced spectacular development. Many of the grape growers have become wine producers, new wine firms have come into being, and new vineyards have been laid out on a big scale, sometimes in valleys completely new to wine. Black grapes are very much in the majority here, and Merlots from Rapel are reckoned the best in Chile.

Visiting Rapel: Wine tourism is still underdeveloped in Chile, but there are a few wine routes. The Valle de Colchagua has the best signposted one.

One of Chile's most famous places to stay is the Hacienda Los Lingues, some 130 kilometres south of Santiago, a luxurious residence in Spanish colonial style, in the middle of a tropical garden, with just ten rooms and two suites. It is affiliated with the prestigious Relais & Châteaux group. For those who can afford it, Los Lingues is a good base for visiting the Rapel region; tel (56-2) 235 5446; fax (56-2) 235 7604.

Health resorts have been established at various times between the Valle Central and the Andes. One of these is the Termes de Cauquenes hotel, east of Rancagua in the Rapel region. It overlooks a ravine on the Río Cachapoal, and has rather austere rooms and medicinal baths. A special *menu degustación* is regularly served in the restaurant. Wines from Viña Santa Mónica, Rancagua, are among those served; tel or fax (56-72) 297 226.

Valle de Curicó

Curicó lies some 200 kilometres south of Santiago, and is a lively provincial town with a population of about 75,000. It boasts the beautiful Plaza de Armas, with its tall palm trees, a busy regional market, what seems to be the greatest number of bicycles per inhabitant, an annual wine festival and a wine cooperative. The country around consists mainly of a plateau, in part flat or gently sloping, and sometimes interrupted by hills. Both grapes and other fruits are grown here.

The biggest concentration of vineyards is found to the south, where Viña San Pedro alone cultivates more than 2,000 hectares. The soils generally are clay and loam, with volcanic material. The mean annual average temperature is around 14°C, and the rainfall is between 400–700 millimetres a year. Every night the temperature drops by 14 or 15°C. Black and white grapes are both grown, in about equal proportions, and yield attractive wines. Lontué, with a population of about 10,000, comes within the sub-region and is advertised as the *capital del vino*. Valle del Lontué, or just Lontué, is a zone name that frequently appears on wine labels.

Visiting Curicó: Just north of Curicó along the Pan-Americana is the most comfortable hotel in the place, the Villa El Descanso. It has a garden with swimming pool, bungalows and a

KEY

Map 5
- Montes
- Cooperativa Agrícola Vitivinícola de Curicó
- Sociedad Vinícola Miguel Torres
- La Fortuna
- Hacienda El Condor
- Viña Valdivieso
- Viña San Pedro
- Viña Echeverría

Map 6
- Agrícola Salve
- Viñedos Terranoble
- Viñedos J. Bouchon y Compania
- Viña Tabontinaja
- Viña Rucahue
- Viña Balduzzi
- Vitivícola Cremaschi Barriga
- Viña El Aromo
- Viña Carta Vieja
- Viña Segú Ollé

Map 5 Valle de Curicó

Map 6 Valle del Maule

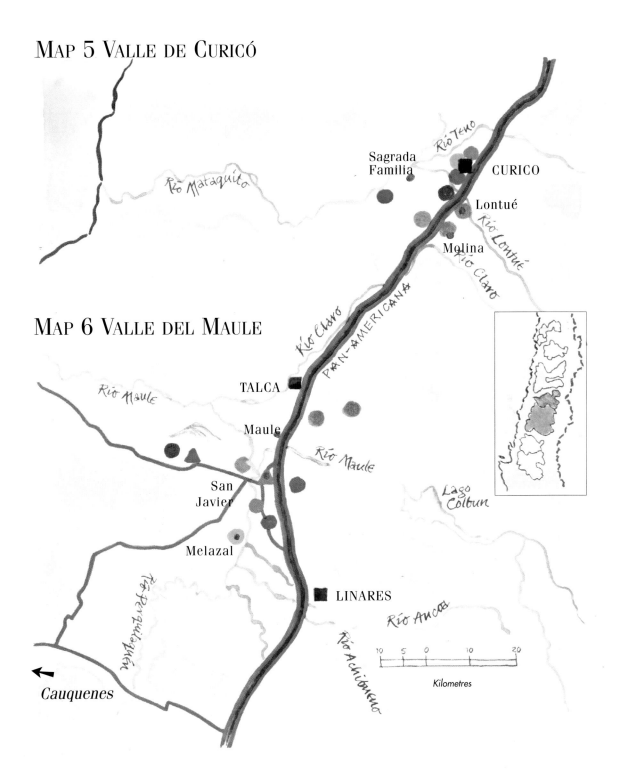

Río Teno

Sagrada
Familia

CURICO

Río Mataquito

Lontué

Río Lontué

Molina

Río Claro

Río Claro

PAN-AMERICANA

Río Maule

TALCA

Maule

Río Maule

San
Javier

Lago
Colbun

Melazal

LINARES

Río Ancoa

Río Perquilauquén

Río Achibueno

| 10 | 5 | 0 | 10 | 20 |

Kilometres

Cauquenes

very decent restaurant with a competent wine list; tel (56-75) 382 238; fax (56-75) 382 239.

Valle del Maule

The southernmost part of the Valle Central takes its name from the Río Maule, a river with a widespread catchment area. Talca is the chief town here: founded in the year 1690, it has two universities and a population of nearly 175,000.

The Valle del Maule has the most vineyards in the whole of Chile, and a long history of wine. Vines were planted here by the Spaniards from the late 17th century, and a survey in 1831 showed that some 5,000 hectares of vineyard were already being cultivated around the Maule – nearly a third of the present area.

In this broad valley, running mainly parallel to the Andes and the coast, the difference between day and night is 20°C, with a yearly mean average temperature of 14°C. The rainfall is concentrated in the winter, and can be very heavy: the Valle del Maule has an annual average of 750–800 millimetres.

Night frost is a potential danger, so some vineyards – Bouchon for example – have windmills and others, such as Carta Vieja, have bought mobile air-warmers that can be trundled through the vineyards.

The landscape consists of both flat areas and low hills. The soils vary from alluvial, loamy and volcanic to degraded granite. A lot of País is still produced in this part of Chile, but since the end of the 1980s superior black and white grape varieties have made great advances. White grapes, chiefly Sauvignon Blanc and Chardonnay, now predominate,

The Andes, source of vital water.

and Merlot is at present the most important among the black varieties.

Visiting Valle del Maule: Wine tourism is beginning in the Valle del Maule: there is a wine route around San Javier and Villa Alegra – but this can only be followed with the aid of a map, available in a folder from Viña Balduzzi in San Javier, among others.

REGIÓN DEL SUR
Valle del Itata

Winegrowing has been practised in the valley of the Itata, a river that flows to the sea to the west of the town of Chillán, since the time of the *conquistadores*. The relatively large plantings of País and other simple varieties is an inheritance from that period.

Today, the thrust is towards quality: a course that was set with the arrival of Agrícola y Vitivinícola Itata. This firm, financed by the Fundación Chile, is the first in this sub-region to plant and process high-grade grapes. Other wineries are emerging: one such is being built by Francisco Gillmore, of Viña Tabontinaja and other properties.

A semi-humid Mediterranean climate prevails in the Valle del Itata, with an annual rainfall between 650–700 millimetres. The soil often shows a reddish-brown tint: it is partly volcanic in origin, and made up of sand and degraded granite. Itata seems to lend itself well to growing both black and white grapes, so other companies are planning to expand their activities to the area.

Valle del Bío-Bío

Winegrowing is somewhat of a borderline activity in the relatively cool Bío-Bío Valley. The grapes ripen slowly here, and late in the season there is always a chance of autumn rains causing rot. Spring frosts, too, form a real danger.

With a Mediterranean-type mean average annual temperature around 13–14°C, the annual rainfall is between 700–1,200 millimetres, depending on the location. The grapes grown with most success in Bío-Bío are Chardonnay, Pinot Noir, Riesling and Gewürztraminer. In this valley, too, they benefit from a considerable temperature variation of around 17°C between day and night. The soil is often loamy and volcanic.

Chile's most southerly vineyard is situated near Traiguén, 650 kilometres from Santiago. It forms part of the Malalco estate, which belongs to the father-in-law of Felipe de Solminihac, one of the proprietors of Viña Aquitania. The property mostly grows cereals, but Felipe and his father-in-law also have five hectares of Chardonnay, from which an aromatic, fruity and fresh wine is made. Pinot Noir would also lend itself to planting here. So far the wine has been sold in bulk, but will certainly be bottled by the makers in the future.

Flowers abound, as well as vines.

Winegrowing

The natural conditions in Chile are almost ideal for winegrowing. The country has plenty of suitable land, with soils ranging from fertile to poor; there is a lot of sunshine and (away from Santiago with its frequent smogs) there is great luminosity. Light has been found to influence the aroma and colour of grapes more than high temperature. Better yet, the wine regions are cooled down sharply every night – and sometimes by the afternoon – by influxes of colder air from the sea or from the Andes. There is usually a 15–20°C difference between maximum daytime and minimum night temperatures. This cooling promotes the development of real quality in the grapes: they gain especially in aroma, but their sugar content, colour and tannin formation can also be stimulated by this temperature change. Warm days and cool nights enable the grapes to ripen without losing their acidity.

In this viticultural Nirvana, water is the only limiting factor. In most of the wine regions the annual rainfall is too low for growing high-quality grapes, so irrigation is necessary. It is quite exceptional for vineyards growing the superior varieties not to need an extra water supply. The simple black País, however, a grape introduced by the Spanish, does grow well in mostly unirrigated soils.

Irrigation systems

The traditional method of irrigation, dating back to pre-Spanish times, is to flood the ground with water. This water originates in the Andes, and is collected from the rivers that flow to the Pacific, and from reservoirs. Distribution is regulated by law, and there is an often ingenious system of canals, ditches and distribution stations that divide the water flow into measured amounts. The bigger wine estates use pumping stations to direct the incoming water, but frequently it flows over the fields with just the help of gravity – and therefore very often from east to west, from the Andes towards the sea. The measuring out is done with the help of small temporary dams. These block channels running at right angles to the rows of vines, causing a localized flood. Normally a batch of nine or ten rows are irrigated in this way, for about 12 hours at a time.

A more modern version of this intrinsically primitive system is one in which the water runs through underground pipes along the ends of the rows, and is then distributed in measured amounts from these. Viña Los Vascos is partly watered in this way. This method produces a water saving of some 20–25 per cent. Another similar method is one where, instead of underground pipes, large-calibre hoses of synthetic material are used above ground, with small pipes, one to a row, through which the water flows. Some vineyards at Viña La Rosa, for example, get their extra moisture this way.

Where there is insufficient Andean water available – or none at all, as in the whole Valle de Casablanca – drip, or trickle, irrigation is the solution. The water for this usually comes from wells. To lay out such a system, in which the water falls drop by drop from narrow rubber hoses to the soil around the roots of each plant, is not cheap: at least $3,000 per hectare. The advantage of drip irrigation is that the amount of water can be precisely measured out, without the wastage inherent in the two methods above.

A simple system is widely used to ascertain whether wines need moisture. This consists of pushing a tube down between the roots, to a depth of about one metre. To determine the water requirement, some earth is taken from the base of the tube and checked.

In many parts of Europe now irrigation is banned, but in Chile they have no difficulty with it. Or, as a winegrower once put it, 'irrigating here is just using rainwater that didn't reach us directly because it fell in the Andes. Thanks to irrigation we aren't dependent on nature. We don't have to wait for rain to give our vines water, but can water them exactly when they need it – and in the right amounts'.

Without irrigation most Chilean vineyards would not exist, and would end up just as arid as most of the slopes around them. With no additional water the Chilean wine industry would run dry – literally.

A healthy environment

It is of course important to time and measure the supply of water carefully. Irrigation is essential for the growth of the vines during the dry Chilean summer, when not a drop of rain falls for four or five months. Extra water is however certainly not wanted in the period before the harvest: then, it would produce watery grapes and therefore wines that were too thin. The limited rainfall in most of the Chilean wine regions – 250 millimetres per annum in the Valle del Aconcagua, and 750–800 millimetres in the Valle del Maule further south – means that the growers have to take the water supply very much into account.

The dry season, which lasts until well into the harvest period, makes irrigation necessary but it does have advantages, including the prevention of a large number of fungal diseases, such as rot and mildew. This is further helped by the low summer humidity which prevails in many wine valleys: in the region of Rengo, for example, it averages only 40–50 per cent. One result is that Chilean vineyards need only a small amount of preventative treatment. Spain's Miguel Torres, who also produces wine in Chile, recalls how Professor Boubals of Montpellier University in France was always very positive in his references to Chile's healthy vineyards. The scientist, a specialist in viticultural pathology, told his students that the fungi, viruses and insects that plague grape-growers around the world are largely absent from Chile, which makes the vineyards there 'the best in the world'.

No phylloxera

Chile is the only important wine country where phylloxera has not – so far – appeared. This louse, which destroyed practically all vines in Europe and Australia in the late 19th century, and is at present carrying out its devastating work in California, has never reached Chile. It is therefore possible to plant vines directly here, without first grafting them on to resistant American rootstocks. These directly-planted vines keep their identity completely, and thanks to the freer sap circulation also stay in robust health. They can go on yielding good amounts of good-quality grapes at a great age. This explains why there are many productive vines in Chile that are 50–100 years old. However, quite a few Chilean producers are taking the possible arrival of phylloxera into account, and grafting new vines onto resistant rootstocks as an insurance. With so much foreign travel, there is always the danger that the louse will one day hitch a lift over the splendid natural barriers that encircle the country: the Andes to the east, the ocean to the west, the Atacana desert in the north, and to the south Antarctica. New grape varieties, such as the Tempranillo imported by Viña Canepa, have to spend two to three years in quarantine. Only after the vines have been shown to be free of viruses are they released for reproduction.

Left and right: whole families, from young to old, often join in the grape harvest

Frost danger

In most of the Chilean wine areas winter tem-

peratures keep above freezing, and spring frosts do not take place either. There are, however, exceptions. Springtime frost is a real problem in the Valle de Casablanca, and in the more southerly (and therefore cooler) regions, it can threaten new shoots on the vines. At

Viña Carta Vieja, in the Valle del Maule, they well remember the devastating frost of 1935 and the severe, although less dramatic, cold spells of 1968 and 1979. As a precaution a machine is in use here that blows warmer air over the vines. The cost of this apparatus is covered if just half a hectare can be kept free of frost. In Casablanca, too, devices of this kind are used, and elsewhere there are windmills or small stoves in the vineyards. A special method of protection is under development at Viñedos J. Bouchon. This has the effect of raising the sugar content in the vine, which can then withstand a temperature of minus 6.5°C.

Differences in microclimate are often found in a north-south direction, but they are at least as great from east to west. This is very marked in the Rapel region, for example, where the vineyards stretch from the foot of the Andes to a few dozen kilometres from the sea.

Varied soil types

Alluvial clay soils, soils with sand, loam, lime, gravel or stone: they come in all possible combinations in Chile. More detailed information about them is given in the Wine Valleys chapter, and in the entries on individual producers. The great majority of the Chilean vineyards are on relatively flat or gently-sloping terrain, although there is now something of a trend towards planting on the sides and tops of hills – with all the extra costs involved, including drip irrigation. Viña Errázuriz has been something of a trailblazer in this. Some other producers have invested considerably in land on the slopes, or are going to do so, among them Viña Francisco de Aguirre, Viña Luis Felipe Edwards, Viña Montgras and Viña Santa Rita.

Vigorous growth

Soil, sun, light and water in Chile lead to vigorously growing vines. A young shoot planted in June can be a metre high by December. Young vines develop quickly, giving amazingly good wines after just three to four years. Often with young vines a year's difference in age is readily recognizable in the wine.

Leaf formation is also abundant, sometimes too much so. Increasingly, Chilean winegrowers are removing a percentage of the leaves in the latter stages of ripening, partly to give the grapes more sunlight. Canopy management is also often applied, especially when new plots are being developed.

Different planting systems are also being tried out in order to better manage the growth of the vines. Various wine producers have chosen the lyre method for some of their vines. In this, the upper parts of the vines are grown in a V-shape, which gives the foliage and bunches of grapes the maximum exposure and ventilation.

Many grapes are also produced on vines grown in the pergola form. These are mostly table grapes, or are meant for the distilled wine used in making Pisco. This mode of planting, called the *parronal* system in Chile, can produce a very high yield. It is also used for wine grapes, one advantage being that it protects the fruit against night frosts. Harvesting, though, demands extra effort, with pickers having to stand on boxes and reach up to remove the grapes.

Abundant yields

The auspicious combination of natural and man-made factors leads on the one hand to generally very sound, aromatic grapes and on the other to considerable yields. In Chile there is no problem in harvesting 90–100 hectolitres per hectare – and then making wines of quality nevertheless: wines with intense aromas and good concentration. This is not to say that quantities of this order are garnered everywhere. Many conscientious producers deliberately limit the yield – or poor land or old vines may enforce this. At Viña Luis Felipe Edwards, for instance, there is a ban on harvesting more than 10 tons per hectare, which amounts to 68–70 hectolitres. And there are many yields even lower than this.

Night picking

Picking by machine is widespread in Chile, and goes on not only by day but by night as well. Harvesting continues right around the clock. Generally it is the white grapes in particular that are machine-picked, as these benefit most from being processed when fresh and cool. If picked by hand the grapes are either collected in bins holding some 400 kilograms, or in plastic boxes with a capacity of 15 to 25 kilograms. For quality wines the smaller containers are preferable, as the fruit suffers less damage in the boxes.

The fast pace kept up during the grape harvest results from the system for paying the pickers. Often they are given a plastic disc representing a small number of *pesos* for every load they tip out. The more grapes they bring in, the more they are paid.

In the traditional method of irrigation the water can be directed around the vineyards through the making and breaking of small, temporary earth dams.

Everything – including
vines – grows vigorously in
Chile's benign environment.

Grapes

Despite the fact that the country was a
Spanish colony, most of the grape varieties grown in Chile are French. This is
due to those wealthy Chileans who travelled to
Europe in the mid-19th century, discovered the
French wines there, and then took the appropriate varieties back home with them. They
favoured the Bordeaux grapes, such as Cabernet
Sauvignon, Merlot, Malbec, Sauvignon Blanc,
Sémillon – and Carmenère, which has since
practically disappeared from Bordeaux itself.
In about 1880 Alberto Valdivieso became the
first to plant Chardonnay and Pinot Noir in
Chile – with the aim of making a sparkling
wine *à la Champagne*.

The most obvious viticultural inheritance
from the Spaniards is the País grape, identical
to the Mission grape of California. This black
variety was planted originally for communion
wines; later, however, it was used for simple
everyday wines on the Chilean home market.
In recent years the area growing País has
tended to decrease somewhat, through uprooting – or grafting. A different variety is grafted
on to the sawn-off rootstock; the País vine
remains in the ground, roots and all. Various
producers – Viña Carta Vieja and Viña Segú
Ollé are examples – have their own nurseries
for raising young vines. Viña Morandé does
this on a big scale, and supplies other firms.

Chardonnay is the white grape that has seen
the biggest increase
in plantings in the
1990s, and there is a
chance that this variety will in the long run
prove more important

than Sauvignon Blanc. The reason is world demand. This is increasingly focusing on Chilean red wines; if a white wine is wanted, the preference among export customers is usually for Chardonnay.

The Sauvignonasse affair

How pure is Chilean Sauvignon Blanc? Recent research has shown that some of the vines are in fact Sauvignonasse. This grape is related to Sauvignon Blanc, but gives grapes and wines with less extract, less aroma, and less quality. Natural mutations of both Sauvignon Blanc and Sauvignonasse occur, as well as crosses of these varieties with Sémillon. Older vines are mainly involved here: recent plantings, since the beginning of the 1990s, have been of pure Sauvignon Blanc.

Since the identification of the Sauvignonasse vines many producers have been grafting Sauvignon Blanc on to its rootstocks, thus remedying the problem in their vineyards. It is quite possible, however, to make attractive dry white wines from Sauvignonasse alone, as is shown by the Cooperativa Agrícola Vitivinícola de Curicó. This concern has a pleasing wine, fermented with oak chips, which they call Sauvignon Vert – this is the correct name for Sauvignonasse.

Merlot or Carmenère?

A similar vineyard confusion exists over Chile's 'Merlot' vines – of which it is possible that more than half are in fact the old Bordeaux variety Carmenère. Here, though, the problem is only one of nomenclature and identification: to the Chilean winegrower, the Carmenère vine's drawback is its vulnerability, not its quality. See the Merlot and Carmenère entries below.

Grapes grown in Chile, first white and then black, in order of importance:

WHITE VARIETIES
Sauvignon Blanc
Sauvignon Blanc probably originated in Bordeaux, where it has certainly been cultivated since the first half of the 18th century and where it now yields the Graves and other white wines. Characteristic of the dry versions of its wine are a fresh acidity and an aroma that can contain elements both of fruits, such as gooseberry, citrus or tropical, and of fresh-mown grass and such vegetables as asparagus, green pepper and fennel. In Chile, as in Bordeaux, this grape is also used for sweet wines.

Muscatel Alejandría
This type of Muscat grape – its names elsewhere include Muscat of Alexandria, Muscat d'Alexandrie, Muscat Romain – gives sweet or semi-sweet wines in Chile, usually of a simple quality and meant for the home market.

Chardonnay
This favourite of grape growers, winemakers and wine lovers is of Burgundian origin, has spread around the world, and thrives in Chile. Its wine is usually typified by an accessible, rounded, supple taste with relatively smooth acidity, its fruit being mango, passion fruit, pineapple or other such exotic notes. Crisper versions are also made: in these the fruit has a more citrus character. Other features can be a certain nuttiness, a hint of honey and oak aspects – many of Chile's better Chardonnays are partly or wholly fermented and matured in oak casks, or made with staves or chips of oak (see Winemaking).

Sémillon

The Sémillon variety can generally be grown here without problems and, like Sauvignon Blanc, comes from Bordeaux – where it was mentioned as early as 1711. In Chile today it mostly serves for low-priced everyday wines – but just recently a few producers have exploited the potential of this quality grape, making really good wines from it.

The Chilean Sémillon vines are generally quite old: for years there has been no replanting, so the area growing it has shrunk. The great age of the vines is an advantage for those who want to make quality wine. Wine from ripe Sémillon can have a lemony aroma, with sometimes a hint of melon, liquorice and spices. Maturing in cask flatters this wine greatly, as is shown by the Sémillon Oak Aged from Viña Canepa. If the grapes are not fully ripe, the wine has a strongly herbaceous aroma.

Torontel

A white grape from which smooth, dry white wines with a Muscat-style character are made for the Chilean home market. In Argentina this Spanish-origin variety is called the Torrontés.

Riesling

In Chile this superior German grape gives a modest number of floral and fruity wines, dry or semi-dry, and sometimes slightly flinty. They are seldom commercially successful. Or as Emilio de Solminihac of Santa Mónica put it: 'Why do I make Riesling? Not because I sell much of it, but because I like it.'

Chenin Blanc

Wines made from Chenin Blanc, which originated in the Loire, are hardly ever exported.

The best Chilean ones taste dry, with a fresh fruitiness – pear, apple, and sometimes melon.

Gewürztraminer

Various wine estates have proved able to make successful wines from this grape. They are striking in character, due to a sultry spiciness and an aroma that may contains elements of lychee, orange and roses.

BLACK VARIETIES
Cabernet Sauvignon

Since 1997 the total area growing Cabernet Sauvignon has overtaken that for País, which makes Cabernet the most-grown variety. Cabernet Sauvignon originated, of course, in Bordeaux – where it is the most important grape for the great Médocs. Among the qualities of wines made solely or principally from Cabernet Sauvignon are a deep colour and an elegant firmness with tannins, usually ripe and smooth in Chile, giving them backbone. It has berry fruit, with blackcurrant, blackberry and the like in particular. Quite a few Chilean Cabernet Sauvignons, especially from the Maipo area, also have a touch of menthol or mint – sometimes the reference is to eucalyptus. If these grapes are not fully ripe, herbaceous notes can appear in the taste. Many Chilean Cabernets are matured in oak casks.

In Bordeaux, Merlot is used to soften Cabernet's noticeable tannins. But as Paul Pontallier of Viña Aquitania and Château Margaux says, 'Chilean Cabernet already has the texture of a Merlot, and so needs no softening.'

País

The quality of red País wines is often so uninteresting that Chilean producers never allow foreign visitors to taste them. But if this variety, first planted by Spanish colonists, comes from old vines and is vinified with care, it can produce a really pleasing wine, with jammy fruit – blackberry – and a supple texture. The firm of J. Bouchon demonstrates this with its Convento Viejo. There are no new plantings of País, so this grape is slowly decreasing.

Merlot

Bordeaux is the home of Merlot. It is probably related to Cabernet Sauvignon, and so many Merlots have an aroma of black fruit – berry, cherry, and others. The grape also has characteristics of its own, which appear in its wine. Compared with a Cabernet Sauvignon a Merlot tastes rather rounder, more filled out and juicier. Other characteristics are its nuances of bayleaf, brushwood, fur and leather. Of the 5–6,000 hectares of 'Merlot' grown in Chile

a considerable proportion – perhaps over half – is in fact Carmenère. For generations these two very similar varieties have been regarded as identical. It was not until the 1990s that French experts distinguished between Merlot and Carmenère in a number of vineyards. The two kinds sometimes grow side by side in the same plot, or are even intermixed. Unless and until no clear official distinction is made, wines from Carmenère grapes may still be labelled as Merlot. This also applies to wines made largely, or even exclusively, from Carmenère.

Carignan

A few producers in Chile make agreeable, slightly spicy, but seldom remarkable wines from the Spanish Cariñena, or Carignan.

Malbec

Spicy black and red fruit characterize Malbec, a variety from south-west France which is

The lighter leaf is Carmenère, the darker Merlot. Right: Cabernet Sauvignon is the most common vine.

today regarded as a speciality of Argentina. In Chile very successful wines are being produced from it, with and without cask-ageing.

Pinot Noir

There is increasing interest in Pinot Noir, the famous Burgundian grape. It is especially successful in the rather cooler wine subregions, such as Casablanca and Bío-Bío. A good Chilean Pinot Noir can be recognized by its supple, reasonably full taste with nuances of raspberry, strawberry, plum and cherry, and sometimes oak notes.

Carmenère

'It may not have been a goldmine, but it was the next best thing!' This was the reaction at Viña Santa Ines when Carmenère was discovered in the vineyard, for in Chile this grape is regarded as superior to the closely-related Merlot. Until the arrival of phylloxera in Bordeaux, Carmenère was a much-grown variety there, but it hardly figured at all in the replanting after this scourge. This was because of the rather low yield of the Carmenère vine on the one hand, and its vulnerable character on the other. It is a variety susceptible to mildew, root infections and pests, and to problems with its flowering in spring.

Phylloxera, however, did not manifest itself in Chile and the Carmenère continued to grow. But it was rather lost sight of, often being planted and propagated in with Merlot. It therefore came to be looked on simply as a Merlot – see Merlot's entry above – and is frequently still sold as such. It was only in 1994 that the French expert Jean-Michel Boursiquot was able to identify Carmenère definitively in Chile. Four years earlier the Californian winemaker

Robert Mondavi, Eduardo Chadwick of Viña Errázuriz and his vineyard manager, Pedro Izquierdo, sampled grapes in the Merlot plot at Errázuriz and noticed that the fruit from certain vines had a greater intensity of taste than the others. The tasters believed that they were dealing with a special clone of Merlot, when in fact they had met with Carmenère.

The identification process continued after 1994, and there were new plantings of the Carmenère. Probably most examples of Carmenère have not yet been recognized, however, and are still registered as Merlot. Yet the two varieties are easy to tell apart. The Merlot has a darker-coloured leaf, and the tips are not symmetrical at the leaf stalk. The Carmenère has a denser leaf formation, larger grapes and

Small boxes are used to collect the ripe grapes for transport to the winery.

a ripening period two to three weeks longer. Young Merlot stolons are white, those of the Carmenère brownish pink to red. Differences also exist between the wines. The bouquet of a Carmenère often has something herbaceous about it, especially green pepper, an element you would expect more in a Cabernet Sauvignon – to which it is also related. The taste is smoother, more generous than that of a Merlot, with less acidity. Besides elements of ripe black fruit there is often a touch of chocolate, sometimes with a hint of coffee too. And since nowhere else in the world is so much Carmenère grown, it could be regarded as a typical Chilean speciality. What the Zinfandel is to California, and the Pinotage to South Africa, the Carmenère is to Chile. The number of wines that go out into the world labelled as Carmenères is still limited, but the quantity will undoubtedly grow as more of the vines are identified and planted.

Syrah
From the Middle East, and by way of the Rhône Valley, Syrah eventually arrived in Chile. This is a variety that does best in a warm, sunny climate and in not overly fertile soil. Its vines have to be severely pruned, since if the yield per hectare is too great, the grape loses aroma, acidity and character. As Viña Errázuriz, for example, has shown, excellent wines can be made in Chile from Syrah. Sometimes Syrahs are very fruity (red and black soft fruits), sometimes spicy and peppery, sometimes dark-toned with leather, truffles, chocolate, game; and sometimes these varied facets become combined.

Cinsaut
Here and there, wines made purely from this Mediterranean grape are to be found, but are not remarkable. In a good Cinsaut there is often a suggestion of nuts such as almond, with some fruit – blackberry, cherry – and spices.

Cabernet Franc
In Bordeaux Cabernet Franc is seen as a secondary, supporting grape, after Cabernet Sauvignon or Merlot, whereas in the Loire wines, for example, it has a solo role. It is used in both ways in Chile. By itself the Chilean Cabernet Franc has aspects of berries and/or strawberries, along with hints of chocolate, bayleaf with menthol, and elements of oak if it spends time in cask. Worthwhile examples are the Gillmore from Viña Tabontinaja and the Reserve from Viña Valdiviesa.

Alicante Bouschet
A Mediterranean variety that gives wines rich in alcohol and colour, at a simple level.

Zinfandel
This south Italian Primitivo, or its rootstock, is abundant in California, where it is the most-

grown type of grape. A variety of styles are made there, including semi-sweet rosés, but the modest plantings of the grape in Chile produce red wines exclusively. For a long time Viña Canepa was Chile's only supplier of Zinfandel. Characteristics are a generous character and an intense, peppery, berry-like fruitiness.

Noble rot

The 1990s have brought great interest in Chile itself in dessert wines. These, often called Late Harvest, are usually made *à la Sauternes*, from white grapes picked very late that have undergone *pourriture noble*, or noble rot.

This is a natural phenomenon in which the fruits are affected by the *botrytis cinerea* bacterium. They shrivel, often losing half their moisture, which increases their sugar content, and they gain a special aroma that rather calls to mind stewed plums. The acidity is concentrated too, along with the aromas. Sauvignon Blanc and Sémillon are mainly used in Chile for these late harvests.

CHANGES IN PLANTING

The make-up of Chile's vineyard has changed drastically since the mid-1980s, as is shown by a comparison with 1997:

	1985	1997
País	29,384	15,241
Cabernet Sauvignon	8,143	15,995
Sémillon	6,195	2,427
Sauvignon Blanc	4,961	6,576
Merlot/Carmenère	1,000	5,741
Chardonnay	245	5,563
Pinot Noir	103	411

Figures in hectares

Chardonnay and Merlot (including Carmenère) have had the biggest proportional increases.

GRAPE VARIETIES RANKED BY AREA PLANTED

White	Hectares
Sauvignon Blanc	6,576
Muscatel Alejandría	5,956
Chardonnay	5,563
Sémillon	2,427
Torontel	1,083
Riesling	338
Chenin Blanc	98
Gewürztraminer	84
Pinot Blanc	11
Other varieties	1,593
Total	**23,729**

Black	Hectares
Cabernet Sauvignon	15,995
País	15,241
Merlot	5,411
Carignan	557
Malbec	501
Pinot Noir	411
Carmenère	330
Syrah	201
Cinsaut	178
Cabernet Franc	64
Alicante Bouschet	22
Zinfandel	22
Mourvèdre	10
Sangiovese	9
Petit Verdot	4
Verdot	2
Other varieties	863
Total	**39,821**

These figures date from 1997 and come from the Catastro Vitícola Nacional of the Chilean ministry of agriculture. The 10,009 hectares of grapes for Pisco are not included.

The total area in Chile growing grapes for wine comes to 63,550 hectares according to these 1997 figures. However, new plantings on a large scale mean that the area is estimated to have increased by more than 10,000 hectares.

Winemaking

During the final decade of the 20th century, the whole of Chile's wine-growing belt resembled a building site. Everywhere, new wineries were being erected, or existing ones enlarged or modernized. For five years running Chile was the biggest importer of European winemaking equipment. Seldom in the history of wine has a whole country carried out so many changes in so short a time. In the space of little more than a single decade the Chilean wine industry has completely made up a long-standing techno-logical deficit. It can now be said without exaggeration that today this industry is one of the best-equipped in the world.

Pioneering work

In the making of white wine in Chile, pioneer-ing work has been carried out by the Catalan Miguel Torres. Torres was the first in the coun-try to employ slow, low-temperature fermenta-tion in stainless-steel tanks. That was in 1979, and Torres had to have all the necessary plant and equipment sent from Spain. He demon-strated that even in generally warm, dry Chile it was quite possible to produce fresh, fruity white wines, eminently suited to modern tastes. Full use of the potential of such grape varieties as Sauvignon Blanc and Chardonnay, brought to Chile in the 19th century, could at last be made.

Today stainless steel gleams everywhere you look, and nearly all the better white wines are vinified in temperature-controlled steel tanks, usually at 15–18°C. The design of the tanks can vary greatly. Besides the conventional upright type there are horizontal rotating ones, and flat, squat models with a system for programming the immersion of the black grape-skins.

Presses and filters

Anyone walking around Chilean wineries will come across modern presses, especially pneu-matic ones, along with stainless-steel fermen-tation tanks and cooling equipment. The filters are also modern. Most companies use drum-shaped vacuum filters for cleaning the must or removing fermentation sediment from the wine.

Made to measure

Many Chilean wines – the better white ones in particular – are made with the measured appli-cation of various techniques. Grapes may be macerated with their skins for some of the wine but not for the rest. Part may be fer-mented in tanks, with or without oak chips or staves; a further percentage in cask. The per-centage that may undergo malolactic fermen-tation is also carefully judged. Increasingly, Chilean winemakers work like composers, carefully bringing together consciously created elements into a harmonious and attractive whole.

Fermentation and acidity

Most facets of white-winemaking in Chile are now in line with modern principles. After the grapes have come in, they are pressed – some-times with the bunches still intact, sometimes after the fruit has first been crushed and de-stalked. The dry climate and the many unsur-faced roads mean that there can be relatively large amounts of dust on Chilean grapes. At

Viña William Fèvre Chile there was found to be twice as much dust as in the firm's home district of Chablis in France.

Pressing may be preceded by macerating the crushed grapes, so that the flesh draws aromatic elements from the skins.

To get the fermentation started, yeast cells, carefully selected and usually cultivated, are added. There are also wineries that use only the 'wild' or natural yeasts present in the skins: an example of this kind of wine is the Wild Ferment from Viña Errázuriz. For a white wine – or for part of it – alcoholic fermentation can be followed by malolactic fermentation: this converts the rather sharp malic acid into the softer, creamier lactic acid. In Chile this technique is as a rule used only for the best examples of Chardonnay, as most white wines from this warm-climate country benefit from as much acidity as possible.

White grapes are sped on their way to the crusher by a giant screw.

Oak casks, chips and staves

White wines of better-than-average quality are often given contact with oak, wholly or partly. This can be done in various ways. The most traditional method is for the wine to go into cask for fermenting, for ageing, or for both; however, this is also the most expensive method – especially since the best results are achieved with entirely new (and very costly) oak barrels. So, to keep the cost within reason, two other ways of achieving contact with oak are used, both originally devised in Australia.

The first entails using small pieces of oak, often referred to as 'chips'. These go into a sort of outsized tea-bag, which is then suspended in the fermenting wine. With intelligent (i.e. not excessive) use of these chips, the wines can acquire a pleasing oak effect while still young. However, the effect of fermentation and storing in cask can be more closely approximated by using oak staves (known as 'planks' or 'inner staves' in winemaking jargon). These are about two metres in length, 20 centimetres wide and one centimetre thick. They can be suspended, stacked or arranged like spokes of a wheel, inside the stainless-steel fermentation tanks.

The oak that is used for these planks must not be of any lesser quality than that used for barrels, and so may be four to five years old. Both French and American oak is used in Chile. (A major French cooper, Nadalié, has even set up a joint-venture business there.) The degree to which the wood is charred, or 'toasted', can be decided in the same way as for actual barrels. 'Especially with the best staves, you have to be an expert to distinguish a wine made with them from one that has been in cask', comments New Zealand winemaker Kim Craford.

Tanks containing these staves really function as large barrels – and the system works far quicker than cask-ageing. Ten to twelve days' contact with staves gives about the same result as an entire six months spent in cask. A wine enriched in this way is hardly distinguishable from one kept in a *barrica*, which is by definition more expensive.

The effects of oak

A wine that is put into casks – in Chile the prevailing capacities are 225 and 300 litres – gains added dimensions thanks to oaky, often spicy aromas, aspects of toast, chocolate, coffee, cocoa, and vanilla. Fermenting white wines in cask provides them with smoother and at the same time more nuanced tastes, with in the best instances a sound balance between the oak elements and the fruit.

With red wines the malolactic fermentation is sometimes carried out in cask, because this makes their taste more supple. Oxygen gets to the wine through pores in the wood, which boosts the ageing process, and the tannin present in wood also has a certain influence. This oxygenating effect does not occur when oak chips and staves are used in tanks. Devices have therefore been developed which blow oxygen bubbles through the wine in the tank. The technique in question is called *microboulage* or micro-oxygenation; its application in Chile and elsewhere is limited as yet.

Classic vats

The making of red wine has also undergone changes, albeit less drastic ones. Much red Chilean wine today is fermented in stainless steel tanks, but concrete tanks are also in

Grapes arrive at the winery; a rauli-wood vat; appraising wine.

use and so too are, to
a limited extent, the
traditional vats made
of rauli wood (a South
American beech, *nothofagus procera*). Some
producers use the open rauli barrels only for
simple everyday wines, or the bulk varieties.
Others, however, use them for quality wines.
The precondition is that the vats are kept well
cleaned and maintained.

An advantage of these vats – which are
sometimes a century old – is their wide shape,
which ensures good extraction when the wine
is fermented with its skins.

A la Bordeaux

After their fermentation is completed many
red wines – especially those from Bordeaux
grape varieties such as Cabernet Sauvignon,
Carmenère and Merlot – are left in contact
with their skins. Domaines Barons de
Rothschild, the group that owns Château
Lafite Rothschild, introduced this method to
Viña Los Vascos in 1989, not long after taking

it over. (The Chilean winemaker resigned – he
did not wish to be responsible for wine made
this way.) After initial scepticism, the method
has been fully accepted – not least because
wines rich in colour and extract enjoy great
popularity worldwide. Malolactic fermentation
always takes place in red wines, whether in
tank, barrel or vat. Just as with white wines
(see above), the Chilean reds acquire oak aromas by various means: from casks, chips,
staves, or from combinations of these.

Macération carbonique

Macération carbonique (in Spanish *mace-
ración carbónica)* is applied to red wines on a

limited scale in Chile. In this method of fermentation black grapes are not de-stalked and crushed, but tipped as intact as possible into the tanks. These are then filled with carbon dioxide and closed off. Literally translated the process is 'soaking in carbon dioxide'.

Juice from the bursting grapes at the bottom of the vat begins to ferment. The fermentation then spreads to the juice of intact grapes: in this way fermentation is started inside the skins. The carbon dioxide released during fermentation combines with what has already been added to the tank to form a cover which guards against oxidation and acidification, and raises the temperature of the must.

The aim of this method, which is widely used in France in the Beaujolais, Languedoc and Rousillon areas, is to create aromatic, fruity and supple wines. And wines from certain grapes, such as the Carignan, can also gain in structure by this means. One of the most remarkable Chilean wines achieved by *macération carbonique* is the standard Merlot from Viñedos Terranoble.

Other wines

Besides its dry white and red wines Chile also produces rosés, although on a limited scale. More popular, certainly on the home market, are the semi-sweet whites and the dessert wines, usually called Late Harvests.

This country certainly has ample potential for producing high-priced sparkling wines, particularly in cooler districts like Casablanca, but it has hardly been exploited yet. Miguel Torres is one of the very few making a clean, refreshing effervescent wine by secondary fermentation in the bottle, in the manner of Champagne or Cava.

Qualifications and Consultants

In Chile you can only study to become an oenologist after qualifying as an agricultural engineer. All Chilean oenologists are therefore doubly qualified. Many producers make use of consultants – either Chilean or foreign, and most of them oenologists. Two well-known Chilean consultants are Ignacio Recabarren, who is himself part-owner of Viña Quebrada de Macul, and Aurelio Montes, a partner at the Montes estate. Viña Francisco de Aguirre, Viña Echeverría, Agrícola y Vitivinícola Itata, Viña Santa Ines and Viu Manent are among wine firms that Montes has advised, after first having worked for Viña San Pedro. Foreign consultants include Jacques Bassenot, Jacques Lurton and Michel Rolland, all based in Bordeaux. Rolland designed Casa Lapostolle, and Jacques Lurton played a key role in the planning of Viña San Pedro's new vinification centre.

The Wine Law

In May 1995 details of new wine legislation were published, including the *denominaciones de origen* that were to be used. Four categories were defined, from large and comprehensive to small and very local.

Región vitivinícola: five large areas that cover a considerable part of the cultivable land. Only one of these regions appears frequently on wine labels: Valle Central, the Central Valley.

Subregión: A total of 13 sub-regions are distinguished within the five main regions. Their names are used by most producers as indications of origin. Well-known sub-regions within the Región del Valle Central are Valle de Curicó, Valle del Maipo, Valle del Maule and Valle del Rapel. In all cases the English word 'valley' may also be used. Omitting 'Valle' or 'Valley' from the label is also allowed.

Zona: There are *zonas* in three *subregiónes* within the Valle Central region. These may be used on wine labels without reference to their region or sub-region. Of the seven *zonas*, those most frequently seen on labels are Valle del Cachapoal and Valle de Colchagua within the Valle del Rapel sub-region, and Valle del Lontué in the Valle de Curicó.

Area: Finally there are areas in all except three of the sub-regions. These are usually towns or villages, or sometimes groups of these. Their names do not often appear on wine labels, partly because people outside Chile hardly know of them, and cannot locate them. Non-Chileans generally have difficulty with the valley names, let alone those of individual places within them.

Viñedos Torreón de Parades is one of the producers who does consistently use the area of origin, however: the name Rengo appears on the labels.

The wine laws also specify which grape names should appear on labels. If a single grape variety is named, the wine should be at least 75 per cent from that grape (but see Merlot under Grape Varieties, above). The same ruling applies to the origin of the grapes. The producer is free to use 25 per cent of the grapes from districts other than the one stated. A total of three grape varieties may be indicated on labels. In this case no other varieties must have been used. There is a minimum of 15 per cent for the grape of which least is used. If the vintage year is stated then at least 75 per cent of the wine must be of that origin.

Other information

The wine laws also state what terms may be used on labels to indicate quality. In this case, however, no standards are specified. Each producer is therefore free to use the following terms at his own discretion: *Gran reserva, Gran vino, Reserva, Reserva especial, Reserva privada, Selección, Superior.* Translations of these terms are also permitted.

Permitted grape varieties

The wine law specifies which grape names, or their internationally accepted synonyms, may appear on Chilean wine labels.

White grapes Chardonnay, Chenin Blanc, Gewürztraminer, Marsanne, Moscatel de Alejandría, Moscatel Rosada, Pinot Blanc, Riesling, Roussanne, Sauvignon (Vert), Sauvignon Blanc, Sémillon, Torontel, Viognier.

The Pedro Jiménez (Ximénez) does not

appear in this list. However this grape, used especially for Pisco, is named on a wine label from Viña Francisco de Aguirre.

Black grapes Cabernet Franc, Cabernet Sauvignon, Carmenère, Malbec/Cot, Merlot, Mourvèdre, Nebbiolo, Petit Verdot, Pinot Gris, Pinot Noir, Sangiovese, Syrah, Verdot, Zinfandel.

The Pinot Gris should really be included with the white varieties, but is listed with the black grapes. Among the varieties not yet included is the Tempranillo. Viña Canepa, however, has applied for permission to use it.

THE CHILEAN DENOMINACIONES DE ORIGEN

Región Vitivinícola	Subregión	Zona	Area
REGIÓN DE ATACAMA	Valle de Copiapo Valle del Huasco		
REGIÓN DEL COQUIMBO	Valle del Elqui Valle del Limarí Valle del Choapa		Vicuña, Paihuano Ovalle, Monte Patria, Punitaqui, Río Hurtado Salamanca, Illapel
REGIÓN DE ACONCAGUA	Valle del Aconcagua Valle de Casablanca		Panquehue
REGIÓN DEL VALLE CENTRAL	Valle del Maipo Valle del Rapel Valle de Curicó Valle del Maule	 Valle del Cachapoal Valle de Colchagua Valle del Teno Valle del Lontué Valle del Claro Valle de Loncomilla Valle del Tutuvén	Santiago, Pirque, Puente Alto, Buin, Isla de Maipo, Talagante, Melipilla Rancagua, Requínoa, Rengo, Puemo San Fernando, Chimbarongo, Nancagua, Santa Cruz, Palmilla, Peralillo Rauco, Romeral Molina, Sagrada Familia Talca, Pencahue, San Clemente San Javier, Villa Alegre, Parral, Linares Cauquenes
REGIÓN DEL SUR	Valle del Itata Valle del Bío-Bío		Chillán, Quillon, Portezuelo, Coelemu Yumbel, Mulchen

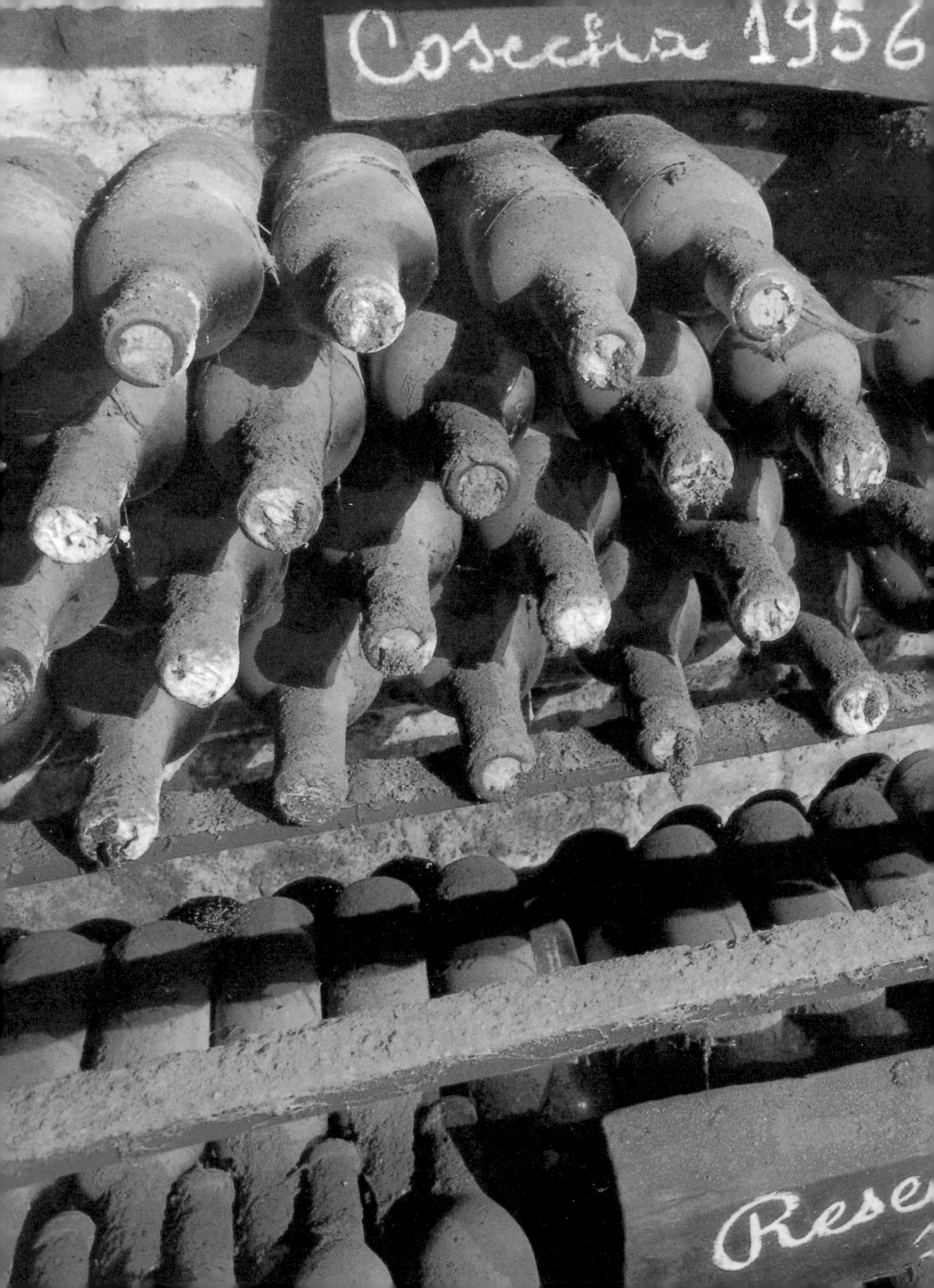
Cosecha 1956

THE PRODUCERS

The following chapters are devoted to profiles, in alphabetical order, of 66 producers and their wines. During the 1990s the number of Chilean wine producers increased greatly, while many existing wineries went over from bulk to bottles. For much of the decade Chile was the world's biggest importer of European fermentation tanks, cooling apparatus, presses, bottling lines and other equipment: investment in new vineyards, oak barrels and modern cellar equipment has been on an incredible scale.

Another positive development has been the advent of producers working exclusively, or mainly, on an estate basis and using grapes from their own vineyards. This enables total control and monitoring of the grapes, essential for making quality wines. All this has led to a spectacular rise in the number of good, very good and excellent wines; the best from each firm are named and described here.

Key to the chapters

Producer names: Each chapter is headed by the main company name (all are listed on the Contents pages, 4–5, at the start of the book). 'SA', 'limitad' and other such terms are omitted.

Wine names: Immediately below, in italics, are the names that appear on the labels: many producers have several wines/ranges/brand names – especially where export markets are concerned. (There is an index of these on pages 6-7). In all cases these are wine names as provided by the producers. Own-brands used by supermarket chains and other importers are not generally given. Each chapter has a sample label: further labels are shown at the end of the book.

Facts and figures: this table tells you, in the following order:-
▶ Owner(s) ▶ Year established ▶ Area of own vineyards in hectares ▶ Annual production, calculated in cases of 12 standard wine bottles (nine litres per case) ▶ Address of head office ▶ telephone ▶ fax ▶ E-mail address (if applicable).

The best wines: a personal selection, based on the author's extensive tastings at the wineries. The *denominación de origen* follows what is on the label, where one is given: the Chilean wine law allows, for example, 'Valle del Maipo', or its translation 'Maipo Valley' – or just 'Maipo' (see pages 50-51).

Viña Francisco de Aguirre

Tierra Arena, Doña Gabriela, Palo Alto, Piedras Altas, Tierras Altas

Facts and figures
▶ Pisquera Elqui
▶ 1993
▶ 500 ha, about half in production
▶ 70,000 cases; this is planned to rise to 1.6 million
▶ Camino a Punitaqui, km 12, Ovalle
▶ Tel: (56-53) 731 075
▶ Fax: (56-53) 731 085
▶ E-mail: vfcoag@ctcreuna.cl

Additional labels
Vina Francisco de Aguirre uses some other brands besides those above. These are Oliva, La Serena (especially in the United States) and Santa Andrea, which is an importer's label for Germany and Japan. On the home market Tetra-pak wines are sold with the labels Grosso, Nuestro Valle and 1000 Grande.

The grape brandy Pisco is tremendously popular in Chile. But, at around 5.5 million cases a year, it has reached saturation point on the home market and, being unfamiliar abroad, is hard to export. So its biggest producer, Pisquera Elqui, owner of Capel, Control and other brands, began to look for products with more growth potential – preferably related ones, such as table wines, that could be made in the Pisco region.

The region as a whole covers some 10,000 hectares (with 7,000 of them controlled by Capel) and lies far to the north of Santiago and the Central Valley. At about 400 kilometres north of the capital, its position is that much closer to the Equator: this means a low rainfall. Where the Pisco grapes grow – mainly around the little town of Ovalle – the rainfall is only 40–80 millimetres a year. Grapes and other crops are only made possible by the use of drip irrigation, supplied from three vast reservoirs. Excellent table grapes, and grapes for distilling, are produced; but could the area also grow finer, more delicate varieties for more expensive table wines?

Research in collaboration with the Fundación Chile, a body that encourages new enterprises, led Pisquera Elqui, a cooperative, to become a wine producer in 1993. The first 100 hectares was bought in the Limarí valley, some 12 kilometres south of Ovalle. Here they planted vines, installed irrigation, and built an ultra-modern cellar complex. Viña Francisco de Aguirre was chosen as the name for the enterprise, after the Spaniard who in 1549 rebuilt La Serena, the harbour and resort 100 kilometres to the northwest, and brought the first vines to Chile.

Metamorphosis

The Limarí valley, for centuries dry and parched like the surrounding hills, is now green and fertile. Much of the valley floor is covered with vines, and the vineyards climb the slopes to 160 metres. The lower plots have a soil of stony clay, but the slopes are much more rocky: dynamite had to be used when this vineyard was laid out.

The climate in this part of Chile is amazingly moderate; tropical temperatures are seldom reached. In summer the daytime temperature only occasionally rise above 27°C. Sea fogs are a feature here, often blanketing the whole area in the early mornings – the ocean is only 40 kilometres away as the crow flies. The maximum winter temperature is 18°C. The night-time drop in temperature, so typical of the wine districts further south, occurs here too: in the summer it goes down to 9–10°C, and to about 4° in winter. Frost is never a problem.

Taking care of appearances

Stainless-steel tanks, cooling systems, modern presses, air-conditioned halls: technology is the order of the day at this winery. Nevertheless they have tried to make Francisco de Aguirre look attractive. The entrance boasts a white gateway in Spanish colonial style (Robert Mondavi, too,

The best wines

All these have the denominación de origen Coquimbo Region, Limarí Valley

- Pedro Jiménez, Tierra Arena
- Sauvignon Blanc, Palo Alto
- Sauvignon Blanc, Piedras Altas
- Chardonnay, Palo Alto
- Chardonnay, Tierras Altas
- Cabernet Franc, Palo Alto
- Cabernet Sauvignon, Palo Alto
- Cabernet Sauvignon, Piedras Altas
- Cabernet Sauvignon, Tierras Altas
- Merlot, Palo Alto

Also noteworthy: a recently-developed Cabernet Sauvignon/ Cabernet Franc/Merlot blend, and the fruity, nutmeggy Late Harvest: a sweet white wine made from Moscatel grapes slightly affected by noble rot.

The arched entrance, in Spanish colonial style, frames the estate buildings; behind, vineyard-clad slopes rise to the horizon.

Cool-climate grapes

Not all the grapes for the Aguirre wines come from the Pisco region. The firm brings in white varieties from vineyards in and around Cerillos de Tamaya, a village 28 kilometres in from the coast. It is too cool there for Pisco grapes, but Chardonnay, Sauvignon Blanc and Viognier, for example, thrive.

Reduced yield

Between 30-50 metric tons of Pisco grapes per hectare can be harvested whereas the average for the Francisco de Aguirre wines is 11 tons.

> ❝ **Our wines are less serious than those from the Central Valley** ❞
> ~ *Carlos Andrade,*
> *oenologist and manager of Viña*
> *Francisco de Aguirre*

took his inspiration from this style for his Napa Valley winery). Many flowers have been planted around the site, and a vaulted cellar has been hewn out of a nearby granite hill for visitors. When they enter they first hear music by Vivaldi, after which atmospheric lighting appears.

Clean, fruity, supple and charming

After beginning, in 1995, with wines in Tetra-pak cartons, Francisco de Aguirre launched its first bottled wines in 1996. There are four lines, in

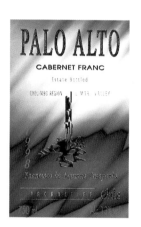

rising order of quality: Tierra Arena (and the similar Doña Gabriela), Palo Alto, Piedras Altas and Tierras Altas. The better wines not only have the best grapes but, increasingly, contact with wood. Nearly all bottled wines have classic grape varieties as their basis, but the range also includes a dry white wine from a Pisco grape: the Pedro Jiménez in the Tierra Arena line. This is gently fresh, with pleasing fruit, and sometimes a light bread-crust aroma.

The Francisco de Aguirre style may be described as clean, fruity, supple and charming. Most of the vines are still quite young, and so the wines do not yet have their maximum depth or intensity, but this is simply a matter of time. Most are already exceptionally attractive, as international tasters have found: the Chardonnay Piedras Altas 1997 won a gold medal at the Brussels Mondial. Half of this is fermented in American oak casks, some new. Ageing lasts 8–10 months, and 15 per cent of the total undergoes malolactic fermentation. Among the elements that go to make up its taste are toast, oak, tropical fruits, a slight butteriness, a hint of honey and a touch of caramel. The richest white in the range is the entirely barrel-aged Chardonnay Tierras Alto. Two Sauvignon Blancs are worth discovering: the Palo Alto with jammy gooseberry and tropical fruit, with some spice; and the Piedras Altas, partly barrel-fermented and offering generous fruit and a little toast.

The red wines

The first thing to strike the taster about the red wines is their opaque colour. The Cabernet

Above: the firm boasts the most up-to-date equipment, including these stainless-steel fermentation tanks.

Left: La Serena, founded in 1544, is the most important city in this part of Chile. The cathedral dates from the mid-nineteenth century.

 Memorable moments
Not far south of Coquimbo fishing port, on a marvellous bay, is Las Tacas, a luxurious resort in Spanish style. In the excellent restaurant, with its view over the beach and the blue ocean, I ate fresh sole and shrimp sauce with the Chardonnay Palo Alto: in all respects a delightful combination.

Sauvignon Palo Alto has abundant fruit – blackcurrant and other berries – and great suppleness. Just 10 per cent of it goes into cask, for six months. Currant, strawberry and other red fruits show on the aroma of the Cabernet Franc Palo Alto, a wine that also has some Carmenère, Malbec and Pinot Noir in the blend. Oak is more to the fore in the Cabernet Sauvignon Piedras Altas, which spends a year in American *barricas*. Besides toast and vanilla, this meaty charmer of a wine offers notes of blackcurrants and black cherries, as well as some smoky spiciness.

Only French barrels are used for ageing the Cabernet Sauvignon Tierras Altas. This wine has more breeding, more energy, more power and more concentration than the Piedras Altas. Its year in cask adds a chocolaty element to its taste, alongside the prominent fruit. The Merlot Palo Alto, with 10 per cent going into cask, is usually typified by its fruit. It is supple and rounded, with some bayleaf and succulent black fruit.

VIÑA ALMAVIVA
Almaviva

Facts and figures
▶ Viña Concha y Toro and Baron Philippe de Rothschild (50/50)
▶ 1997
▶ 41 ha
▶ 3,600 cases (to increase to 25,000)
▶ Avenida Santa Rosa 821, Paradero 45, Puente Alto
▶ Tel: (56-2) 852 9300
▶ Fax: (56-2) 852 5405
▶ E-mail: bprchilerdc.cl

The best wine
• Almaviva
(the only wine this estate produces)

Balance is the keynote at Viña Almaviva, a Franco-Chilean enterprise in Puente Alto, a southern suburb of Santiago. Balance is the aim not only in the wine here, but also in the vineyard. This extends over just 41 hectares, which consist of poor, very stony soil with a top layer that is predominately gravel.

The first vines were planted here in 1978 by Concha y Toro, the Chilean giant that owns the land. Then, in January 1997, a joint venture agreement signed between Baron Philippe de Rothschild SA and Concha y Toro brought Viña Almaviva into being. Since then, the two partners have carried out a great deal of work in the vineyard.

Research made it clear that irrigation and weedkillers had compacted the soil. The vine roots remained too much on the surface – which not only rendered them vulnerable, but also resulted sometimes in grapes with too little acidity. The problem was solved by installing drip irrigation and by loosening the soil to a depth of about 60 centimetres. As a result the grapes not only had riper tannins, but also a better balance between sugars and acidity.

With the rather higher degree of acidity the fruit could now ripen for longer, with all the advantages that this brought. In the next stage, further grape varieties were added to the Almaviva palette: Malbec and Petit Verdot were planted in addition to the Cabernet Sauvignon, Carmenère and Cabernet Franc already there. This was to give future vintages rather more breadth.

All this care and investment by the Viña Almaviva partners, Chilean and French, goes into the production of a single, splendid red wine.

This chalet-style building serves as an office and as a place to receive guests.

A distinctive bodega

Investment by the two partners – each owns half of the shares – was not restricted to the vineyard. Behind the office and the reception building, which is graced by a small tower, a

remarkable cellar complex was erected. Its undulating silhouette echoes the Andean skyline, and a generous use of wood gives the whole a very Chilean cachet. The bodega works principally by gravity; this is so as to disturb the wine as little as possible. The architect, Martin Hurtado, designed these distinctive buildings so that they can be extended without problem in the future, as the estate grows. The intention is for production at Almaviva to be greatly increased. Their first vintage, in 1996, delivered 3,600 cases; the partners hope that the production will eventually reach between 20,000 and 25,000 cases.

Bordeaux-style

The wine is made entirely in the Bordeaux manner and is treated as a *premier cru classé*: a yield of only 35–50 hectolitres per hectare, picking by hand, fruit at optimum ripeness, long fermentation plus macerating (28 days for the 1998), and ageing for 16 months in French casks, about 90 per cent of them new. It is usually 75 per cent Cabernet Sauvignon, together with (at least) Carmenère and Cabernet Franc. Its smooth tannins make Almaviva pleasantly drinkable after just two years, though the wine has sufficient backbone to develop for at least eight to ten years. Other characteristics are its solid colour, spicy oak, a stylish, complex taste with elements of berries, blackcurrants, liquorice, bayleaf, a firm structure, a finish lasting minutes – and that flawless balance.

Trade via Bordeaux

Except for Chile and the USA, all Almaviva is sold through Bordeaux. The first vintage, 1996, went entirely on subscription. In France, it was already on some wine lists (at La Tour d'Argent in Paris for example) while it was still on the boat. In the shops Almaviva sells at around $60 a bottle.

> 66 *Let us be clear: the obvious, brilliant, joyful pleasure you experience when drinking Almaviva has little in common with the almost religious emotion felt when tasting the greatest Bordeaux* 99 ~ *Michel Piot, in the French newspaper Le Figaro*

The Figaro link

'Almaviva' comes from Le Mariage de Figaro, by de Beaumarchais. This character, also brought to life in Mozart's opera, is one of the most important in the work. The name Almaviva appears on the labels in Pierre de Beaumarchais' own handwriting, while other design elements are Chilean symbols taken from the pre-Columbian period.

Viña Anakena

Anakena

Facts and figures
▶ Jorge Gutierrez
▶ 1984
▶ 70 ha (a further 100 ha will be added gradually; planting has already begun)
▶ 60,000 cases (will increase greatly with new plantings)
▶ Avenida El Bosque Norte 0140, Suite 23, Las Condas, Santiago
▶ Tel: (56-2) 233 2311
▶ Fax: (56-2) 232 8677
▶ E-mail: anakena@cepri.cl

 The best wines
• Chardonnay Reserva, Valle del Cachapoal
• Cabernet Sauvignon Reserva, Valle del Cachapoal
• Merlot Reserva, Valle del Cachapoal

 **New varieties**
The further 100 ha of vineyard will be mainly planted with black grapes. Besides the Cabernet Sauvignon and Merlot, varieties such as Carmenère, Malbec and Syrah will also go in.

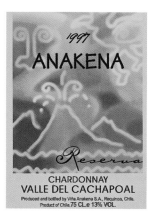

In 1978 the civil engineer Jorge Gutierrez bought the La Cabra estate at Requínoa, a town about 120 kilometres south of Santiago. The land was planted with alfalfa, but Gutierrez decided to grow fruit: apples, pears, table grapes. The fruit trade, however, proved to be risky because of the freshness factor; so, in 1984, he decided to plant wine grapes as well. Producing wine, he thought, would spread his risks. At first Gutierrez wanted to sell his wine just in South America: the first consignment went to Peru – but was never paid for. After this setback he abandoned exports, at least temporarily. For a few years he supplied wine in bulk to other Chilean producers. It was not until the early 1990s that his foreign sales got under way, particularly to Japan, Britain and the United States. It was then that he thought up the names for his business and his wines: Viña Anakena and Anakena respectively. At present 90 per cent of the production goes out of the country.

Late picking

When Jorge Gutierrez started looking into how he could move from wines in bulk to wines in bottle, he brought in a consultant from California. The first thing the expert said was 'limit the yield'. This alarmed the Chilean, for as a fruit grower he was of course used to producing as much as possible. The debate went on: quantity or quality? After much deliberation Jorge chose the latter, after which the yield per hectare was reduced to 70 or 75 hectolitres. The vineyard soil is sandy, with a stony subsoil. Since the valley here, sandwiched between the Andes and the coastal ranges, is very narrow, a relatively cool microclimate prevails. The grapes therefore ripen two to three weeks later than elsewhere. Picking at Viña Anakena often only begins when other producers have finished, usually in May ('which makes us rather nervous'). The advantage is, however, that the Anakena grapes are much more aromatic. Viña Anakena has continued to make use of Californian consultants, among them Bernard Portet of Clos du Val.

Below: at La Cabra rooms that once did duty as a school and a chapel have been refurbished as living quarters.

Right: the owner, Jorge Gutierrez.

The wine that flows from the functional, fairly compact cellar, separated from the main buildings of Viña Anakena by a railway track, is mostly red: 85 per cent of the vines in the vineyard today are black varieties. The best white wine is the Chardonnay Reserva, Valle del Cachapoal. Some 40 per cent of this is fermented and matured in casks (about 40

Easter Island

The name Anakena comes from one of the finest beaches on Easter Island. Jorge Gutierrez did not want to become the umpteenth 'Santa' of Chile's wine industry, yet wished to create a truly Chilean identity.

Other interests

Jorge Gutierrez also owned the Viña Porta brand, which he created in 1990 and sold to Viña Gracia in 1997. One of the reasons for selling was to concentrate wholly on Viña Anakena. Gutierrez was contracted to supply wine to Dallas Conte, a brand belonging to an Australian firm; the wines were sold in the United States and Britain. He is interested in Australia, California and the south of France: 'Because I think that the real competitors for the surge of new Chilean wines are to be found there.'

Proprietor Jorge Gutierrez has assembled a splendid art collection at Viña Anakena.

per cent are new) for at most four months. About 10 per cent of the Viña Anakena wine goes through a malolactic fermentation.

Freshness is usually a distinct feature of this Chardonnay, and you can taste citrus fruit particularly, as well as some mango and discreet toast from the oak-ageing. This is a Chardonnay which has a distinctive style, a true personality all its own.

Red Reservas

Since most of the Cabernet Sauvignon Reserva (80–85 per cent) goes into cask to mature for about 13 months, this wine does not have to be filtered. Viña Anakena uses both French and American oak, and a third of the *barricas* are new. This dark Cabernet Sauvignon has considerable oak and toast in both bouquet and taste, as well as notes of berry fruit and a dash of spice. It is a fairly lively wine, with reasonable substance, without being unduly heavy or tedious.

Jorge Gutierrez has specifically chosen only American oak for maturing his Merlot Reserva, and this wine spends a relatively short six months in the barrel. Like the Cabernet Sauvignon, this too is a wine with vitality; bayleaf and dark fruits are among the elements here, with some oak and toast in the background.

Viña Aquitania
Domaine Paul Bruno

A visit to Viña Aquitania nearly always begins with a climb up to the little tower atop the main building, because from this *mirador* not only can you see the whole estate laid out before you, but you also realise exactly where it is situated. The Santiago skyline looms to the north-west, and the first suburbs can be seen just a few hundred metres beyond the vines. The Andes rise to the east; Viña Aquitania lies close to the foot of the Cordilleras.

The 25-hectare estate forms the highest part of the Quebrada de Macul, one of Chile's oldest and best-known wine districts (though one which is greatly threatened by the onward creep of urbanization: see also Viña Cousino Macul). The soil here consists of a fairly sandy top layer with stones beneath. The distance between the lowest and highest parts of the vineyard amounts to 800 metres; as you travel between the two points the land rises by 40 metres.

Facts and figures
▶ Bruno Prats (40%)
Paul Pontallier (40%)
Felipe de Solminihac (10%)
▶ 1990
▶ 25 ha
▶ 122–130,000 cases
▶ Avenida Consistorial 5090, Penalolén
▶ Tel: (56-2) 284 5470
▶ Fax: (56-2) 284 5469

Development and growth
Two eminent French wine men spent four years looking for this site. Back in 1984 Bruno Prats, the former joint-owner and manager of Château Cos d'Estournel in St-Estèphe, and Paul Pontallier, the manager of Château Margaux, hatched the idea of developing a wine project together in Chile. They discovered what they were looking for in 1988, and bought the land two years later. The site was planted in phases, beginning in 1990. The cellar was ready in 1993, a rectangular brick building near the middle of the vineyard (a further cask cellar was added in 1999). The first vintages, 1993 and 1994, were made with bought-in grapes. It was only in 1995 that their own vineyards began to produce fruit. By 1998 the whole estate was in production, and the desired output,

The eastern part of the estate gradually rises up towards the Andes.

Large casks
In Bordeaux and elsewhere the usual cask capacity is 220 litres, but at Viña Aquitania 300 to 350 litres is the chosen cask size; this is to prevent the influence of the wood becoming too dominant. Only some of the wine goes into barrels and it spends at most six months there.

Washed grapes
After the grapes have been picked they are first washed, on a perforated conveyor belt, then the bunches pass through a drying tunnel. This removes the dust on the fruit. Viña Aquitania was the first Chilean firm to apply this practice.

Bottling by hand
Bottling at Viña Aquitania is done by hand, one bottle at a time, and the same applies to labelling.

Chilean oenologist Felipe de Solminihac is one of the partners. Left: the watchtower atop the winery gives a splendid view.

12,000 to 13,000 cases, was achieved. Bruno Prats and Paul Pontallier are always there to help with the grape harvest, and work very hard at it. The day-to-day running of Viña Aquitania rests with minority shareholder Felipe de Solminihac, a very talented oenologist – voted the best in Chile in 1993 – who also advises various other producers.

Balance of fruit and oak
The grapes are generally picked late, often at the beginning of April: this is so as to give them both ripe tannins and a good concentration of sugar, with a potential 13–13.5 per cent alcohol. Fermentation takes place in stainless-steel tanks: these have equal height and width for maximum extraction. The three partners do not want too much of an oak aroma in their Domaine Paul Bruno (the label chosen) and so half of it at most goes into barrels, and then for not more than six to ten months.

1997

Domaine
PAUL BRUNO
Cabernet Sauvignon

Mis en Bouteille au Domaine

Yet oak, with the associated notes of vanilla and the 'roasted' elements of toast and coffee, are generally clearly noticeable. However, these aspects balance nicely the sun-dried fruit with dark berry notes. This Maipo wine has style, is firm of constitution with a pleasant, sometimes slightly smoky, aftertaste and smooth tannins. 'Our wine', says Felipe de Solminihac, 'is aimed at wine collectors and connoisseurs.'

Viña El Aromo
Aromo, Catedral

Bottles – from 20 centilitres to 1. 5 litres – cartons in two sizes, bottles in baskets, 5-litre plastic containers: Viña El Aromo uses them all. The company is very much oriented to the home market, which is where 85 per cent of the output goes; and since the Chileans mostly drink the simpler wines, these are what El Aromo specializes in. It is hardly surprising therefore that this firm, situated in Talca, Valle del Maule, has not a cask in its cellars. The few wines that do have some wood aroma owe this to oak chips or staves. It is chips that give a hint of oak together with slight vanilla to the Aromo Cabernet Sauvignon Sello Reserva Privada, a mellow, rounded wine with some ripe blackberry fruit. Wooden staves are used for the deep-red Merlot Sello Gran Reserva, a markedly supple wine that has vanilla and a slightly herbaceous touch from about 25 per cent of Carmenère in its blend. Viña El Aromo designates some of its wines as Gran Reserva within one year, which is prodigiously fast by European standards.

French origin
In origin Viña El Aromo is French, for it was established in 1922 by the French concern Estansan y Cía. In 1940 Victor Henríquez added El Aromo to the vineyards his family already owned. The present owners are Arturo and Manuel Henríquez, Victor's sons. They have nearly 160 hectares, which supply about a third of their needs. They buy in the remainder, either as grapes or as wine.

Arturo Henríquez, who runs Viña El Aromo with his brother Manuel.

Facts and figures
▶ Arturo and Manuel Henríquez
▶ 1922
▶ 158 ha
▶ 120,000 cases of 75-centilitre bottles, plus 8.3 million litres in other sizes of bottle and in cartons
▶ 17 Oriente 931, Talca
▶ Tel: (56-71) 242 438
▶ Fax: (56-71) 245 533

 The best wines
• Cabernet Sauvignon Sello Reserva Privada, Aromo, Valle del Maule
• Merlot Sello Gran Reserva, Aromo, Valle del Maule

VIÑA BALDUZZI
Balduzzi, La Marina

Facts and figures
▶ Jorge L. Balduzzi
▶ 1906
▶ 100 ha
▶ 50,000 cases (due to more than double, with the stress on Cabernet Sauvignon)
▶ Avenida Balmaceda 1189, San Javier
▶ Tel: (56-73) 322 138
▶ Fax: (56-73) 322 416
▶ E-mail: www. balduzzi.cl

The best wines
• Sauvignon Blanc Reserva, Maule Valley
• Chardonnay Reserva, Maule Valley
• Cabernet Sauvignon Reserva, Maule Valley

The main facade of the Balduzzi villa, which dates from 1906.

BALDUZZI

CABERNET SAUVIGNON

RESERVA 1996
OAK BARREL AGED
Estate Produced & Bottled by Balduzzi
Vineyards in Maule Valley
PRODUCE OF CHILE
12 % Vol.   75 cl e

The village of San Javier sits on the south bank of the Río Maule, close to the point where the tributary Río Loncomilla joins it. By one of the roads out of the village, next to the church of La Merced which dates from 1875, lies the Viña Balduzzi wine estate. It was established by Albano Balduzzi, grandfather of Jorge L. Balduzzi, the present owner.

Albano Balduzzi came from Carezzano, a village in Piemonte, about 50 kilometres from Turin. His family had been making wine there since the 18th century. In 1906, the year that Albano arrived in San Javier, he built a splendid white house on his new property with a wine cellar extending underneath the whole living area. This relatively cool space has remained in use until today – at present for storing maturing barrels. The floors above are occupied by Jorge, his wife Lisette and their children. In front of the villa there is a shady garden, with American oaks and other trees that were planted back in those early years at the beginning of the 20th century. The office, the vinification building and part of the vineyard lie behind the house; and here too there is a fully-equipped, comfortable guest-house.

Investment for quality

Jorge – who studied economics as well as wine technology – took over the running of Viña Balduzzi in 1986. The firm did not then have its own production facilities: the wine was made elsewhere and sold in bulk. Today Viña Balduzzi supplies exclusively bottled wine – 90 per cent of it going abroad. This turnaround was achieved through a quality-driven policy, and through continuous investment. Jorge also began to develop the export markets right from the start. The present *bodega* took shape around 1990. About a third of the capacity consists of stainless-steel fermentation tanks, a further third of concrete vats, and the rest of vats made of Chilean rauli wood. These vats are lined inside with glass fibre and are used only for storage: 'they are just like giant bottles', says Jorge.

Washing the maturing casks just before the new harvest.

White wines with and without oak

Besides steel tanks and concrete vats, some of the 250 casks are also used for fermenting. Jorge ferments between a fifth and a quarter of his Sauvignon Blanc Reserva in brand-new American oak barrels. The fruitiness of this wine thus gains a spicy aspect: oak and vanilla can also be tasted, along with a correct acidity. The standard rises again with the Chardonnay Reserva; a quarter of this is fermented in new French oak. The grapes for this wine are picked early in the morning in order to ensure that they keep their freshness. Notes of passion-fruit and smoky toast often typify Balduzzi's Chardonnay; besides plenty of aroma the wine has a certain generosity and a good balance. The estate has developed a fresh white unoaked wine especially for the Chilean market, based on the Sauvignon Blanc. This is labelled La Marina.

Solitary red

Viña Balduzzi's only red wine is a Cabernet Sauvignon Reserva. Before bottling this spends ten months in American and French oak casks, then matures a further six months in bottle. Ripe fruit, with some blackcurrant, mild vanilla and a creamy suppleness make the taste quite mellow; a few years after the vintage the oak sometimes dominates.

All the grapes that Jorge Balduzzi vinifies come from his own land. The total estate covers 100 hectares: 30 sited around the cellar, and 70 elsewhere. This 70-hectare area, planted only since the mid-1990s, is entirely Cabernet Sauvignon; so the amount of Cabernet wine produced here is set to increase greatly. There are, however, no plans to add more varieties to the three – two white, one red – currently planted. In his vineyard Jorge Balduzzi uses as little herbicide or pesticide as possible, and is aiming to go almost entirely organic in the future.

Memorable moments

The Balduzzi villa has a dining room with colourful painted panels in modern style. Here Lisette Balduzzi, who was born in Ecuador, served as a first course a fantastic carpaccio of Chilean salmon. She had frozen the fish, sliced it very thinly, and then sprinkled it with lemon juice, olive oil, salt, pepper and grated cheese. Its partnership with the Chardonnay Reserva was a stunning success.

Visitors welcome

Viña Balduzzi has an open-door policy. All are welcome from Monday to Saturday, between 9 am and 6 pm. Visitors can count on a guided tour of the cellars and the small museum, and a tasting. There is no charge – though bottles of wine can be bought.

> ❝ *We grow only three kinds of grapes here. We are not aiming to increase the number of varieties, just the quality* ❞
> ~ *Jorge L. Balduzzi*

Viña Bisquertt

Bisquertt, Château La Joya, Casa La Joya, Don Osvaldo, Viña Las Garzas, Los Pedrones, Soleca, Doña Sol, Bellíssima

Facts and figures
▶ The Bisquertt family
▶ 1970
▶ 600 ha
▶ 500,000 cases
▶ El Comendador 2264, Providencia, Santiago
▶ Tel: (56-2) 233 6681
▶ Fax: (56-2) 231 9137

Judged the best
The 1998-99 Guía de Vinos de Chile declared the Cabernet Sauvignon Gran Reserva 1996, La Joya, to be Chile's best Cabernet Sauvignon.

Calixto Bisquertt de la Barrera, from the French Basque country, began producing wine in Chile at the end of the 19th century. The Bisquertt family carried this on into the early years of the 20th century, but then for two generations they moved into other forms of farming. It was not until 1970 that they revived their wine traditions. This came about through Osvaldo Bisquertt, who planted new vineyards on a considerable scale in the Valle de Colchagua, which is part of Rapel. At the same time, Osvaldo bought a two-centuries-old farm beside the road that follows the winding Río Tinguiririca and links San Fernando with the coast. The farmhouse was restored, and wine-making facilities installed. Today this establishment, between the villages of Palmilla and Peralillo, has a palm-lined drive and, to the front, a broad terrace with ferns and tubs. Flowers grow round the lawn in the inner courtyard, adorned with a fountain and sculptures.

From their own land
For almost two decades the whole grape harvest was sold in bulk to other producers. Viña Bisquertt began to do its own bottling and exporting in 1991, after Osvaldo had noted that considerably more was being paid for the wines made from his grapes because of their palpably superior quality. Bisquertt wines come exclusively from their own land: 600 hectares altogether, by far the greater part now planted. The five vineyards making up the estate are all in the neighbourhood of the *bodega*, the farthest being ten kilometres away. Although trials are being carried out with Malbec, Syrah and other varieties, the portfolio of grapes used is conventional in

Picking white grapes by machine at night.

character. Cabernet Sauvignon, Merlot, Carmenère, Chardonnay and Sauvignon Blanc predominate, along with Sémillon – also very common elsewhere in Chile. The black grapes are hand-picked by day; the whites, except for the Chardonnay Reserve, at night by machine.

Well-equipped

A walk through the cellars makes it clear that Viña Bisquertt is outstandingly well-equipped. For fermenting there are mainly stainless-steel tanks: these are made here to their own design – and also produced for other winegrowers. To a lesser degree the estate also uses concrete vats, lined with resin. The wooden vats still here are empty and serve only as decoration. Wood from more old vats has been made into doors.

A portfolio of labels

Viña Bisquertt has quite a number of different labels. Some are meant for certain markets only, or are little heard of. Bellísima for example, in stylish half-litre bottles, has so far only been seen on the home market; Soleca – fairly light and easy wines, usually a blend of two grapes – was created specially for Britain. Don Osvaldo, Viña Las Garzas, Los Pedrones and Soleca are all in the range, but have received relatively little attention in recent years in comparison to Château La Joya (called Casa La Joya in Britain) and Bisquertt itself. There is a good chance, however, that the firm will be turning the spotlight onto some of these hitherto secondary labels. In late 1998, for example, the Don Osvaldo Sauvignon Blanc was launched in London: a well-structured, clean wine

The best wines

• Chardonnay Gran Reserva, Château La Joya
• Cabernet Sauvignon, Château La Joya
• Cabernet Sauvignon Gran Reserva, Château La Joya
• Château La Joya Merlot
• Merlot Gran Reserva, Château La Joya

All are denominación de origen Colchagua Valley.

Behind the names

There is no castle behind the Château La Joya name. Originally the name was Casa La Joya (still used in Britain), but the American importer insisted on the word 'château'. Another label, Soleca, is named after Osvaldo Bisquertt's wife. She is called Soledad, but is known as Soleca.

The attractive and shady colonnaded walk at the front of the winery houses a collection of ferns.

The stainless steel tanks at Bisquertt are made to their own design – and also sold to other wineries.

with a lively fruitiness. The exciting Château La Joya Sauvignon Blanc, more crisp and flinty, is marked by its citrus fruit.

European-style Chardonnay and impressive Merlots

One of the stars of the La Joya range is the Chardonnay Gran Reserva. This wine does not taste very mellow or rich; however, it does have a complex, vivacious taste, with fresh tropical and citrus fruit, nuts and a dash of honey – all nicely framed by toasty oak. The style of the wine is European rather than New World. It ferments in casks (half of French oak, half of American) and it undergoes complete malolactic fermentation. This Chardonnay has repeatedly been awarded gold medals in a number of countries. The Chardonnay Selection, a fifth of which goes into cask, is of a generally correct quality. The red wine that stays longest in cask is the Cabernet Sauvignon Gran Reserva from Château (or Casa) La Joya. This lasts for a year, and all the barrels (again, half American, half French oak) are new. A delightful wine, this boasts plenty of colour, good concentration, a lot of fruit (blackberry, black cherry), toast, chocolate and spicy oak. Usually all these elements are nicely balanced. The standard Cabernet Sauvignon Selection contains 20 per cent of the Gran Reserva, and is an elegantly firm wine that develops quite quickly; it has a spicy, fruity character.

Even more impressive than the two Cabernets, perhaps, are the La Joya Merlots. As the Merlot Selection actually consists mainly of Carmenère, its bouquet is somewhat herbaceous. On the palate the wine comes across as very supple, with spices that include bayleaf, and black fruit such as plum. The Merlot Gran Reserva, matured for eight months in new French and American oak, combines the generous, smooth qualities of ripe black fruits with elements of bayleaf, toast and vanilla. Not particularly fat or rounded, this Merlot nevertheless has substance and backbone. There is no point in laying it down for a long period, however: this Gran Reserva tastes at its best four to five years after the vintage.

Millennium wine

Bisquertt has put a Cabernet Sauvignon-Merlot 1996 into six-litre bottles especially for the millennium. This special wine has been named La Joya 2000, and the number of bottles is also 2,000.

Concentration

To give the Gran Reservas Cabernet Sauvignon and Merlot more contact with the grapeskins, and thus more colour and concentration, about one-fifth of the must is drawn off from the vats.

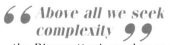

❝❝ Above all we seek complexity ❞❞
~ *the Bisquertt winemaker and consultant Mario Geisse in the newspaper El Mercurio*

Viña Casas del Bosque
Viña Casas del Bosque, Gredas Negras

If you drive from Santiago to Casablanca and turn left in the village square, it is then another kilometre to Viña Casas del Bosque, the wine estate started by Juan Cuneo in 1992. This dynamic entrepreneur, whose interests range from department stores to the Banco de Chile, owns about 1,000 hectares of land in this part of the Casablanca valley. Of this, 135 hectares have been identified as suitable for winegrowing. The grape varieties for this new vineyard were selected with the help of a French consultant: Chardonnay (40 hectares), Sauvignon Blanc (25 hectares), Carmenère (10 hectares; the clone came from Bordeaux), Merlot (30 hectares), and Pinot Noir (30 hectares).

Cabernet Sauvignon is absent, but a small estate may eventually be created for it in Maipo; the fear is that this variety might not ripen fully in this part of the Casablanca valley.

High ambitions

Cuneo has considerable ambitions for his wine business. He wants, merely, to make 'the best wines in Chile' here, in small quantities and geared from the start to the British market. The grape harvests of the first few years were sold in bulk to other producers, and Casas del Bosque did not make its first wine until 1998. This took place at TerraMater, with which the firm shared an Australian consultant, David Morrison. In 1999, however, del Bosque's own cellar complex was built. Since the aim is simply to produce top-quality wine, only the best is selected to carry the firm's own brand names; the rest of the production is sold in bulk. This care is carried through to the vineyards – at Viña Casas del Bosque, only certified drinking water is used for the vines when drip-irrigating.

First impressions

A small proportion of the Sauvignon Blanc – some 12 per cent – is fermented in barrels that have been used just once. This wine is generally fragrant and distinctly fruity (a mixture of gooseberry and exotic

Facts and figures
► Agrícola Casas del Bosque (Juan Cuneo)
► 1992
► 135 ha
► 10,000 cases (and increasing fast)
► Nueva de Lyon 96, Of. 303, Providencia, Santiago
► Tel: (56-2) 232 4315
► Fax: (56-2) 252 0346
► E-mail: cdelbosq@entelchile.net

The best wines
All have Casablanca origin on their labels

• Sauvignon Blanc, Viña Casas del Bosque
• Chardonnay, Viña Casas del Bosque
• Chardonnay Reserve, Gredas Negras
• Merlot, Viña Casas del Bosque

The number of good wines will undoubtedly increase as other grape varieties come to maturity.

The Valle de Casablanca, where Casas del Bosque has been producing high-quality red and white wines since 1998.

Animal lover

Owner Juan Cuneo loves animals as well as vines. He owns a herd of pedigree cattle and is chairman of the Chilean horse-racing association.

fruit), with a clear hint of vanilla and a good level of acidity.

First impressions of the Chardonnays – both the standard wine and the Reserve version – are similarly positive. The first red wine that was produced here was a Merlot. Eighteen per cent of this is fermented in American oak casks, 16 per cent in French ones, and the rest in stainless-steel tanks. The wine that has been fermented in cask then has nine months in wood. In bouquet and taste smoky oak, toast and related aspects complement the dark, and at the same time fruity, aroma of this supple wine.

As the vines at Viña Casas del Bosque are still rather young the first vintages have somewhat lacked depth, but with time this estate will undoubtedly be increasing its reputation – both the potential and the will to make high-quality wines are here in full measure.

VIÑEDOS J. BOUCHON Y COMPAÑÍA
Chicureo, Las Mercedes, Convento Viejo, J. Bouchon

To reach J. Bouchon's wine estate of Santa María de Mingre you drive from San Javier, a village about 20 kilometres south of Talca, in the Maule region, along the highway to Constitución on the coast. At first the road crosses low, mostly pine-clad hills. Then the hills give way to a broadening valley. Follow a dirt road northwards across this valley, and soon to left and right vineyards begin to appear, and in the distance large, square white buildings come into view, together with the low out-line of a *hacienda*.

The house at the Santa María de Mingre estate dates from the middle of the 19th century. Then, the whole property covered 3,400 hectares, compared with 800 today (including hills and land lying fallow). The average height above sea level is 750 metres. When Julio Antonio Bouchon bought this land in 1976, there were already vines here: 100 hectares planted with the black País variety and with Sauvignon Blanc. The greater part has now been converted to other varieties, chiefly Chardonnay, Cabernet Sauvignon, Malbec and Merlot. Syrah is being experimented with, but Julio Antonio does not yet know whether this grape will be a success here: 'besides, the varieties we already have are very good, so why should we plant others?'

Bouchon has 350 hectares of vineyard, divided between Santa María de Mingre and another property 100 kilometres further north, near San Fernando in the province of Colchagua. All the wines sold in bottle come from the company's own land. At a second firm, El Porvenir Talca, Viñedos Bouchon produces wines in bulk for Europe and Canada.

Australian methods
Bouchon's winery in Maule has a markedly Australian character, revealing its design by Australian expert Ron Potter. He imported rotating fermentation tanks from Australia in 1991. These horizontal tanks are used both for

Facts and Figures
▶ Julio Antonio Bouchon
▶ 1892
▶ 350 ha
▶ 100,000 cases plus 1.3 million litres of wine in bulk
▶ Evaristo Lillo 178, Of. 23, Las Condes, Santiago
▶ Tel: (56-2) 246 9778
▶ Fax: (56-2) 246 9707
▶ E-mail: jbouchon@netup.cl

Scant irrigation
At the Santa María de Mingre property about 80 per cent of the vines are cultivated without irrigation. This keeps the yield relatively low. For example, between 8–12 tons per ha of Malbec is harvested. Every night the temperature drops to around 15°C. In order to profit from this cooling down the white grapes are picked early in the morning, and sometimes in the early evening as well. All picking is carried out by hand.

The wine estate is very modern, but the hacienda has all the ambience of times gone by.

Versatility

The owner Julio Antonio Bouchon has a diploma in agronomy, and studied oenology in Bordeaux under the legendary Professor Emile Peynaud. He is also a polo player and a pilot – which is why the Santa María de Mingre estate has its own airstrip.

French founder

The origin of the establishment goes back to 1892, when the 22-year-old Guillaume Bouchon from Saint-Emilion arrived in Chile and set up the Casa Silva wine firm in San Fernando (which see).

1998

J.BOUCHON

GRAN RESERVA

MERLOT

CHILEAN RED WINE
MAULE VALLEY

750 ML.   ALC. 12.5% VOL.

ESTATE GROWN AND BOTTLED BY JULIO BOUCHON

red wines, to give them as much colour and extract as possible, and for certain of the whites, the fruit for which undergoes an eight-hour maceration to soften the skins. Before the bunches of grapes reach the tanks they are first checked for quality.

As well as these rotating tanks, the firm has square, vertical, stainless steel ones, also of Australian design, and concrete vats lined with synthetic resin. The casks – about 250 of them, a fifth to a quarter of which are replaced each year – are housed in an old, traditional building with thick walls. Bottling, and storage of bottled wine, on the other hand, takes place in a modern, temperature-controlled building which also accommodates offices and the laboratory.

White varieties

At Bouchon the accent lies on red wines, but attractive whites are also produced. One of these is the Chicureo Sauvignon Blanc, a refreshing, supple wine with often a slight spiciness, and occasionally a passion-fruit aroma. The Chardonnay Las Mercedes has more depth. This wine ferments in new barrels and is then pumped into tanks, without having undergone malolactic fermentation. Las Mercedes is marked by agreeable freshness, firm structure and a juicy, though restrained, fruitiness with hints of grapefruit, tropical fruits and bananas, while notes of oak and toast complete the whole.

A surprise from the País

One of the most suprising red wines made here is the Convento Viejo Mission, for this is from the much-maligned País, the basic grape for

Top: Julio Antonio Bouchon. Left: poplar trees border a vineyard at Santa María de Mingre.

In 1991 Viñedos Bouchon installed these horizontal rotating fermentation tanks from Australia.

Chile's simplest mass-market wines. With his Convento Viejo, Julio Antonio Bouchon shows that a thoroughly pleasant wine can be made from the País grape (which in California is called the Mission, as it was first planted by Spanish missionaries). Bouchon's Mission has a good amount of jammy fruit, especially blackberry, and a very supple taste which is at its best if the wine is served young and cool. The grapes for this wine, which has something of a simple Beaujolais about it, come exclusively from old vines.

Splendid Malbec

Another speciality is the Las Mercedes Malbec: this is one of the very best in the whole of Chile. It tastes meaty, reasonably concentrated, supple and fruity (notes of plum are very clear). It is not aged in cask. This is in contrast to the Las Mercedes Cabernet Sauvignon Reserva, which matures on average six months in barrels of French oak. Generous vanilla, some toast and ripe berry fruit contribute to a satisfying whole. The Chicureo Merlot is usually very agreeable, with hints of chocolate, cherry, bayleaf and cloves. Recent additions are wines with the label J. Bouchon Gran Reserva: a Cabernet Sauvignon which spends eight months in new oak, as does the Merlot (one-third new barrels). These were launched in 1999, with 1997 the first vintage.

The best wines
All the wines have Maule Valley as their denominación de origen

- Chicureo Sauvignon Blanc
- Chardonnay Las Mercedes
- Chardonnay J. Bouchon Gran Reserva
- Convento Mission
- Cabernet Sauvignon Reserva Las Mercedes
- Cabernet Sauvignon J. Bouchon Gran Reserva
- Malbec Las Mercedes
- Malbec J. Bouchon Gran Reserva
- Merlot Chicureo
- Merlot J. Bouchon Gran Reserva

LAS VIÑAS DE LA CALINA

Viña Calina

Facts and figures
▶ Jess Jackson,
Barbara Banke,
Donald Harford
▶ 1994
▶ None
▶ 80,000 cases
▶ 1 Poniente no.
1360-A, Talca
▶ Tel: (56-71) 235 810
▶ Fax: (56-71) 239 316
▶ E-mail:
vicalsa@entelchile.net

The best wines
• Chardonnay,
Valle de Casablanca
• Chardonnay,
Valle del Itata
• Cabernet Sauvignon,
Valle del Rapel
• Merlot,
Valle del Maule
• Merlot Selección
de Las Lomas,
Valle del Maule

Barrels of barrels
A relatively large
number of barrels –
2,000 – are used for
Viña Calina. About 70
per cent of these are of
French oak.

La Calina's first winery is next to that of Viña Tabontinaja.

In 1993 Jess Jackson, owner of the very successful Californian Kendall–Jackson winery, commissioned the setting up of a Chilean subsidiary. Winemaker James Randy Ullom, given the management of the project, undertook exhaustive research and came up with a fairly revolutionary concept. Ullom decided not to buy any land. Instead, grapes would be bought from a large number of vineyards spread across the whole country. Strict conditions were laid down concerning the age of the vines, the yield per hectare, and the intrinsic quality of the fruit itself. In total he picked some 30 different locations, from Casablanca in the north to Itata in the south. At first all the vinification was contracted out; today, however, the firm – Las Viñas de la Calina is its official name – has its own modern winemaking centre. It stands next to the Viña Tabontinaja cellars (which see) in the Maule district.

Irresistible fruit

Calina can finance its own winery, thanks to the reputation its wines enjoy – especially in America. The Rapel Cabernet is a well-balanced wine, at once supple and concentrated, with an irresistible berry fruitiness and some oak from nine months in cask. Better still is the Selección de Las Lomas, which spends some 18 months in barrel. The Merlots show the same class. The standard Merlot, from Maule, is generous and well-balanced, with notes of chocolate, cherry, toast from seven months in oak. The Merlot Selección de Las Lomas oozes with fruit, including blackberry and blackcurrant, has plenty of toast and is generosity itself. Three-quarters of the grapes for it come from Maule, the rest from Rapel, and it has 16 months in cask. The Chardonnays, too, should not to be overlooked: a spicy-fruity wine from Itata and an energetic one from Casablanca with some vanilla.

Viña Caliterra
Caliterra

Wednesday 25 March 1998 was a red-letter day for Viña Caliterra. It was when the first grapes – Merlot – were ceremonially picked at La Arboleda, Caliterra's brand-new centre for the production of red wine. La Arboleda, a quiet, remote corner of Rapel's Valle de Colchagua district, occupies a valley surrounded by low hills, near to the Río Tinguiririca. This isolated landscape lay uncultivated until 1996, but was then speedily planted and a drip irrigation system installed. Of the 1,000 hectares available, 300–400 proved suitable for vine-growing. Caliterra had some enormous problems to overcome in carrying out this project, among them the building of an access road, some of it over steep hillsides, and the construction of a pipeline to bring in water from a spring seven kilometres away. The valley now holds a complete red-wine vinification centre, with a capacity of 6.3 million litres. White wine production is wholly concentrated in the Casablanca district.

Facts and figures
▶ The Chadwick and Mondavi families
▶ 1989
▶ About 430 ha, more than half of it planted
▶ 600,000 cases (will increase greatly)
▶ Avenida Nueva Tajamar 481, Torre Sur, Of. 503, Las Condes, Santiago
▶ Tel: (56-2) 203 6900
▶ Fax: (56-2) 203 6346
▶ Email: jmasot@caliterra.cl

International collaboration

This kind of investment was possible for Viña Caliterra thanks to Chilean–U.S. collaboration. The firm is an equal partnership between the Chadwick family, of Viña Errázuriz – among others – and the Mondavis, of the Robert Mondavi Winery in California. The two families had known each other since 1991, and in January 1995 decided to collaborate. Eduardo Chadwick, the president of Viña Caliterra, describes this as 'a true partnership: from the grape-growing to the winemaking and the international marketing of our wines, this is a joint venture between families that is going to last for decades.' There had been a Californian connection even before the Mondavis came into the picture. Viña Caliterra was set up in 1989, and this came about through the efforts of the Chadwick family

Further vineyard planting is planned in the valley where the new winery buildings stand.

By bringing in water, via a pipeline some kilometres long, Caliterra has conjured up an oasis of green out of a previously uncultivated valley.

and Augustín Huneeus, the Chilean-born owner of Franciscan Vineyards. This partnership lasted two years; then in 1991 the Chadwicks bought all the shares. Huneeus continued with his own estate of Veramonte.

Accessible wines

Viña Caliterra was already making good to very good wines, partly under the direction of the well-known winemaker Ignacio Recabarren, before the arrival of the Mondavis, and today they are achieving quality of at least the same level. Accessibility and drinkability are two of the characteristics here, as well as great purity, a firm but not overly heavy structure and a good balance, with the Reservas offering rather more body, power and depth than the ordinary wines. As early as 1991 wine writer Tom Stevenson was noting in the London *Daily Telegraph*, 'If Chile had 100 Caliterra-type wineries, its wines could conquer the planet.'

Made to measure

Winemaking is always a matter of measure. In making the Chardonnay Reserva, 80–100 per cent is fermented in cask; it matures for five months; and nearly 10 per cent of natural yeast cells are used along

with cultivated yeasts. One-fifth of the barrels are new, and malolactic fermentation is limited to 25–30 per cent of the wine. The choice of casks is a very careful matter.

Another example of Caliterra's approach is the standard Merlot: grapes for this are selected from the Curicó, Maipo and Rapel regions, including some 15 per cent Cabernet Sauvignon which is added to give the wine rather more tannin and backbone.

Contact with wood is deliberately limited to three to four months, exclusively in used *barricas*. During the period of the grape harvest there is a great deal of consultation between the two

The best wines
- Sauvignon Blanc, Valle Central
- Chardonnay, Valle Central
- Chardonnay Reserva, Casablanca
- Cabernet Sauvignon, Valle Central
- Cabernet Sauvignon Reserva, Maipo Valley
- Merlot, Valle Central
- Merlot Reserva, Valle Central

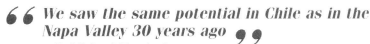

❝ *We saw the same potential in Chile as in the Napa Valley 30 years ago* **❞**
~ R. Michael Mondavi,
President of the Robert Mondavi Winery

partners' technicians – a Mondavi winemaker spends about a month here at vintage-time in support of his Chilean colleague.

This equation of investment, know-how and care make the Caliterra Sauvignon Blanc a wine with fruit, floral elements and a clean freshness. About half of the Sauvignon for it comes from Casablanca, and the rest from a cool part of Maipo. Roughly half of the Chardonnay, too, comes from Casablanca, and of this nearly one-seventh undergoes cask fermentation – which explains why this supple, rounded wine has toast as well as fruit notes. Oak is even more generously in evidence in the more substantial, balanced Chardonnay Reserva, which is of pure Casablanca origin.

Among the red wines, the Merlot's charm lies in its generous, lively black fruit and earthy aspects; bay, chocolate, and a herbaceous touch may be perceptible, with a hint of oak. The Cabernet Sauvignon, from three valleys, offers some toast – a fifth of it spends six months in barrel – and also elements of black cherry, blackberry and menthol. This can also be tasted in the Cabernet Sauvignon Reserva, albeit less intensely and sometimes with a suggestion of cedar-wood and significantly more oak: all of this wine spends 12–16 months in American casks.

Viña Canepa

Canepa, Peteroa, Rowan Brook, Las Taguas, Montenuevo

Facts and figures
▶ Luciana Garibaldi de Canepa
▶ 1930
▶ About 1,000 ha (only partly planted)
▶ 1,400,000 cases plus bulk wine
▶ Camino Lo Sierra 1500, Cerillos, Santiago
▶ Tel: (56-2) 557 9121
▶ Fax: (56-2) 557 9186

The best wines
• Sauvignon Blanc, Cachapoal
• Sémillon Oak Aged, Rapel
• Gewürztraminer, Maule
• Chardonnay Private Reserve, Rancagua
• Zinfandel, Maipo
• Pinot Noir, Maipo
• Malbec Private Reserve
• Cabernet Sauvignon Private Reserve
• Cabernet Sauvignon Finísimo, Lontué
• Cabernet Sauvignon Magnificum, Curico
• Merlot Private Reserve, San Fernando

At Viña Canepa it is not unusual for foreign visitors to be asked whether they speak Italian. Within the owners' family it is spoken perfectly – better than English, for example. The firm was founded by José Canepa, an Italian who came from Liguria. As a 15-year-old he journeyed from the hills near Genoa to the Chilean port of Valparaiso. That was in 1914, on the eve of the First World War. After working for years in a compatriot's firm, José decided to become a winegrower. With his savings he bought, in 1930, about 450 hectares of land in three different valleys, and planted it with top-quality European grape varieties.

José's work was continued by one of his sons, also called José (but known as Pepe). Like his father, he was an entrepreneur with vision. After looking around overseas, in 1982 he set up a firm that six years later was being described by the American trade magazine *Wines & Vines* as 'the most modern in Chile, and probably in South America'. It had a capacity of 6.2 million litres, and its stainless-steel fermentation tanks came from California.

Partly as the result of family problems which seriously affected him, José Canepa died in 1992. Since then the business has been managed by his widow Luciana Garibaldi de Canepa, also a Ligurian by birth.

Priced above rubies

The wine firm that Luciana took over consisted only of the *bodega*, the 18-hectare vineyard around it and the various brands. A division of the estate had meant that the larger part went to another branch of the family (see TerraMater). 'I had two options', as Luciana said with a smile, 'spending everything on jewellery or on vineyards.' Her decision means that at present Viña Canepa has more than 1,000 hectares planted, or about to be planted. The largest estate is called Trinidad and lies near the hamlet of Trinidad in the Colchagua valley (not far from Marchihue in Rapel). Eventually 540 hectares will be under cultivation, and since the beginning of 1999 a whole new cellar complex has stood here. The climate in the large, open valley of Trinidad is relatively cool, thanks to the sea breeze that usually blows in from around 11 a.m. Besides the conventional grape varieties Syrah, Tempranillo and Viognier have also been planted. All the vines are drip-irrigated; the water for this comes from five wells.

Lolol is another Rapel area where Vina Canepa owns land. In time 300 hectares will be producing mainly white grapes here. A third holding, also in Rapel, is behind Casa Lapostolle. It covers 150 hectares of mostly hilly terrain, not all of which can be planted.

Eventually the origin of some of the wines will change, as increasingly the grapes for each will come from a particular Canepa estate.

Investment in the original estate

Investments have not been confined to the new vineyards: a great deal of money has been put into the original holding at Cerrillos, beneath Santiago's smoke. The capacity in stainless-steel tanks has risen from 7.3 to 8.5 million litres, a new bottling-line has been installed, and an attractive entrance, a reception suite with a tasting area and a small museum have been specially built for visitors.

Besides wine in bottle, Viña Canepa also supplies a considerable quantity of wine in bulk – to Norway, for example. Viña Canepa is also a significant player on the home market, both with its own wines and as a distributor of imported wines, beers and mineral waters.

White surprises

The Canepa wines are exceptionally reliable in quality – as shown by the fact that that the firm supplies the wines for numerous own-brands

Luciana Garibaldi de Canepa: she has invested a fortune in new vineyards, extending to nearly 1,000 hectares, and in a new cellar complex to complement the original bodega.

Unaccented

In the pronunciation of Canepa, the stress comes on the first syllable. In Spanish this means that there should be an accent on it. It does not have one because the name Canepa is Italian in origin.

An artistic family

On the Canepa coat of arms are the words 'Vitam exolvere per Artes' – 'a life dedicated to art'. The family is in truth artistic. Canepa's owner Luciana has studied art, and her daughter is a professional pianist. Do art and winemaking have a connection? Luciana believes so: 'to make wine you need artistry – and a certain madness'.

> *"* *Anyone who invests a great deal as a winegrower lives poor but dies rich* *"*
> ~ *Luciana Garibaldi de Canepa*

sold by many British stores. One notable white wine in the range is the Sémillon Oak Aged, from Rapel. About 60 per cent of this is fermented in new French barrels and matured for five months. Toast, spices, liquorice and citrus notes give it a very agreeable taste, and there is a good balanc between the oak and the alcohol. The herbaceous quality that characterizes some Chilean Sémillons is entirely absent. This is due to the great age of the vines – from 50 to 60 years old. The Gewürztraminer from Maule is also noteworthy, a sultry and spicy creation with an aroma of Muscatel grapes and lychees. The first harvest was in 1998.

A more usual style of white wine is the Sauvignon Blanc from Cachapoal, generous in its fruit and with a touch of asparagus. The Chardonnay Private Reserve from Rancagua is classic and serious in style; half of it is fermented in new French casks. This is a muscular, mouth-filling wine with elements of tropical fruit such as mango alongside toast, vanilla and smoky oak. The standard Chardonnay Rancagua, too, has merit.

Rare Zinfandel

A red wine that is rare for Chile is the Canepa Zinfandel. The vines for it were brought back from California in the early 1980s by José Canepa himself, and planted round the cellar, which was then newly built. These 4.5 hectares of Zinfandel vines demand special care. Every year there has to be a preliminary picking in which whole unripe bunches of grapes are removed to let the plants breathe. Without this intervention, the grapes will not ripen. For a long time Viña Canepa was Chile's only producer of Zinfandel. The wine has a generous character and a somewhat intense, peppery, berry-like fruitiness.

Private Reserve

Pinot Noir Private Reserve has also been part of the Viña Canepa range since 1997, a smooth wine with mild fruit, including plum, and some oak – from fermentation in new French casks, and ageing for five months in used barrels. The Malbec Private Reserve is marked by fresh fruit, especially berries, with some liquorice, a hint of vanilla and a fairly elegant structure. This wine is given a month in wood.

Like many Chilean wine producers, Viña Canepa uses vacuum filters for cleaning the must.

Unfiltered Cabernets

Naturally, Cabernet Sauvignon and Merlot feature among the reds. The standard wines are of a very decent quality, but those from the Private Reserve line are more interesting. After 12–14 months in used barrels the Cabernet Sauvignon has berries, spices and spicy oak in both aroma and taste. The Merlot, made the same way, is somewhat more supple, with black fruit, woodland scents and toast. Finísimo, a special version of the Cabernet Sauvignon, goes into cask for two years. This has a velvety taste: hints of menthol and eucalyptus are often alongside the ripe fruit and oak. Cabernet Sauvignon Magnificum is quite different: much fruitier, with plenty of blackberry, cherry and plum. The grapes for this are grown without irrigation, giving a very low yield. Toast and chocolate are also present, for the Magnificum goes into new French oak casks for a year. Like the Private Reserve and the Finísimo Cabernets, it is not filtered.

Different brands, similar quality

The 'Reserve' level in all the ranges produced is, in principle, equal in quality to that of the Canepa Private Reserve. (Other wines made at Viña Canepa may well differ according to brand.)

VIÑA CARMEN

Carmen, Viña Carmen, Sierra de los Andes

Facts and figures
▶ Viña Santa Rita
(Ricardo Claro)
▶ 1850
▶ 740 ha owned or
leased
▶ 350,000–400,000
cases
▶ Apoquindo 3669,
Piso 6, Las Condes,
Santiago
▶ Tel: (56-2) 362 2122
▶ Fax: (56-2) 263 1599
▶ E-mail:
aotten@carmen.cl

Viña Carmen was named after the wife of Christian Lanz, who started the company in 1850. After passing through various owners, Viña Carmen, the oldest wine brand in Chile, was acquired in the mid-1980s by Ricardo Claro, who already owned Viña Santa Rita. Claro gave Carmen a second youth, a new élan: in 1992 he built an entirely new, very modern and extremely efficient vinification centre. For the site of the new Carmen premises he chose Buin, the commune where Viña Santa Rita is also situated. The two concerns are not far apart, and are separated only by vineyards.

This showcase winery stands at the bottom of a hill, the gleaming modern equipment hidden behind sand-coloured walls. The building houses rows of stainless-steel fermentation tanks and their attendant apparatus, plus casks for storage. The wines here are moved largely by gravity through the various phases of production.

The cellar is the brainchild of the Viña Carmen winemaker, the oenologist Alvaro Espinosa, whose practical training, after college, was at estates that included Château Margaux. Alvaro's starting-point is that the quality of the wine comes at least 80 per cent from the quality of the grapes. The Carmen team accordingly takes enormous care with all aspects of the

Viña Carmen has some 3,000 casks, of which 500 are new each year. Two-thirds are of American oak, the rest are French.

grape cultivation in the vineyards – their own, the ones they rent and those under contract. Clonal selection, grafting on American rootstocks (to guard against any possible arrival of phylloxera), canopy management and soil treatment . . . all are painstakingly monitored; the team are, more and more, introducing organic methods.

In order to gain the greatest possible control over the grapes, Viña Carmen has been steadily increasing the area of vineyard it owns or leases. The firm now has 250 hectares divided among the valleys of Maipo, Casablanca, Rapel and Maule; when all the vines planted on this land are bearing fruit, they will be supplying at least 60 per cent of the grapes the firm needs, and 100 per cent for the Reserves.

The character of the grape

Viña Carmen achieves almost all its sales abroad, marketing some 20 different wines. The high average standard of the range is clear from wide critical acclaim, and a number of gold medals. In making the single-variety wines they aim to bring out the clearest expression of that particular grape, that particular land. Thus the Sauvignon Blanc Valle Central typically has a fresh, flinty taste with spicy fruit, where the lively Sauvignon Blanc Reserve Casablanca is more aromatic and luscious, thanks to its pineapple and citrus notes.

Carmen's Chardonnays are usually delicious. Leading the field is the Chardonnay Winemaker's Reserve from Casablanca. Fermented in casks in which it then stays for eight months, this wine resounds with mango, almond, toast and other nuances. A little less exuberant, and less typified by oak, is the Chardonnay Reserve from Maipo, a fine, full-bodied wine that also boasts fresh tropical fruit; 40 per cent of this is barrel-fermented. Natural yeasts are used to ferment four-fifths of the Chardonnay Nativa from Maipo. This wine often shows a slightly flinty touch, citrus-fruit notes and considerable oak – it is wholly fermented in casks, followed by seven months' maturing, again in barrels. The rare Sémillon Late Harvest is a honey-and-peaches sweet white wine.

Velvet fist

The Cabernet Sauvignon Gold Reserve is the show-stealer among Carmen's red wines. This comes from vines nearly 40 years old and yielding less than 30 hectolitres per hectare. After about a month fermenting and macerating, and nearly 18 months in French barrels, two-thirds of which are new, a dense, dark wine emerges with a very smooth texture, plenty of structure, formidable intensity and a finish lasting long minutes. In addition this fist-in-velvet holds lots of blackcurrant and other black fruits, as well as spices and toasty oak.

Ripe blackberry and eucalyptus, together with plenty of toast – from six months in cask – define the Cabernet Sauvignon Nativa, for which only natural yeasts are used. Very creamy, with deep, ripe, almost lavish fruit, the complex Cabernet Sauvignon Reserve with its eight months in

The best wines
• Sauvignon Blanc Reserve
• Chardonnay Reserve, Maipo
• Chardonnay Nativa, Maipo
• Chardonnay Winemaker's Reserve, Casablanca
• Sémillon Late Harvest Reserve, Maipo
• Cabernet Sauvignon Reserve, Maipo
• Cabernet Sauvignon Gold Reserve, Maipo
• Merlot Reserve, Rapel
• Grand Vidure Cabernet, Maipo
• Petite Sirah, Maipo
• Pinot Noir, Maipo
• Syrah Reserve, Maipo
• Winemaker's Reserve Red Wine, Maipo

CARMEN
Founded in 1850

Wine Maker's Reserve

Chardonnay
1997
CASABLANCA VALLEY
Produced and Bottled by Viña Carmen S.A
PRODUCE OF CHILE
ALC. 13.5% BY VOL.   75cl℮

Efficiency

Although the Carmen bodega has a considerable capacity – nine million litres – only nine people are needed to run it.

Home market

The simplest wines for the home market bear the name Viña Carmen and are made by Viña Santa Rita. The better wines are called Viña Carmen Insigne. and are of the same quality as Carmen's export varieties.

> **I want the wines to demonstrate the uniqueness of the fruit, the soil and the climates**
> ~ *Alvaro Espinoza, winemaker*

wood is similarly impressive. The Merlot Reserve offers a comparable standard: with 10 per cent Cabernet Sauvignon, it is a generous Rapel wine with luxurious black fruit, toast and smooth tannins, 80 per cent of which goes into cask for eight months. The Grand Vidure Cabernet Reserve is an exciting blend of 60 per cent Carmenère and 40 per cent Cabernet Sauvignon: a rounded wine with toast, ripe berry and sometimes red fruit, bayleaf and other nuances. The lively Pinot Noir – 1998 was its first vintage – deserves mention, as does the powerful Syrah Reserve, rich in fruit and toast.

Masculine and feminine

The Petite Sirah came about through a mistake by the nursery – Carmen had in fact ordered Syrah vines. This wine, which is one-fifth Merlot, has massive colour and tastes even more intense than the Syrah. It has more tannin, too, alongside its peppery fruit.

Petite Sirah is one of the components of the red Winemaker's Reserve, for which 1997 was the first vintage. The other grape varieties are 40 per cent Cabernet Sauvignon, 20 per cent Carmenère and 20 per cent Merlot. The wine has nine months in new French *barriques*, which account for a third of the firm's stock of casks. It is a wine with breadth to it, with tobacco, notes of a variety of of black and red fruit, toast, spices, a silky character, power and generosity.

Three months were taken up with putting together this blended Winemaker's Reserve wine. There were sometimes quite intense discussions with the French consultant winemaker Jacques Boissenot. Boissenot believed that you could not mix what he considered a 'feminine' grape variety such as Petite Sirah with 'masculine' ones like Cabernet Sauvignon. However, it was included in the end.

The fermentation and storage tanks at Carmen have a total capacity of nine million litres.

VIÑA CARTA VIEJA

Carta Vieja

Villa Alegre, a village 285 kilometres south of Santiago in the Maule wine district, is as famous for the orange-trees in its main street as for its wines. The land around the village is mostly vineyards; the soil here consists of a sandy top layer with stony sub-soil. Carta Vieja is the biggest wine concern, with 500 hectares of vines. Its cellars and part of its land lie along the road in from the east. The fine large villa amid gardens, shown on the Viña Carta Vieja labels, dates from about 1880 and belongs to the del Pedegral family, owners of the winery. The del Pedegrals came to the valley from Asturias in Spain in 1825, planting vines in that first year. The firm is now run by the seventh generation.

From growers to businessmen

For some 160 years practically all the Carta Vieja wines were sold in bulk – so profitably that there was simply no need to start bottling them on any scale. It was only 1986 that the state of the market encouraged exports, and therefore the selling of wines in bottle. Alberto del Pedegral was very much involved in the change-over: 'from being growers living quite comfortably we had suddenly to become businessmen. But I'm glad we took the step.' After a cautious start the amount exported rose in 12 years to 700,000 cases, and this is expected to go up to 1,500,000 by the year 2005. At the same time the number of casks will grow tenfold, to 5,000.

Since 1997 Carta Vieja has had a number of stainless-steel fermentation tanks. Many concrete vats are still in use alongside these, but nearly all the old wooden vats have disappeared. With this equipment the firm makes its red wines, representing 70 per cent of the output. Between one-tenth and one-eighth of this total is produced as Reserve, which

Facts and figures
▶ The del Pedegral family
▶ 1825
▶ 500 ha
▶ 700,000 cases (eventually rising to 1,500,000)
▶ Avenida Francisco Antonio Encina 231, Villa Alegre
▶ Tel (56-73) 381 612
▶ Fax (56-73) 381 681
▶ E-mail Vicar@Ctc–Mundo.net

The best wines
• Cabernet Sauvignon Reserve, Maule Valley
• Merlot Reserve, Maule Valley

Since 1999 Carta Vieja has also made a Gewürztraminer and a Late Harvest (from Sauvignon Blanc plus a percentage of Sémillon).

A plot of Merlot vines in the five hundred hectares of Carta Vieja vineyards.

Coaches

There are models of coaches in the family residence. These are reminders of a collection of real coaches that belonged to the grandfather of José Manuel del Pedegral, the general director. The whole collection was sold after his grandfather's death. One of those coaches is now used by the Chilean president on official occasions. In the 1930s the same grandfather gave a plot of land beside his cellars to Villa Alegre village for a small hospital to be built, and this is still in use today.

means that it has been in contact with oak. This contact, however, is deliberately limited: these red wines spend 12 months at most in cask. The style that Carta Vieja strives for across its whole range is that of wines that are enjoyable when relatively young, easy to drink, and also reasonably priced.

Impressions of fruit and oak

The standard Sauvignon Blanc and Chardonnay are both better than merely correct: they are characterized by fresh fruit – citrus and tropical respectively – and offer very good value for money. This freshness and fruit are also found in the Reserve versions, although here the oak and toast elements deepen the aroma. A proportion of these wines – a half at most – is fermented in new French barrels. The Cabernet Sauvignon matures for eight months in casks that have first been used for the white Reserves. This is why its taste holds elements of vanilla and cedarwood alongside the ripe fruit, the black and red berries. In the standard Merlot there is more of a taste of ripe blackberry; in essence, this is a pleasant, supple, mouth-filling wine.

Grapes from the oldest vines are used for the red Reserves. The Cabernet Sauvignon Reserve has reasonable concentration, reasonable fruitiness, with a judicious amount of toast and creamy vanilla. Notes of leather, bayleaf, chocolate and black fruit, along with oak aromas, determine the character of the Merlot Reserve.

Some of the fermentation tanks: the firm has invested large sums in stainless steel.

VIÑA CASABLANCA

Casablanca

In 1990 Viña Santa Carolina vinified grapes from the Casablanca area separately for the first time, and with great success. The hoped-for quality potential proving attainable, the decision was taken to set up a new winery in the area: the first Viña Casablanca vintage to come on to the market was the 1992. These wines, a Sauvignon Blanc, a Chardonnay and a Gewürztraminer, won medals in Australia, Britain and France. Wines from the subsequent vintages also received favourable comment and won awards. Viña Casablanca's turnover grew along with its reputation: at present more than 90,000 cases are being sold annually – compared with only about 1,000 in 1993, the first year of sales. And as Viña Casablanca developed, so the district began to flourish: the firm has played a pioneering role here. The great man behind the firm is L. Ignacio Recabarren, a talented, passionate winemaker with an

Facts and figures
▶ Fernando Larrain (also owner of Viña Santa Carolina)
▶ 1991
▶ 60 ha (plus 220 under long-term contract)
▶ 90,000 cases
▶ Roderigo de Araya 1431, Santiago
▶ Tel: (56-2) 450 3000
▶ Fax: (56-2) 238 0307
▶ E-mail: beckdor@santacarolina.cl

Viña Casablanca makes some remarkably aromatic wines from Sauvignon Blanc grapes. They are among Chile's best.

Thin soil

*The Santa Isabel
Estate, Viña
Casablanca's own
estate, lies in the
western, coolest part
of Casablanca, about
350 metres above sea
level. The fertile top-
soil here is usually
only 40 centimetres
deep, with hard rock
below. To give the vine
roots more room to
grow extra soil has
been added in
various places.*

CASABLANCA
**SAUVIGNON
BLANC**
SANTA ISABEL ESTATE
1997
PRODUCE OF CHILE

CASABLANCA

66 *The best wines in the
world are made in marginal
conditions: Chablis has frost,
Bordeaux has frost,
Casablanca has frost* 99
~ Ignatio Recabarren, winemaker

impressive record. In 1990 he travelled to New Zealand and Australia. There he became familiar with techniques that were new to him. From New Zealand producers he learned how Sauvignon Blancs of world class can be made in a relatively cool climate – like that of Casablanca.

In Casablanca the energetic, talkative Recabarren manages 280 hectares; 60 owned by the winery and 220 under contract. In addition he processes the grapes from other valleys for a few red wines. The range of wines has been gradually increased to around fifteen. The top of the list consists of wines labelled as coming from the Santa Isabel Estate. These are from the firm's own land in the Casablanca valley.

Clones from Sancerre

The Santa Isabel Sauvignon Blanc is an outstanding wine. Its vitality, its freshness, its vigorous fruit – especially gooseberry – and its balance make it everything a Sauvignon Blanc can be. Clones brought in from Sancerre were used exclusively for the vines which yield this wine. Nor is the standard Sauvignon Blanc from the Casablanca valley a wine to be looked down on, given its fragrance, its lovely fruit and its lively character.

The Chardonnays, too, are splendid. The Santa Isabel is aromatic and supple, fresh and firm, fruity with mango and lemon, and it also has a little oak. A fifth of the volume is fermented in casks of French oak, 20 per cent of them new, and matures in them for a further ten months.

Going up the quality scale, the Chardonnay Barrel Fermented has yet more depth and complexity. Besides mango, in this wine you can taste pineapple, nuts, honey (a proportion of the grapes are picked over-ripe), and a considerable measure of toast: 70 per cent of the wine is fermented in the barrel, it all spends a year in wood, and about 50 per cent undergoes malolactic fermentation.

The Neblus is a special and very unusual style of Chardonnay. Recabarren bases this on grapes of which most are affected by *pour-riture noble*, and ferments the wine in casks, where it stays for 20 months. The result tastes slightly sweet, firm, with distinct oak – plus an aroma of chocolate mints and toffee. The Gewürztraminer is made at the Santa Isabel Estate from very ripe grapes. This wine offers an intense aroma of lychees, spices and roses, and displays a lively, stylish taste in which these same elements are echoed.

Mastery in red

Viña Casablanca makes two Merlots, both coming from Casablanca. Small proportions of other grape varieties are added to the Merlot to enhance complexity. The standard version, for example, has Carmenère and Cabernet Sauvignon to add to its 80 per cent Merlot. This mixture ages for eight months in cask. Smoky oak, bayleaf, leather and black fruit dominate its aroma and taste. Still more concentration is offered by the Merlot Santa Isabel, impressive in every respect and with 10 per cent of Cabernet Sauvignon; it is loaded with black and red fruit, and chocolate, toast and red fruit are there too. It spends a year in *barricas*, all of them new.

Three fine Cabernets

The Cabernet Sauvignon from the Miraflores Estate in San Fernando has elements of chocolate, cigar boxes, toast from five months in cask, and fruit. In quality, however, it is surpassed by the Cabernet Sauvignon from the El Bosque Estate in Maipo. This is not fined, filtered or stabilized, has a year in new French oak casks, and comes from vines that are around 80 years old. Very ripe fruit – berries and plums – chocolate, menthol, toast and herbs are among the nuances of this substantial wine. Finally there is the brilliant Cabernet Sauvignon Santa Isabel, a wine that is rich in taste, concentrated and with a lingering finish; it has spicy woodland fruit, fine tannins, and noble, but not exaggerated, oak and chocolate. The 1993 Santa Isabel was the first Cabernet Sauvignon wine to be produced in Casablanca. It comes from vines which are growing in a relatively sheltered plot: this corner has a warmer microclimate than elsewhere on the estate.

The best wines
- Sauvignon Blanc
- Sauvignon Blanc, Santa Isabel Estate
- Chardonnay, Santa Isabel Estate
- Chardonnay Barrel Fermented, Santa Isabel Estate
- Chardonnay Neblus
- Gewürztraminer, Santa Isabel Estate
- Cabernet Sauvignon, Miraflores Estate, San Fernando
- Cabernet Sauvignon, El Bosque Estate, Maipo
- Merlot
- Merlot, Santa Isabel Estate

The denominación in most cases is Casablanca

Billboard in the Valle de Casablanca.

Viña Concha y Toro

Concha y Toro

Facts and figures
▶ Listed on the Chilean stock exchange (the Guilisasti and Alfonso Larrain families are major shareholders)
▶ 1883
▶ 3,300 ha
▶ 11,000,000 cases
▶ Avenida Nueva Tajamar 481, Torre Norte, Piso 15, Las Condes, Santiago
▶ Tel: (56-2) 821 7000
▶ Fax: (56-2) 853 0024
▶ E-mail: pkonar@conchaytoro.cl

At Pirque, which is separated from Santiago by the Maipo valley, the wealthy 19th-century mine owner Ramón Subercaseaux laid out an extensive vineyard. This was, perhaps, returning to his roots: Subercaseaux was of French origin, and for his vineyard he took advice from a French expert. Ramón's daughter, Emiliana, married Melchor de Concha y Toro, Marqués de Casa Concha, and together they built a fine country house at Pirque in 1875, with a 25-hectare park stretching to the banks of the Maipo.

Melchor de Concha y Toro was a politician – among his other roles – and served as Chile's minister of finance. In 1883, eight years after the family's house, the Casona de Pirque, had been built, he decided to become a winegrower, and together with his wife he founded Viña Concha y Toro. The concern grew quickly and, to add to Subercaseaux's vineyard in Pirque, another was planted at Peumo, not far from Rancagua; the vines for this new enterprise came directly from France.

Thanks to the efforts of successive generations, who took the business onto the Santiago stock exchange in 1923, and to New York's in

Left; small baskets are used so as not to damage the grapes. Below: the garden. Right: this giant cask is dated 1883.

1994, Concha y Toro became Chile's biggest wine producer. The firm sells about eleven million cases a year, 55–60 per cent of them abroad.

The company's main centre is still in Pirque. The cellar buildings there are wholly functional, but the Casona de Pirque still has the same Chilean and French furniture, paintings and tapestries as when it was built at the end of the 19th century. A portrait of Melchor de Concha y Toro hangs prominently in the dining room.

Melchor de Concha y Toro, the wealthy marquis after whom the estate is named.

Modernization

Concha y Toro has been able to carry out a big modernization programme in its cellars, thanks to around $50 million raised on the New York stock exchange. Half of the storage capacity, which amounts to 110 million litres, now consists of stainless-steel tanks. The area of vineyard owned has been extended to 3,300 hectares, divided over more than ten locations, eight of them with their own cellar facilities. At the same time great attention has been paid to improving wine quality, a process begun in the mid-1980s. The firm has also created new lines of specific types of wine for particular segments of the market, under the Explorer, Sunrise and Trio labels.

Explorer and Sunrise

Concha y Toro's Explorer concept aims to surprise, with wines from relatively unknown grapes, from blends of two grapes, or from comparatively unknown areas. The Pinot Noir from Casablanca is an excellent example: a smooth, firm wine with some oak and strawberry and plummy fruit. The Explorer series also includes a Syrah from Rapel: rounded, with juicy red fruit and mild vanilla; a pleasing Cabernet/Syrah (75 per cent and 25 per cent respectively, and seven months in cask) from Maipo; a Bouchet from Maule; a Malbec from Rapel; and a Sauvignon

The best wines
- Sauvignon Blanc Explorer, Casablanca Valley
- Chardonnay Trio, Casablanca Valley
- Chardonnay Casillero del Diablo, Agoncagua/Casablanca
- Chardonnay Marqués de Casa Choncha, Maipo Valley
- Chardonnay Amelia, Casablanca Valley
- Cabernet Sauvignon Trio, Maipo Valley
- Cabernet Sauvignon Casillero del Diablo, Maipo Valley
- Cabernet Sauvignon Marqués de Casa Concha, Maipo Valley
- Cabernet Sauvignon Sunrise, Valle Central
- Merlot Sunrise, Valle Central
- Merlot Trio, Peumo Valley
- Cabernet/Syrah Explorer, Maipo Valley
- Pinot Noir Explorer, Casablanca Valley
- Syrah Explorer, Rapel Valley

The Devil's Cellar

To prevent thefts from the Casona de Pirque wine cellar by his staff, Melchor de Concha y Toro put about the story that the Devil lived on the premises. So it was that the Casillero del Diablo or 'Devil's Cellar' label came into being.

Guided tours

The Pirque headquarters runs guided tours, with commentary in Spanish and English. These last about an hour. Booking in advance is required: tel (56-2) 821 7069, fax (56-2) 853 0063.

The barrels

A total stock of 13,500 casks is distributed among the Concha y Toro cellars. Of these, 60 per cent are made of French oak. About a third of them are replaced every year.

Blanc from Casablanca, rich in fruit with a touch of herbaceousness.

The brand name Sunrise, with annual sales of more than a million cases, refers to wines that come 100 per cent from one particular grape variety and have had little cask-ageing or other contact with wood. Most of them carry the denominación de origen Valle Central. The Chardonnay generally has a little sweetness – five grams of residual sugar is not uncommon – and its fruit can vary from pear with melon and tropical notes to a taste that is almost Muscatel-like. Among the reds, the Cabernet Sauvignon is easy to enjoy – a wine with good tannins; and the Merlot is notable for its firm structure, its spicy red-cherry fruit, and its agreeable suppleness.

A vinous trinity

Behind the three wines of the Trio series lies the vinous trinity of soil, climate and winemaker – all combining to optimize the potential of particular grapes in particular areas. The winemaker engaged for the job was Ignacio Recabarren (see also Viña Casablanca), who carried out his task wonderfully well. The Chardonnay, a wine from Casablanca, sees no wood and combines lively citrus with some mango and a firm structure.

The Cabernet Sauvignon, from Maipo, spends a year in French oak casks, a quarter of which are new. This wine, with its jammy berry and

other fruit, also has a minty, menthol note in its aroma. Chocolate, liquorice, black fruit and oak elements are offered by the Merlot, a Rapel wine. This wine, with one-eighth Cabernet Sauvignon blended in for extra backbone, has eight months in contact with French oak – 90 per cent of it in the form of barrels, the rest staves.

Casillero del Diablo

One of Concha y Toro's oldest labels is Casillero del Diablo – the Devil's Cellar. The range at present consists of four single-grape wines, from the districts considered best for each of the varieties; thus the Chardonnay is from Casablanca. A quarter of this wine is fermented in cask, and

Early exporter
Viña Concha y Toro had started exporting by 1933, when the first consignment arrived in Rotterdam.

Highest price
When Christie's auctioned some Chilean wines the highest price went to a case of Don Melchor 1988: it fetched $2,500, or one million Chilean pesos.

malolactic fermentation is limited to 5 per cent. This is a reasonably generous wine with mango-like fruit. In the Cabernet Sauvignon from Maipo, menthol with eucalyptus is often distinctly there in smell and taste, with blackberry and oak – 60 per cent goes into cask for at least six months. The Merlot from Rapel is well endowed with fruit – cherry, plum, bramble – and also offers roasted notes, including chocolate.

Marqués de Casa Concha

Quality and price increase with another, still older, label: Marqués de Casa Concha. These wines undergo longer contact with wood: 40 per cent of the Chardonnay is barrel-fermented, and in aroma and taste the wine has noticeable toast along with aspects of fruit and nut. Ripe black-currant, menthol, chocolate, spicy oak, vanilla and toast are to be found in the Cabernet Sauvignon – all adding up to a generous whole. The Merlot is characterized more by feral aspects, although spices are not lacking. Both the red wines go into cask for a year.

Amelia and Don Melchor

Concha y Toro's top white is called Amelia. Chardonnay grapes from Casablanca serve as its basis, and 80 per cent of their must ferments in French oak, followed by seven or eight months in cask. This is a broad-shouldered, concentrated wine with sweet elements of vanilla, along with the crackling citrus and tropical fruit so characteristic of Casablanca. Don Melchor leads the red wines in quality. It is a Cabernet Sauvignon that spends 12 months in French *barriques*, 60 per cent of them new; the result is an impressive wine with solid colour, a tremendous intensity and a lush texture. Chocolate, rich berry, ripe black cherry, menthol, toast and vanilla are among its nuances.

Finally there are the bread-and-butter wines sold simply as Concha y Toro. These are simple, decent products with a good price-to-quality relationship; part of the output is sold in 1.5-litre bottles.

The firm also makes sparkling wines, but beyond the (undemanding) home market these are not rated very highly.

As the grapes arrive at the winery, they are transported into the crusher by a rotating screw in a stainless-steel hopper.

HACIENDA EL CONDOR
Millamán, Campero

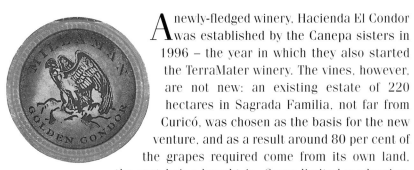

A newly-fledged winery, Hacienda El Condor was established by the Canepa sisters in 1996 – the year in which they also started the TerraMater winery. The vines, however, are not new: an existing estate of 220 hectares in Sagrada Familia, not far from Curicó, was chosen as the basis for the new venture, and as a result around 80 per cent of the grapes required come from its own land, the rest being bought in. Some limited modernization work means that the winery now has stainless-steel fermentation tanks with a capacity of 100,000 litres – five per cent of the total. The *hacienda* itself is a farm in the traditional low-built style.

A notable blend
In tasting, the wines – Millamán is the brand-name under which they are marketed – clearly show that they are meant for a somewhat lower price bracket than those from TerraMater. They are supple and easy, generally with a firm core of alcohol, and fruit that is adequate without being sensational.

The leading wine here is the Cabernet Sauvignon/Malbec. This comes from vines at least 40 years old. The two varieties were planted together in the vineyard, and both kinds of grapes are thus picked and vinified together. The end result probably works out at about 60 per cent Cabernet and 40 per cent Malbec. This wine is fairly aromatic, and besides its blackcurranty, juicy fruit it also has elements of bayleaf, leather and vanilla – half of it sees some wood. Of the other wines here, the Cabernet Sauvignon Reserve achieves the highest standard.

Golden name
The brand name Millamán is derived from the native word for 'golden condor'. Exactly the same wines are sold under Hacienda El Condor's second trade name, Campero.

Facts and figures
▶ Gilda, Antonieta and Edda Canepa
▶ 1996
▶ 220 ha
▶ 200,000 cases
▶ Luis Thayer Ojeda 236, 6° Piso, Santiago
▶ Tel: (56-2) 233 1311
▶ Fax: 56-2) 231 6391

The best wine
• Millamán Cabernet Sauvignon/Malbec, Curicó

International advice
The consultant brought in when the firm began was a Scotswoman with winemaking experience in Australia, and now living in Spain.

VIÑA CONO SUR
Cono Sur, Isla Negra, Tocornal

Facts and figures
▶ Viña Concha y Toro
▶ 1993
▶ 300 ha
▶ 500,000 cases
▶ Nueva Tajamar 481,
Torre Sur, Of. 1602, Las
Condes, Santiago
▶ Tel: (56-2) 203 6100
▶ Fax: (56-2) 203 6732
▶ E-mail:
query@ConoSur.com

Other brands
Viña Cono Sur supplies
wines to British chain
stores under their own
private labels. These
brand names include
Alto Plano, Altura and
Las Cumbres.

Cono Sur is a fairly common name in Chile (there is, for example, a bank so named); it is a reference to the conical shape of the South American continent. But the name Viña Cono Sur belongs to a very unusual wine firm. This subsidiary of Concha y Toro, established in 1993, not only uses coloured synthetic corks (among the first wine firms in Chile to do so), but also has its website address printed on them. What's more, the bottles carry labels of strikingly contemporary design.

As far as the wines are concerned, the company puts great stress on using the best possible grapes. To this end, meticulous attention is paid to the management of the firm's vineyards – 300 hectares that provide three-quarters of the grapes required – and the wines are made with the help of the most up-to-date technology. During the second half of the 1990s an existing cellar complex at Chimbarongo, just south of San Fernando, was totally renovated and enlarged. That this investment of millions of dollars was justified has been borne out by Viña Cono Sur's commercial success. So far it has been exclusively an exporting firm and in 1994, its first year of sales, 30,000 cases of Cono Sur and 120,000 with the Tocornal label were shipped; since then the production has increased to 500,000 cases.

Three kinds of Pinot Noir
The wines sold under the Tocornal name are the inexpensive end of the range. The quality rises with the Cono Sur label, in which the Pinot Noir is prominent. The standard version, 20 per cent of which goes into cask for five months, offers leather and tobacco notes as well as its red Pinot fruit. About a fifth of its grapes come from Rapel, the rest from Bío-Bío. There is more oak in the Pinot Noir Reserve, 60 per cent of which goes into cask for seven months; and the Pinot Noir 20 Barrel combines a measure of ripeness with velvety fruit, earthy aromas and oak. This wine comes from relatively low-yielding vineyards – about 55 hectolitres per hectare – and it spends a year in medium-toasted, once-used barrels of French wood.

The same three variants of the Cabernet Sauvignon are made. Blackcurrant and some green pepper are usually to be found in the standard wine; spicy wood and a charming fruitiness in the Reserve; toast together with berries and spices in the nuanced 20 Barrel. There are

❝ We never want to lose fruit – in any of our grape varieties ❞
~ *Constanza Vicent, manager of Cono Sur*

also Merlot versions of the same trio of quality-levels. These wines, rich in extract and visually striking by reason of their opaque colour, display black fruit, bayleaf, woodland and feral scents in their aroma and taste – sometimes together with a hint of green pepper, for most of the grapes are Carmenère. The Merlot 20 Barrel is usually a rich, delicious wine, with notes of fruit that include ripe blackcurrants. Normally the Merlots are not matured in cask, but acquire some oak through the use of staves.

White wines and special selections

Of the white wines, the Cono Sur Viognier should perhaps come first: a well-balanced wine with notes of dried apricot, peach and mint. Then from Bío-Bío there is a Gewürztraminer, with spices, roses, lychees. The standard Chardonnay, sourced from Rapel fruit, is slightly creamy as well as fruity. The character becomes fresher, nearer to citrus fruit, in the Reserve Chardonnay, which also offers some oak; its district of origin is Casablanca. Finally there is the Isla Negra range, which includes Argentinian as well as Chilean wines. These are special selections, with the concentrated, meaty, spicily fruity Cabernet Sauvignon as the star.

The best wines

- Gewürztraminer Cono Sur, Bío-Bío/Mulchen
- Viognier Cono Sur, Casablanca
- Chardonnay Cono Sur, Rapel
- Chardonnay Reserve Cono Sur, Casablanca
- Cabernet Sauvignon Cono Sur, Rapel
- Cabernet Sauvignon Reserve Cono Sur, Rapel
- Cabernet Sauuvignon Cono Sur 20 Barrel, Rapel
- Cabernet Sauvignon Isla Negra, Rapel
- Merlot Cono Sur, Rapel
- Merlot Reserve Cono Sur, Rapel
- Merlot Cono Sur 20 Barrel, Rapel
- Pinot Noir Cono Sur, Rapel
- Pinot Noir Reserve Cono Sur, Rapel
- Pinot Noir 20 Barrel Cono Sur, Rapel
- Zinfandel Reserve Cono Sur, Cachapoal

Irrigation is essential in most of Chile's vineyards. When vines can stretch to the horizon, a bicycle comes in useful.

CÓRPORA VINEYARDS & WINERY
Viña Gracia, Gracia de Chile, Viña Porta, Porta

Facts and figures
▶ The Ibañez family
▶ 1989
▶ 1,000 ha
▶ 350,000 cases (still growing strongly)
▶ Asturuias 280, Suite 402, Santiago
▶ (56-2) 206 7868
▶ (56-2) 206 7862

The best wines
• Chardonnay Viña Gracia, Cachapoal Valley
• Chardonnay Casa Porta, Central Valley
• Chardonnay Viña Porta, Valle del Cachapoal
• Chardonnay Reserva, Viña Gracia/Viña Porta Cachapoal Valley
• Cabernet Sauvignon Viña Gracia, Maipo Valley
• Cabernet Sauvignon Casa Porta, Valle del Cachapoal
• Cabernet Sauvignon Reserva, Viña Gracia/Viña Porta, Cachapoal Valley
• Merlot Viña Porta, Valle del Cachapoal
• Merlot Reserva, Viña Gracia, Aconcagua Valley
• Pinot Noir Viña Gracia, Bío-Bío Valley

The Chilean Córpora group, which belongs to the Ibañez family, owns companies producing everything from preserves, fresh fruit, instant drinks, salmon and tin to – since 1989 – wine. Viña Gracia was set up in that year, and the first vintage was 1993. Some four years later, in December 1997, Viña Porta was taken over and integrated with Viña Gracia. Vinification of all the wines takes place in the hamlet of Totihue, where a modern winery has been built. Córpora's ambitions in the wine realm are considerable. Eventually it wants to become the fifth-largest producer in Chile – this in the knowledge that the 1,000 hectares of vineyard it owns could be further enlarged to 5,000.

Land in four valleys

The grapes for Córpora's wines come entirely from the company's own land, which is gradually coming into production. Around the cellar buildings in the Cachapoal valley there are at present 145 hectares, with about 160 in Maipo (in the north of the Aconcagua valley, where the soil is covered with boulders and pebbles), and nearly 120 in the south of the Bío-Bío valley. Córpora is proud of being one of the Bío-Bío pioneers, along with Concha y Toro. So far exclusively Chardonnay and Pinot Noir have been grown here. During the vintage, grapes from the more distant areas are transported entirely by night, to keep them fresh.

Grapes take centre-stage

About 60 per cent of the wine carries the Viña Gracia or Gracia de Chile names; the rest goes out into the world as Viña Porta. The basic wines in the Gracia line are primarily fruity, whereas the Portas are rather more classic in style, with a touch of oak. Taking over Viña Porta was quite logical: its wines complemented Viña Gracia's perfectly. On the Gracia labels only broad indications of origin are given, such as Central Valley and South Valley. With Viña Gracia, the grapes take centre-stage: in each wine the firm tries to reflect to the full the variety used. They succeed with the fresh, mango-like Chardonnay, and even better with the Chardonnay Reserve. In the latter the mango is augmented by passion fruit, generous vanilla and oak. Some of this wine is fermented and stored in casks, and all of it undergoes malolactic fermentation. Still more oak is noticeable in the Select Reserve.

The standard Cabernet Sauvignon is by far the top seller among the Viña Gracia reds. It has charm, a creamy suppleness, and black- and other berry fruit, with nearly always a touch of mint. The Pinot Noir from South Valley (in this case Bío-Bío) is not very deep or full, but shows the red-fruit character of the grape, some fresh acidity, and the merest hint of oak. There is also a Reserve variant of this. The Reserve is the most appealing of the Merlots, a reasonably generous wine with a good measure of black fruit, spices and oak aromas. For the Viña Gracia and Viña Porta ranges, Carmenère, Syrah and Viognier wines are planned.

The terroir concept

Respect for *terroir* – the sum of soil, terrain, climate and grape – is the common denominator for the Viña Porta wines. Their origins are shown as precisely as possible on the labels. The best Chardonnay is the Porta Reserva from Requínoa in the Cachapoal valley. This offers tropical fruit in plenty, sometimes apple and melon too, plus buttery, oaky, toasted fullness. The Pinot Noir Porta Reserva from Bío-Bío is an extremely agreeable red with smoky oak, spicy red fruit, mellow suppleness. The standard Cabernet Sauvignon from the Maipo valley is rich in extract, with a meaty structure, slight spiciness and a good deal of berry fruit. More depth, and in particular more oak, mark the Select Reserve, Special Reserve and Limited Edition versions – the latter only sold after four to five years. The equivalent Merlots, too, are worth discovering, but the standard one, with liquorice, bayleaf, black fruit and a little green pepper also gives pleasure.

For the Viña Porta and Viña Gracia Reserve wines over 600 casks, nearly all French, a quarter of them new each year, are used.

Water tunnel
Creating the vineyard in Aconcagua Valley took tremendous effort; not only thanks to the many stones and boulders, but also because a 5-km tunnel had to be dug to carry water.

Picked by hand
All grapes for the Reservas are picked by hand, and there is no mechanical harvesting at all in Bío-Bío.

Majestic mountains fill the horizon around the Corpora Winery's vineyards.

VIÑA COUSIÑO-MACUL

Cousiño-Macul

Facts and figures
▶ Cousiño family
▶ 1856
▶ At present 550 ha
(of which 250 ha are
in Macul)
▶ 250,000 cases
▶ Avenida Quinlín
7100, Peñalolén,
Santiago
▶ Tel: (56-2) 284 1011
▶ Fax: (56-2) 2841 509
▶ E-mail:
expcousi@ia.cl

That all or part of the original Cousiño-Macul vineyard is going to disappear is certain; the only question is when. This 250-hectare estate, where grapes have been grown since the mid-16th century, once lay within the boundaries of the peaceful village of Macul, south-east of the capital. Today, however, the site is increasingly becoming hemmed in by residential developments – and simultaneously this encroaching urbanization has pushed up the price of land to astronomic levels.

It also poses a threat to the water supply. By the early 1990s this was already such a problem that Cousiño-Macul had to spend eight months boring holes before at last finding a spring at a depth of 150 metres. But now the Cousiño family, the estate's owners since it was founded in 1856, are planning to leave the old vineyard: so much is apparent from their purchase of 300 hectares in Buin. A large part of this new estate had in fact been planted by 1996, and the building of a new *bodega* there was already under consideration.

Bulwark of tradition

For many producers such a move might have seemed quite logical – but not for Cousiño-Macul. If there is one thing this firm cherishes it is tradition, and it has done so through succeeding generations. Until about 1990 it was still using the same large American maturation casks that had been installed in the 19th century: this can be seen as entirely typical. It was only in the course of the following decade that these were replaced by 3,200 of the smaller *barricas*. And although the last decades of the 20th century have brought investment in, for example, new stainless steel tanks for fermentation, many wooden and concrete vats – for fermenting and storing respectively – are still to be seen in the buildings here. A walk through the site, surrounded by shady trees,

Cousiño-Macul's best wines are aged in this impressive barrel cellar, 300 metres long, which dates from 1872.

Strong wines with a good body and tannin in their youth
~ one of the winemakers on Cousiño-Macul reds

In the Cousiño family's private cellar the vintages date back to 1927.

brings the visitor to one of the finest wine cellars in Chile: a vaulted space 300 metres long, with brick entrances. Built in 1872, it lies six metres below ground and has an ingenious ventilation system whereby the temperature varies by no more than one degree throughout the year. The family's own wine collection is kept in an area behind this cellar, with bottles going back to at least 1927.

Classic style

This feeling for tradition is reflected in the character of the Cousiño-Macul reds – classic in style, without the prominent fruit that marks most other Chilean wines. In the whites, too, the fruit is seldom obtrusive. The standard Chardonnay is a smooth, rounded wine with a modest amount of mango in its aroma, while the Chardonnay Antiguas Reservas are dominated by spices, with some underlying toast and tropical fruit. Sixty per cent of the Antiguas Reservas is fermented in casks (mainly American; a third of them new), then aged for a year in wood; half undergoes malolactic fermentation.

Right hand

The word Macul comes from the Inca language and means 'right hand'. It is a reference to a fortification from which the representatives of the emperor – his right-hand men – exercised authority and collected taxes.

Wine in reserve

Cousiño-Macul has on average 1.2 million bottles in its cellar.

Cellar visits

The Cousiño family home and its surrounding park are not open to the public, but the cellars can be visited: an average of 40 to 50 visitors a day do so. Wine can be bought in the shop and tasting-room. An old coach makes a focal point.

The best wines

• Chardonnay Antiguas Reservas
• Cabernet Sauvignon Antiguas Reservas
• Finis Terrae

The denominación de origen of these wines is Valle del Maipo.

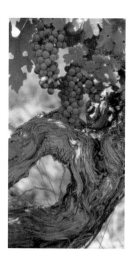

Some people wax lyrical about the red wines; others are critical. They are made in a style that either appeals greatly, or not at all. Essentially the Cabernet Sauvignon comes from vines at least 30 years old, and goes into casks for a year; of these 70 per cent are of American oak, 30 per cent French. This wine generally has a supple, smooth and juicy taste with berry, spice and mint notes.

A 'secret' blend of Cabernet Sauvignon and Merlot forms the basis of Finis Terrae, a wine in the range since 1992. Oak is apt to be strongly, and often predominantly, present, along with restrained acidity, herbs and spices such as bayleaf and aniseed, and a modest measure of fruit. This is Cousiño-Macul's top red wine, and it is given a year in barrels of French wood, a third of them new. There is one Merlot in the range, a wine described as 'a type of Reserva' as it goes into American casks to mature for a year. It has a distinctive, dark-toned taste that has fruit only in the background, and in which spicy oak notes are to the fore.

European influences

There's a lot of history behind these wines. The family that makes them owns a splendid 45-hectare park alongside the old cellar buildings. Some 150 species of trees grow here, from all corners of the world. These were collected by the founder of Cousiño-Macul, Matias Cousiño, a wealthy entrepreneur whose interests included his own merchant fleet. His son, Luis Cousiño, extended this trading empire further, partly through his marriage with Isidora Goyenechea. They owned copper, silver and coal mines, Chile's first power station, a brewery and other enterprises, and contributed to the building of the country's first railway line.

At first the vineyard at Macul was planted with the humble País grape, but Luis changed this. In 1860 he travelled to Europe, where he bought young vines of superior classic varieties such as Cabernet Sauvignon, Merlot, Pinot Noir, Sauvignon Blanc, Sémillon and Riesling. The País vines were uprooted and replaced by the European varieties.

In 1870, on Luis Cousiño's initiative, French architects began the now historic cellar. Luis himself died unexpectedly in 1873, but under his widow Isidora, the cellar was completed by 1875. Later Isidora, who survived her husband by nearly 25 years, was to engage a Frenchman as winemaker.

Despite inheritance divisions (Isidora had six children) the estate stayed intact. Day-to-day management now rests with the sixth generation, the three sons of chairman Carlos Cousiño. The decisions they have to make are at least as important and far-reaching as those of their 19th-century forebears.

VITIVINÍCOLA CREMASCHI BARRIGA

Cremaschi Furlotti

At the end of 1998 Cremaschi Barriga looked as if a large bomb had struck it: sections of stainless-steel fermentation tanks lay scattered in and around the winery, along with wooden vat staves, heaps of sand, the remains of walls. Like many Chilean producers, this firm was in the throes of renovations and extensions ready for the coming harvest. The winery can now hold 2.5 million litres in stainless-steel tanks, and a further 1.5 million in traditional rauli vats. Some of these needed complete dismantling before they were fit

Gravel and pebbles spell good vineyard soil.

Facts and figures
▶ Cremaschi family
▶ 1978
▶ 100 ha
▶ 25,000 cases plus bulk wine
▶ Estado 359, Piso 4, Santiago
▶ Tel: (56-2) 633 0776
▶ Fax: (56-2) 632 7346

The best wines
• Chardonnay, Maule Valley
• Cabernet Sauvignon, Maule Valley
• Cabernet Sauvignon Ultra Premium, Maule Valley

In the vineyard
In order of importance quality grapes here are Cabernet Sauvignon, Chardonnay, Merlot and Sauvignon Blanc. The Cremaschi family also grows Muscatel grapes, but the entire yield from these is sold and so not processed here.

Long maceration
In the Cabernet Sauvignon and the Merlot, the grapeskins are left to macerate after fermentation to gain the greatest possible extraction.

for use – which led director Christian Cremaschi to remark that it would have been cheaper to replace these 'low-tech' items with stainless steel.

Now, though, the rejuvenated Cremaschi Barriga has excess capacity and makes wine for other producers. Its 100 hectares of vineyards, which lie close to the cellars, not far from San Javier in the Maule region, supply all the grapes for its own wines.

The Cremaschi family arrived by a roundabout route. When Christian's great-grandfather set off in 1890 for 'America' as a 19-year-old, he landed in Argentina. There he became a wine consultant, and later a winegrower.

Above: carefully-restored old vats of rauli wood are in use alongside modern stainless steel..

Right: director Christian Cremaschi, an oenologist schooled in Bordeaux and California.

Since 1940 the Cremaschis have lived and worked in Chile, although a branch of the family, the Furlottis, still have a 3,000-hectare wine estate in Argentina. In the mid-1960s the Argentinian and Chilean possessions were officially separated, although the family ties still continue.

A modest range

Christian Cremaschi, an oenologist who was trained in both Bordeaux and California, regards working in an environmentally-friendly way as important. That is why, for example, by-products from the winery such as grape-seeds, -stalks and -skins are ground up and returned to the stony vineyard. The range of wines includes only five varieties, with a Sauvignon Blanc as the most recent addition, from the 1999 vintage. The Chardonnay offers fresh citrus fruit and apple notes, combined with vanilla and smoky oak. Its fermentation usually lasts about three weeks, as this is carried out at only 13–15°C. The oak elements come from French staves.

The dark-red Cabernet Sauvignon tastes firm but not too heavy, with blackcurrant and other berry fruit, plus a hint of vanilla, adding the finishing touches. A quarter of it has oak contact via casks and staves.

The Merlot receives practically no wood, and along with its elegant strength it sometimes has more herbaceous than fruit elements.

Cremaschi Barriga's highest-quality red, however, is the Cabernet Sauvignon Ultra Premium. Created from 90 per cent Cabernet Sauvignon, plus equal parts of Merlot and Carmenère, half is matured in French oak barrels (half of them new). Berries and black fruit, smoky notes of oak and toast, touches of green pepper and bayleaf marked the first vintage, the 1997. Production started with 25,000 bottles.

COOPERATIVA AGRÍCOLA VITIVINÍCOLA DE CURICÓ
Los Robles, F.J. Correa Errázuriz

The increasing demand for quality wines and the rise of private wine producers have brought challenges for the Curicó cooperative – investment and education are its response. Some 60 years after the winery was established in 1939, only just over a half of its available storage capacity is in use: 10 million out of 19 million litres. Relatively speaking, not much wine is being exported – less than 50 per cent of the production. A considerable part of the turnover comes from simple wines in Tetra-paks and five-litre bottles for the home market.

The picture is not entirely grief and woe, however: after analysing the situation, the 60 or so remaining members and their management decided on a change of course – towards quality. By 1998, about $2 million had been invested in pneumatic presses, stainless-steel tanks and up-to-the-minute equipment. A fine cask cellar has been built, smelling strongly of vanilla from the American and French oak used. And new and better wines have been developed. The *cooperativa* now has the technology well under control – this is clear, since it is now bottling house wines for Sainsbury's: this major UK supermarket chain has very stringent requirements.

Facts and figures
▶ About 60 wine-growers
▶ 1939
▶ 800 ha
▶ 665,000 cases (80 per cent in bottle or Tetra-pak)
▶ Balmaceda 565, Curicó
▶ Tel: (56-75) 310 047
▶ Fax:(56-75) 310 345
▶ E-mail: robles@chilevinos.cl

Quality bonus
What is also striking is that the *cooperativa* members are planting again, so production is increasing. Necessary further education is laid on: there are now meetings every three months at which the growers are given information on such subjects as irrigation, use of pesticides and canopy management. Incentives have been put in place to encourage the delivery of really good, sound grapes: anyone bringing in fruit that is judged to be of superior quality receives a 10 per cent bonus. Average-standard

Curicó's busy market draws people from the countryside around.

Left: the cellar complex. Below: stately palm trees surround Curicó's central square.

grapes attract average rates, and the cooperative now even imposes a 10 per cent fine for grapes of poorer quality. Grapes arrive in 400-kg bins and are tipped onto a conveyor belt, where a last inspection is painstakingly carried out by hand. Well motivated, with a new dynamism and great self-confidence, the Curicó wine cooperative has prepared itself for the 21st century.

Two-variety wines

Besides the wines from single varieties, the cooperative also makes wines blended from two grape varieties, most of them especially for the British market. The Cabernet Sauvignon/ Merlot is an example.

The best wines

• Sauvignon Vert Los Robles Reserva Privada
• Chardonnay Los Robles Gran Roble
• Cabernet Sauvignon Los Robles Reserve

Weighty grapes

The Curicó cooperative can handle a total of 200,000 tons a day. Most of the grapes – nearly two-thirds – are black.

Sauvignon Vert

The self-confidence also shows in the rather daring launch of the Sauvignon Vert, in the Los Robles Reserva Privada range. Behind this name lurks the much-maligned Sauvignonasse, a variant of Sauvignon Blanc regarded as inferior and somewhat rustic. Curicó has managed to make a surprisingly pleasing wine from Sauvignonasse

grapes, using slow, cool fermentation and oak chips. The Sauvignon Vert has a juicy, fresh taste, with a modest dash of citrus and just a little vanilla. A contrasting wine is the Gran Roble, one of the best Chardonnays. This is quite firm and reasonably fruity – including mango notes – and has spicy wood with toast: one-fifth of the wine goes into used casks for four months.

A top red

At the top among the red wines is the Los Robles Cabernet Sauvignon Reserve, released only after two years in cask and one in bottle. This is distinguished by an almost opulent taste with a good amount of toast, ripe berry fruit and supple texture. The fairly extensive range also includes a Gran Roble Cabernet Sauvignon, a correct wine made with the help of American oak chips. Chips are also used in fermenting the comparatively prestigious brand F.J. Correa Errázuriz. Bought by the cooperative in around 1990, this comes from a winery founded in 1875.

VIÑA ECHEVERRÍA

Echeverría, Casa Nueva

When the owner Roberto Echeverría is at home, a visit to his winery is more like a lecture than a guided tour. This erudite oenologist, who also holds a degree in economics, has a phenomenal knowledge of all aspects of winegrowing, and is happy to pass this on. He is, moreover, a man of vision: in the mid-1970s, when half of all Chilean vines had been dug up, Echeverría foresaw a great future for fine wine. But, as he himself put it, to make world-class wines you need first-class grapes. This meant that the vineyard here had to be reorganized, since the various grape varieties were intermingled. They were picked together and vinified together.

Roberto began by selecting the best possible clones of Cabernet Sauvignon, Merlot, Chardonnay and Sauvignon Blanc. Next he took great care in choosing the best possible system of planting: thus some of the vines were trained over wires in a V-shape, with the aim of giving them as much sun and air as possible. He then decided not to manure the vines, but just to apply a compost based on grapeskins, seeds and stalks. Irrigation was to be strictly limited to 'what the plant needs'; spraying was carried out as little as possible. By these methods an 80-hectare model wine estate came into being. Echeverría's only regret is 'that I have concentrated just on these four well-known varieties'.

❝ We put a lot of love into our wines ❞
~ *Roberto Echeverría*

Facts and figures
▶ Roberto Echeverría
▶ Beginning of the 20th century
▶ 80 ha
▶ 100,000 cases
▶ Avenida A. Vespuccio Norte 568, Depto. 701, Las Condes, Santiago
▶ Tel: (56-2) 207 4327
▶ Fax: (56-2) 207 4328
▶ E-mail: echewine@entelchile.net

 The best wines
• Sauvignon Blanc
• Unoaked Chardonnay
• Chardonnay Reserva
• Late Harvest
• Cabernet Sauvignon
• Cabernet Sauvignon Reserva
• Cabernet Sauvignon Family Reserve
• Merlot Reserva

The labels give Molina as the district of origin.

Towers and purple panelling make the winery stand out.

Young wine is transferred from the fermentation tanks to the casks in which it will mature.

Wide-ranging interests

Roberto Echeverría has been an economist at the World Bank. As well as his own wine interests, he was also the founder of Chilevid, a league of smaller, export-oriented wine producers. He was also made president of the Corporación Chileno del Vino, a body aimed at raising the technological standards of the Chilean wine industry.

Tradition and modernity

The original vineyard was laid out by Echeverría's maternal grandfather, who also built the first cellar – part of which is still in use. Roberto likes the effects of wood, and so ferments red wines in the traditional rauli vats, 'because in these the wines get plenty of extract'. Alongside and above the remaining part of the original cellar a modern structure has gone up, with stainless steel tanks, a cooling system, pneumatic presses and a bottling line: since 1992 Viña Echeverría has been bottling its own wine. The brick-towered buildings have purple panelling on the outside; tradition and modernity go hand-in-hand in this establishment.

Total control is exercised throughout the whole winemaking process, from grape to bottle. This starts in the vineyard, where analyses are carried out during the harvest, and where Roberto and his son Roberto Ignacio make frequent tests of the grapes, grading them according to degree of sweetness and acidity. Picking is by hand and, since Roberto regards a grape as a 'bag of enzymes', the fruit is delivered as intact as possible. Then a further check is carried out – again by hand – on the conveyor belt, before the actual preparation begins. Each wine is given its own particular treatment. Even bottling is a painstaking process. This shows in the way the bottles are scrutinized before filling (quite a number are rejected), by the hand-labelling, and by the time allowed for the cork to expand in the neck: eight minutes – twice the usual time.

Liquid fruit

What all the effort has led to is revealed at tastings of the wine, and for this the grounds or the dining-room of the large house beside the cellar are used. The wines are full-fruited, clean, beautifully balanced. The standard Cabernet Sauvignon makes its name with a good, solid colour and an amazing fruitiness. It is just like drinking liquid fruit – a bunch of fresh grapes in the glass. This wine spends no time in wood, but the Cabernet Sauvignon Reserva is given four months in vat, then eight in *barricas*. It is a very well-balanced wine, with vanilla, chocolate, spices and toast besides plenty of fruit, and good tannin into the bargain. Even greater depth is offered by the rare Cabernet Sauvignon Family Reserve – just 300 cases of this: an excellent wine with berry, blackberry, plum and other fruit, nicely set in oak from its two years in French casks. The Merlot Reserva is an exceptionally engaging wine, not only fully endowed with fruit, but also with bayleaf, liquorice, leather and oak from four months in vats, ten months in barrels. Viña Echeverría has planted relatively little Merlot, and so these grapes have to be bought in each year. This wine generally sells out fast.

Distinctive whites

The same distinction is found in the white wines as in the red. The Sauvignon Blanc is a quite full-bodied wine: rounded, with a freshness and a pleasing dose of fruit – gooseberry, citrus and tropical. The range also has a Sauvignon Blanc Reserva, a fairly soft wine (with four grams of residual sugar), fermented in cask. The Echeverrías first made this in 1997, especially for the Japanese market.

The Unoaked Chardonnay treats you to passion fruit and mango: this, too, is a wine with a sound balance. Toast, tropical fruit and balanced acidity characterize the delicious Chardonnay Reserva, a wine fermented and aged in American and French oak casks for six months. Opinion is split about the Chardonnay Family Reserve: 'some people adore it, others hate it', says Roberto Echeverría. After fermentation in casks and a year in vats, this has considerably more oak.

Finally, there is the Late Harvest, which is a Sauvignon Blanc. This Roberto makes from grapes with 'noble rot': he dictates precisely which ones should be picked, and when –

sometimes in three phases. The '97 was so sweet that its fermentation lasted nearly a year. This golden, concentrated wine is in no way inferior to a German or Austrian Trockenbeerenauslese: raisins, honey, apricot and other nuances make each drop of Echeverría's Late Harvest a delight.

Spanish Basques
The Echeverría family came originally from the Spanish Basque country. They moved to Chile after having first lived in Seville.

Viña La Estancia
The property where Viña Echeverría is situated is officially called Viña La Estancia. This estate was originally much bigger, and in Molina it took in all the land which Viña San Pedro now owns there. The attractive, many-roomed hacienda where Roberto and his wife live is about two hundred years old.

The erudite proprietor Roberto Echeverría.

Viña Luis Felipe Edwards

Luis Felipe Edwards, Edwards Ridge

Facts and figures
▶ Luis Felipe Edwards
▶ 1950
▶ 300 ha
▶ 250,000 cases
(and still rising)
▶ Avenida Vitacura
4130, Santiago
▶ Tel: (56-2) 208 6919
▶ Fax: (56-2) 208 7775

 The best wines
• Chardonnay
• Cabernet Sauvignon
• Cabernet Sauvignon Reserva
• Cabernet Sauvignon Bodega Privada
• Carmenère

Colchagua appears on the labels as the district of origin.

With its ochre walls, its delightful terrace, its comfortable rooms and its splendid park Casa Edwards, not far from Nancagua, is a place where the Edwards family likes to gather. Compared with busy Santiago a salutary peace prevails here, and both parents and children (there are seven) enjoy the fresh vegetables that grace the table, most of them from the adjoining kitchen garden. Since the mid-1990s business contacts have also been entertained here since, as from the 1994 vintage, the family has been bottling its wine. In that same year the cellar buildings, within walking distance of the house, were modernized.

The name of the business comes from Luis Felipe Edwards, the man who established it in 1950 and built it up. He is a descendant of George Edwards, who arrived in the north Chilean port of La Serena from London a century and a half ago, and whose marriage is commemorated in the local cathedral.

Two vineyards

Luis Edwards bought the house, and 250 hectares with it, in 1976. The estate, which bears the name Fundo San José de Puquillay, is enclosed by hills on three sides. It lies a few kilometres south-east of Nancagua, in the Tinguiririca valley. Vines grow here not just on the level ground but also up the hillsides; sometimes on specially laid out terraces. At the same time as he acquired the Puquillay estate, Edwards also bought the Fundo Barnadita de Pupilla, some 20 kilometres further west, and therefore closer still to the ocean. Here the terrain is hillier, and grapes have been grown since the 18th century. Not long after the millennium Luis Felipe, assisted by his sister Patricia, will be running 300 productive hectares; this is why the capacity of the winery has been increased from two to four million litres. Stainless steel only was the choice for the vats in this extension, but in the old cellar there are many concrete ones lined with synthetic resin. Some 800 casks are used for maturing the wine, half of them of French oak, half of American.

A striking Carmenère

The only white wine produced so far is a Chardonnay. It is a worthy representative of the variety, having a firm, smoothly rounded taste, good fruit – tropical, some citrus, a little banana – and a somewhat flinty

The Casa Edwards, with its verandah and ochre walls, stands amid a pretty park.

freshness, with no oak and no malolactic fermentation. The Carmenère is the most striking of the reds. This has a deep colour, the slightly herbaceous bouquet characteristic of the grape variety, and a taste in which the nuances include prune, chocolate and coffee, together with a dash of oak and vanilla. It is, too, a wine with vitality, and with smooth, ripe tannins. Half of it goes into new French oak barrels for six months.

A quartet of Cabernets

The other reds from Viña Luis Felipe Edwards are Cabernets, of which the simplest version is labelled Pupilla. This comes from relatively young vines, has no contact with wood and has a taste in which fresh berry is combined with prune. More substance, more fruit and more concentration is offered by the lively standard Cabernet Sauvignon, produced from vines that are at least 15 years old. Sometimes this attractive, supple wine has a hint of tobacco.

The first of the cask-matured Cabernet Sauvignons is the Reserva: 70 per cent of it goes into *barricas*, more than half of them new, for ageing for two years. Black fruit, berry, smoky oak, toast and vanilla are the main impressions made by this succulent, vital, mouthfilling wine.

The top Cabernet Sauvignon is the Bodega Privada, which with its intensity, substance and breadth surpasses the Reserva. It comes from old vines growing in hillside vineyards, and after a year in new barrels it has a further year's maturing in bottle. The sumptuous fruit in this fine wine is amply framed by toast and other aspects of oak.

Memorable moments

After an apéritif on the terrace, a fruity Chardonnay Luis Felipe Edwards was served in the dining room with fresh green asparagus and home-made mayonnaise. The tender spears and the creamy mayonnaise combined wonderfully well with the juicy Chardonnay.

Restricted yields

Maintaining quality is Luis Felipe Edwards' first principle. He has absolutely forbidden the harvesting of more than 10 tons (about 70 hectolitres) per hectare in his vineyards.

Monogram

The monogram on the wine labels comes from a pair of cuff links worn by Luis Felipe's grandfather: Luis's sister Patricia rediscovered them.

Viña Errázuriz
Errázuriz

Facts and figures
▶ The Chadwick family
▶ 1870
▶ 375 ha
▶ 350,000 cases
▶ Avenida Nueva
Tajamar 481, Torte Sur,
Of. 503, Las Condes,
Santiago
▶ Tel: (56-2) 203 6688
▶ Fax: (56-2) 203 6690
▶ E-mail: errazuriz.cl

Nearly all the wealthy Chileans who created wine estates in the second half of the 19th century chose the area south of Santiago. Maximiano Errázuriz, however, bought land in the north, near Panquehue, a hamlet not far from San Felipe. Here in the Aconcagua valley he planted the best possible vines from France, and built a winery with a large underground cellar on the French model. The year was 1870, and great scepticism over this new venture was voiced in wealthy Chilean circles. But Maximiano's contrary choice of location proved to be excellent for winegrowing. The firm, called Viña Errázuriz Panquehue until late in the 20th century, flourished like few others. Under his son Rafael, it grew to around 700 hectares – at that time the world's biggest single vineyard owned by one person. After passing through other hands, the estate was bought in 1983 by Alfonso Chadwick, whose mother was an Errázuriz. And so it returned to the family who founded it.

The Errázuriz winery stands beside its vineyards in the Aconcagua Valley.

A timeless picture

If you drive 100 kilometres north from the capital and arrive in Panquehue, first impressions are of a timeless corner. Just before the railway stands a weathered board with the words 'Viña Errázuriz 4 km', and you then come to a quiet road, frequented only by cyclists and flanked by flower nurseries. Some low-built, simple dwellings stand near Viña Errázuriz; the road becomes an unsurfaced lane, and a few men in wide-brimmed hats stand talking at a corner.

The wrought-iron entrance to Errázuriz is large and impressive, with a monogram over the gate. To the right you see a slope covered with vines, ahead a flatter vineyard with garden in front, brown-grey hills beyond, and to the left the white buildings of the winery. This view can hardly have changed in a century. The visitor who descends the wide stone steps to the cellar with its ranks of casks will be caught in the atmosphere of times past. But then comes the contrast: an ultra-modern vinification hall where most of the red wines, plus Chardonnay from Casablanca, are made. Through just one door, and the visitor passes from the 19th to the 21st century. This is the Errázuriz of today, a very up-to-date business on a solid foundation of traditional values.

Almost fanatical

There is respect for nature at Errázuriz. If the winemakers strive for one thing above all, then it is the expression of *terroir*, that unique combination of soil type, microclimate and grape variety. In a way that is almost fanatical the grapes are therefore not only picked and vinified separately according to vineyard, but also by plot. 'I want to show the fruit as it is', states Edward Flaherty, the chief winemaker. He puts the best reds into many small barrels to complete their malolactic fermentation, rather than into a few large tanks. The individuality of these small batches gives him the widest range of elements for the *assemblage*.

Viña Errázuriz gets around 85 per cent of the grapes it needs from its own or leased vineyards. These are spread over four estates. The Don Maximiano estate is the flagship and consists of four plots ('Max 1',

The oldest part of the cellars dates back to 1870 – and from the outside it seems little changed.

The best wines

- Sauvignon Blanc, La Escultura estate, Casablanca Valley
- Chardonnay Reserva, La Escultura estate, Casablanca Valley
- Chardonnay Wild Ferment, La Escultura estate, Casablanca Valley
- Cabernet Sauvignon, El Ceibo estate, Aconcagua Valley
- Cabernet Sauvignon Reserva, Don Maximiano estate, Aconcagua Valley
- Don Maximiano Founder's Reserve, Don Maximiano estate, Aconcagua Valley
- Merlot, El Descanso estate, Curicó Valley
- Merlot Reserva, Don Maximiano estate, Aconcagua Valley
- Syrah Reserva, Don Maximiano estate, Aconcagua Valley

An eventful life

Maximiano Errázuriz was born in Santiago in 1832. He married Amalia, daughter of Chile's richest man. With his father-in-law he started a copper mine that at one time produced a third of the world's copper. Amalia died in 1861, and Maximiano travelled to Europe to assuage his grief. His discovery of the great French wines led him to plant 300 hectares of vines at Panquehue. He re-married – but sadly his second wife soon died of yellow fever. At 48, Maximiano withdrew from public life – he had been very active politically. He led a sober, devout life, helping the poor, until his death ten years later. The Errázuriz family, one of Chile's most prominent, arrived from the Basque country in 1735. They have given the country four presidents, two archbishops, various politicians, writers and industrialists.

'Max 2', and so on) in the Aconcagua valley, near the original cellar; it covers 70 hectares. The El Ceibo estate, a low-lying vineyard of 50 hectares, is in the same river valley, along with a further 20 leased hectares. Errázuriz has developed the 70-hectare La Escultura estate in the cool Casablanca valley for all its Chardonnays and some of its Sauvignon Blancs. Finally there is the El Descanso estate in the Valle de Curicó, further to the south.

Wines from the individual estates are marketed as such. The only name not to appear on the labels is that of the relatively small wine estate of just 25 hectares in Maipo. In all the Errázuriz vineyards, painstaking attention is paid to canopy management – 'we train all our pruners to examine each plant carefully' – and to limiting the yield of fruit per vine.

Opposite: pretty gardens surround the winery.

Elegance, aroma

Around three-quarters of the harvest consists of black varieties. The majority of these are destined for the Reservas. The standard Cabernet Sauvignon, from the El Ceibo estate, is a wine with both elegance and aroma. Its fruit is black-currant and red cherry, and it often has just a small proportion of Syrah. The Cabernet Sauvignon Reserva comes from the Don Maximiano estate and is richer, fuller, with plenty of black fruit and generous oak. The top Cabernet, though, is the Don Maximiano Founder's Reserve: this spends 16–18 months in French casks, about a third of which are new. Some Cabernet Franc (around 15 per cent) is generally included in the blend. This deep-red wine tastes spicier than the Reserva, boasting generous doses of dark berry fruit and oak, with often some mint, notes of coffee and chocolate, creamy vanilla – and marvellous concentration.

A special Syrah

Grapes from Curicó, from the El Descanso estate, are used for the basic Merlot, which usually contains nearly 20 per cent Cabernet Sauvignon to give the wine a little more structure and acidity. This aromatic wine combines a slightly herbacaeous quality with black fruit and notes of coffee, chocolate and bayleaf. The Merlot Reserva from the Don Maximiano estate also benefits from a little added Cabernet Sauvignon. This is a robust wine, full of character, with a little paprika and soy along with its smoky oak. The ordinary Merlot's only contact with wood is with oak staves, but the Reserva is matured in French barrels for a year. Errázuriz has been producing a Syrah Reserve from the Don Maximiano estate since 1996: this powerful wine also has some Cabernet Sauvignon and spends 10–14 months in casks. It treats the winelover to smooth blackberry and red fruits,

to spices that include pepper and cinnamon, and to leather notes, toast and vanilla.

'Wild' Chardonnay

The best Sauvignon Blanc is one from the La Escultura estate in Casablanca. Grapes for this – which include some Sauvignonasse – are mainly picked at

night, mechanically, and yield a very fruity wine (citrus, gooseberry, peach, melon). The standard Chardonnay from the same estate couples smooth acidity to succulent tropical fruit, a firm core, and subtle elements of wood and toast. A third of it is fermented in cask, and a fifth undergoes malolactic fermentation. The Chardonnay Reserva has still greater distinction, and toast. A wine with refinement, it is also more buttery, more generous. Around 80 per cent of it is fermented in barrels (about one-fifth are new), followed by seven months of maturing in them. The Chardonnay Wild Ferment began as an experiment in 1995. Since then it has developed into the top Chardonnay from Errázuriz. All of it is fermented in casks by means of natural yeasts, and 80 per cent of it undergoes malolactic fermentation, giving it a velvety taste with notes of breadcrust, toast, honeyed fruit and a beautiful balance.

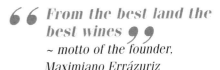

" From the best land the best wines "
~ *motto of the founder, Maximiano Errázuriz*

Viña William Fèvre Chile

La Misión del Clarillo, Don Victor, William Fèvre

It is not unusual to come across newspapers from France in the office at Viña William Fèvre Chile, for the French make the wines here. The eponymous William Fèvre is indeed not only a Frenchman, but the biggest owner of *grand cru* vineyards in Burgundy's Chablis district. He set up his Chilean subsidiary in 1991, together with Victor Pino, who contributed the land. Joseph Henriot, to whom Champagne Henriot and the Burgundy firm of Bouchard Père & Fils also belong, later bought William Fèvre and so he, too, became a joint-owner of the Chilean concern.

The William Fèvre Chile winery dates from 1995 and stands in San Luis de Pirque, beside one of the firm's three vineyards. Ever since it was built the premises have been continuously enlarged. In the short term the aim is to sell 50,000 cases a year, after which a longer-term target of around 80,000 cases has to be reached: 'we will only really be profitable at about a million bottles'.

No concessions

Since William Fèvre makes only white wines in Chablis, obviously that would also be the thrust of the Chile winery. And so it was for the first years, but when the market proved to be more interested in red wines, the emphasis changed accordingly. One result was the adoption of the Australian system of over-grafting: Cabernet Sauvignon on a Chardonnay rootstock, and Pinot Noir on Sauvignon Blanc. At present 70 per cent of production is of red wines. Because of the ties with France, the wines have been created 'in the French style' – which in this case means that finesse is given precedence over strength, and the influence of oak is deliberately limited. Nor are there any concessions made over the taste: none of the wines contain residual sugar, even though certain markets might demand this; and the white wines are given no malolactic fermentation.

Improving Chardonnay

The grapes for the Sauvignon and Chardonnay arrive in 25-kilo boxes. After pressing, the must is left to settle naturally, until it is clear.

Fermentation takes place after this, at 18°C, and lasts for about three weeks. This technique produces a decent Sauvignon Blanc, with a supple roundness, sufficient acidity, some fruit, a touch of herbaceousness. The Chardonnay has become more and more attractive through the 1990s. Since the 1998 vintage it has been given contact with wood, in casks and sometimes through oak chips. It is a restrained, clean wine with some tropical fruit – especially mango – a discreet amount of toast and a slight nutty hint. This wine can mature for three to four years without problem.

A variety of reds

A gradual improvement of quality can also be seen in the red wines since 1998. The current Cabernet Sauvignon has breeding: it is lively, supple and boasts an agreeable amount of fruit, particularly ripe blackcurrant. William Fèvre Chile also produces a Carmenère: this is a thoroughly likeable wine with elements of green pepper, bitter chocolate and black fruit. In addition the range includes a pleasant Pinot Noir: this is usually smooth when still young, and is characterized by red fruit. To give this wine sufficient concentration, 'green' harvesting is used: well before the actual picking, nearly a third of the still-green bunches are removed. Finally there is a Merlot: a sturdy wine with notes of black fruit and chocolate.

Burgundian tanks

Fairly small tanks are used for fermenting the Merlot and Pinot Noir. These make it possible to submerge the skins frequently in the fermenting wine – a system that originated in Burgundy. This gives the wine extra colour and extract.

Below: in the functional cellar complex stand low, wide fermentation tanks designed to boost the amount of extract obtained from varieties such as Pinot Noir and Merlot.

La Fortuna

La Fortuna, Gran Fortuna, Traverso, La Serranía,
Maison Blanche

The broad, tree-lined avenue that leads from a quiet country road in Sagrada Familia to the fruit and wine firm La Fortuna brings you to a courtyard surrounded by low buildings. In its centre stands a curious work of art entitled 'Honor al Trabajo' (Homage to Work). This is made up of bits of agricultural implements, office machinery and other equipment welded together. All were once used here, and they form a permanent reminder of the past. It is the work of Daniel Guëll, who acquired the estate in 1942 and six years later built a new cellar. In the spacious halls where the wine is made – these stand opposite the plant for packing the fruit that La Fortuna grows here – some of the equipment dates back to the firm's beginnings.

Wines are fermented and stored in barrels of rauli wood with a total capacity of 300,000 litres, and also in concrete vats lined with resin. These can hold 800,000 litres. The stainless-steel tanks are more up to date, but their combined capacity is rather less at 200,000 litres. The traditional way in which La Fortuna works is also apparent from the six old hydraulic presses still in use. Director Luis Guëll, Daniel's son, does not keep these presses just for nostalgic reasons, 'but because they work better and quicker than the pneumatic ones'.

For the home market
La Fortuna has been less able than some to invest in modern equipment – and has not wished or needed to – due to its marketing strategy. Until almost the end of the 20th century by far the greater part of the wine produced (some three-quarters of it) was marketed in bulk. And the wines the firm sold in bottle consisted mainly of fairly simple sorts for the home market, including some sparkling and sherry-style ones. In the coming years, however, this situation is going to change drastically. That at least is the plan. Before the year 2005 exports should increase from 35,000 cases a year to 200,000–300,000. The Guëll family hopes to achieve this with the help of Sergio Traverso, a talented Chilean wine-maker who won his spurs in California. Traverso acts as La Fortuna's adviser and frequently visits the firm.

Organic winegrowing

La Fortuna has a total of 700 hectares of land available. Of this, 200 hectares grow fruit and, eventually, 300 hectares will yield wine. This will make the firm self-sufficient in grapes. Part of the vineyard area lies beside, part behind, the winery buildings. Weeds are removed only by plough – sometimes horse-drawn – for La Fortuna believes in using an organic method of winegrowing. Weedkillers and insecticides are taboo, and irrigation is carried out by the traditional flooding method.

Aromatic Malbec

The standard Chardonnay La Fortuna is a pleasant wine with spicy tropical fruit – but it is overshadowed by the Chardonnay Gran Fortuna. This is fermented largely in casks of French oak; its characteristics are an intense mango aroma, a creamy texture and a stylish touch of oak and toast. The Malbec La Fortuna is a speciality among the red wines. It offers plenty of aroma – blackcurrant complemented by black cherry, wild strawberry, leather and spices – and has a generous, smooth, very attractive personality. About half of its grapes come from vines over 40 years old. Malbec also comes in the Gran Fortuna version, but because it matures for at least a year in barrel, the fruit in it becomes dominated by oak.

Show-stealer

The Merlot is as a rule amply provided with juicy black fruit, supplemented by a hint of green pepper. The Merlot Traversa is a special version of this, a lively wine with ripe blackberry as fruit. Its grapes come from a particular plot that yields just 56 hectolitres per hectare.

Of the various permutations of Cabernet Sauvignon it is the Gran Fortuna that steals the show. This is an elegantly firm wine with berry, oak and a hint of toast – it has 12-15 months in cask. The grapes used for it are usually harvested at the low yield of 35 hectolitres per hectare, which explains its good concentration.

Top: director Luis Guëll co-owns this organic estate.

Above: some of the winery buildings at La Fortuna.

Other names, the same wine

The brand name La Serranía is used mainly in Canada; another, Maison Blanche, in Hong Kong. The quality of these wines is the same as the La Fortuna range. Until 1996 the firm of La Fortuna was called Guëll y Borlando, after the families of Daniel Guëll and his wife. A coat-of-arms from this time can be seen in one of the halls, complete with crown.

AGRÍCOLA Y VITIVINÍCOLA ITATA

Carpe Diem, Condor

Facts and figures

▶ Fundación Chile
▶ 1989
▶ 170 ha
▶ 85,000 cases (and increasing) plus bulk
▶ Avenida Parque Antonio Rabat Sur 6165, Vitacura, Santiago
▶ Tel: (56-2) 240 0410
▶ Fax: (56-2) 241 9430

 The best wines
• Chardonnay Reserva
• Cabernet Sauvignon Gran Reserva
• Syrah Reserva

The denominacíon de origen is Valle del Itata.

Immediate success

The firm made its first wines in 1995, and these were an immediate success. Present sales are 65,000 litres of bottled wine, plus 300,000 litres of wine in bulk, both for the Canadian market and for the American concern Las Viñas de la Calina (which see).

The Fundación Chile, an organization financed by the government of Chile and the American ITT corporation, has created more than 30 businesses in Chile. One of these is the only wine producer of any significance in the Valle del Itata area. It was christened Agrícola y Vitivinícola Itata, and its vines were planted at Nueva Aldea, a village near where the Río Nuble flows into the Río Itata. The Spaniards laid out vineyards in and around this location – far to the south in the foothills of the coastal range, about halfway between Chillán and the port and university town of Concepción. In modern times what was left of these vineyards, however, grew mainly simple varieties.

Fundación Chile devoted much time to analysing and evaluating the natural and economic factors in the Itata area, with the help of both Chilean and foreign experts. In 1989 the project was given the green light, and 280 hectares of land were bought. The land was prepared for planting, and drip irrigation was installed. Vines and clones – the best possible of each – were sought in France. This imported plant material was rigorously examined by the Chilean Ministry of Agriculture, and only after it had given its approval did the actual planting begin. This was in 1991; the development of the present vineyard, which covers 170 hectares, took about six years.

The soil in Itata is mostly reddish-brown and sandy, with granite rubble, and is partly of volcanic origin. It also has a lot of blue quartz in places. The southerly location of this wine district gives it a relatively cool climate, which led Fundación Chile to plant the vineyard partly on the lyre system. In this, the upper branches of the vines are trained into a V-form, so that they can absorb the maximum amount of sun.

A first with Syrah

During discussions over what grapes should be planted, the feeling grew that they should not stick just to the usual classics. Less obvious varieties would help the firm to create an image for itself on the market. Studies showed that the Syrah grape had an excellent potential in Itata, and eight hectares were set aside for it. The resulting wine – the first vintage was in 1996, a Syrah Reserva – fully lived up to expectations. It is usually distinguished by an intense colour and an expansive taste, its aroma by red fruit, an earthy note, pepper and some oak together with vanilla: the wine is given three to four months in cask. This was Chile's first Syrah produced as a single-variety wine. Since that first vintage the area growing this grape has been doubled, and the addition of a further five hectares is being considered.

Opaque

The Cabernet Sauvignon Reserva has a good balance between fruit and oak, and plenty of colour. More powerful (usually with more than 14 per cent alcohol), is the Cabernet Sauvignon Gran Reserva. This opaque, substantial wine also possesses plenty of berry fruit, toast and spicy oak. Its cask-ageing is geared to the nature and quality of each vintage: sometimes 80 per cent of the total goes into cask for around 15 months, but it can also happen that the whole lot goes in – then the maturing period depends on the age of the oak. For the 1997 vintage wine in new French *barriques* had eight months, while that in used French and American barrels got a year.

Characteristics of the most interesting white wine, the Chardonnay Reserva, are smoothness of taste with a lot of body, a reasonable degree of fruit (ripe pear, for one), and plenty of toast – a fifth of this wine is fermented in cask, and complete malolactic fermentation usually takes place. Chardonnay grapes ripen so well in Itata that they are generally picked even earlier than in more northerly valleys.

Contracted out
The wines are not made in situ, but at the well-equipped Viña Rucahue (which see) in the Maule area.

Right: Itata's manager Ricardo Poblete.

Below: many vines here are planted in the V-form lyre system to expose them to as much sunlight as possible.

Viña Doña Javiera
Río Claro, Tamarugo, Arlequín

Facts and figures
▶ Francisco Correa
▶ 1992
▶ 80 ha
▶ 22,000 cases (could increase to 100,000)
▶ Fundo San Miguel, El Monte
▶ Tel: (56-2) 818 1470
▶ Fax: (56-2) 818 1815

 The best wines
• Chardonnay
• Chardonnay Reservado
• Cabernet Sauvignon Reservado

Cabernet to the fore
Half of the vines are Cabernet Sauvignon; the Carmenère and Merlot come next. All the grapes are picked by hand and collected in small plastic boxes.

Anyone who takes the road from the village of El Monte, in the west of the Maipo valley, to the Viña Doña Javiera estate will be coming to a place alive with history. Three heroes of Chile's struggle for independence once lived in this *hacienda*, set among flowering plants in a small park: the brothers José, José Miguel and Luis Carrera, along with their exceptional sister, the feisty Javiera. The 250-year-old residence, declared a national monument, has even been depicted on two Chilean banknotes – the five pesos and the 1,000 pesos. After the death of Javiera Carrera at the beginning of the 1870s, the estate was bought by the family of the present owner, Francisco Correa.

Huge investment
Winegrowing is in Francisco's blood – his father and grandfather grew grapes in Molina – and in 1992 he decided to lay out a vineyard in his part of the estate. Within five years 50 out of a possible 80 hectares had been planted. To process the grape harvest a vinification centre had to be built; this was ready in 1996. Inside its totally functional buildings, the equipment includes stainless-steel fermentation tanks from New Zealand: these were specially bought for white wine, and have tops that move up or down according to the volume of must. Thanks to this, contact with oxygen is reduced and the result is a fresher wine. The total investment for a small enterprise has been huge. Or, as Francisco Correa once said with a smile to a group of visitors, 'I've got exactly 500 pesos left in my pocket.'

Agreeably fruity
As the vines were still rather young, the first harvests gave supple, pleasant wines with an agreeable fruitiness, but without much substance or complexity. Wood was first used, on a modest scale, from the 1998 vintage on: this led to the attractive Cabernet Sauvignon Reservado, with plenty of colour and spicy berry fruit; and to the Chardonnay Reservado, a full-bodied wine with fresh citrus fruit and considerable toast. This was fermented in cask – and was by far the best wine Viña Doña Javiera had made so far.

The potential clearly exists here, and seeing the vineyard reinforces this impression. It is all in one piece, partly bordered by poplars, with a

Behind the cellars stands the beautifully-maintained hacienda, which has been declared a national monument.

Brands

Río Claro is the most important brand, although represented by two different labels in circulation. The wines sold as Tamarugo are identical to the Río Claro, and to Arlequín. Bodegas El Monte, Status and Arrayán are brands used in Germany and Holland.

scattering of stones in places – always a good sign – and by afternoon it is often cooled by sea breezes. The growing season for the grapes is lengthened by this drop in temperature, and a richer aroma results.

CASA LAPOSTOLLE
Casa Lapostolle

Facts and figures
▶ Marnier-Lapostolle, with José Rabat
▶ 1994
▶ 300 ha
▶ 180,000 cases (increasing to 200,000)
▶ Benjamin 2935, Of. 801, Las Condes, Santiago
▶ Tel: (56-2) 242 9774
▶ Fax: (56-2) 234 4536
▶ E-mail: lapostol@ctcruena.cl

Stress on French oak
On average 3,600 casks rest in the cool (15°C) cellar at Casa Lapostolle – 90 per cent of them French oak. Every year a quarter of the barrels are replaced by new ones.

Looking to diversify, in 1989 the directors of Marnier-Lapostolle, makers of the famous Grand-Marnier liqueur, commissioned a search for an attractive business in the realm of wine. The mission ended up in Switzerland with Alexandra de Bournet, *née* Marnier-Lapostolle (which name she uses for work). She went on the trail not only in France, where Marnier-Lapostolle already owned the Château de Sancerre, but also in Spain, Portugal and Italy. Repeatedly, however, the price asked was too high, or the required wine quality was just not there.

It was due in part to a meeting with the Bordeaux-based international wine expert Michel Rolland that Alexandra travelled to Chile. There she met José Rabat, who has an excellent wine estate with winery in the Colchagua valley in the Rapel district. From this estate comes the wine for his own Viña Manquehue, very much geared to the Chilean market. In 1994 the Marnier-Lapostolle families agreed that they should acquire a majority share in Colchagua, after which the company name was changed from Viña Manquehue to Casa Lapostolle. Subsequent investments, when added to the purchase price, meant that over $20 million had been committed to the enterprise before the turn of the century.

Vineyards owned and leased
In this way the area of vineyard under the firm's control was greatly extended; by about 2002 Casa Lapostolle will have at its disposal 487 hectares of productive vines. About 300 hectares of this are its own land, with long-term contracts drawn up for the rest. In working with these contracted growers Casa Lapostolle lays down strict conditions. Before they started working with the French, the Chilean growers had been harvesting 12,000–20,000 kilograms per hectare; today, the yields are limited to between 5,000 and 7,500 kilograms. Some of these suppliers under contract have Cabernet and Merlot vines which are 50–80 years old. In all the vineyards picking is carried out by hand only, and the fruit is collected in 12-kilogram boxes.

Mastery of Merlot
Michel Rolland was engaged as adviser. He visits Chile four times a year, often with Alexandra Marnier-Lapostolle. Just before the harvest he sets the date for picking to start, and he is involved in the vinification, the

Alexandra Marnier-Lapostolle and wine consultant Michel Rolland. The house, right, belongs to co-owner José Rabat.

composition of the wines, the purchase of the cellar equip-ment including the types of cask. Rolland has his own châteaux in Pomerol, Saint-Emilion and elsewhere, and began his winemaking career in these Bordeaux dis-tricts. Merlot is the predominant grape there, and Rolland has made it his speciality. Since Merlot is also probably the most successful grape in the Valle de Colchagua, it is hardly surprising that Lapostolle should produce some masterly Merlots. The Merlot Cuvée Alexandre is dense in colour, with an unbelievable amount of extract – a knock-out, with ripe black fruit, ample oak from 14 months in American casks, and an aroma that includes chocolate. This is Merlot in all its glory: a wine which has the generosity of a Pomerol, enriched by the strength of the Chilean sun. The standard Merlot, too, is a delightful wine. Its nuanced and charming taste holds copious amounts of black fruit set in toast and oak – half of this goes into barrel.

A super-premium version of Merlot was launched in 1999: the Clos Apelta is a magnificent, concentrated wine that almost stuns the senses with its fruit, its oak and its power.

Sundrenched intensity

There is also a Cuvée Alexandre made from Cabernet Sauvignon. This comes from very old, un-irrigated vines and goes into French *barriques* for a year. It has great intensity of colour and taste, and it often has even more alcohol than the Merlots – 13.7 per cent, for example. Sun-drenched blackberry, cedarwood, spices and toast are among the nuances of this noble, usually mellow, wine.

 The best wines
• Sauvignon Blanc, Rapel Valley
• Chardonnay, Casablanca Valley
• Chardonnay Cuvée Alexandre, Casablanca Valley
• Cabernet Sauvignon, Rapel Valley
• Cabernet Causignon Cuvée Alexandre, Rapel Valley
• Merlot, Rapel Valley
• Merlot Cuvée Alexandre, Rapel Valley
• Merlot Clos Apalta, Rapel Valley

Marnier-Lapostolle

The Marnier-Lapostolle family have been producing distilled drinks for six generations. In the year 1827 Jean-Baptiste Lapostolle founded the firm, beginning by making fine liqueurs on the outskirts of Paris. It was his son, Eugène, who moved the business down to the Cognac area, and it was there that Eugène's son-in-law, Alexandre Marnier, created the world-famous Grand Marnier liqueur, which blends Cognac with orange. The Marnier-Lapostolle family are not newcomers to winemaking, however: the first wine estate that they bought, back in 1919, was the Château de Sancerre, which lies in the centre of the famous Loire village.

Near the winery is the Apalta estate, the largest of the firm's vineyards. Merlot and other black-grape varieties do well here.

The standard Cabernet Sauvignon is apt to be full of blackcurrant, supplemented by spices, generous vanilla and some toast – half of it has eight months' ageing in barrel. It is a wine with substance, although it has less alcohol, and is less full, than the Cuvée Alexandre.

White wines from Casablanca

Some 80 per cent of all the white grapes Casa Lapostolle processes come from the Casablanca valley. The firm has 70 hectares of vineyard here. The Sauvignon Blanc and the Chardonnay both spend six to eight hours macerating before the grapeskins are removed and fermentation begins, to give their juice some extra aroma.

The fermentation of the Sauvignon Blanc takes place in stainless-steel tanks. Half of the Chardonnay remains in tanks until bottling, with the rest going into cask and receiving a maturation period of five months.

The Chardonnay Cuvée Alexandre, by contrast, is entirely fermented in barrels, and then spends a year maturing in them. The *barricas* used for this wine are a mixture of new ones and one-year-olds.

The Sauvignon Blanc is full rather than crisp, with a wealth of fruit – gooseberry, melon, tropical – and a dash of spice. The standard Chardonnay is highly aromatic, and striking in its generous, exotic fruit, with toast and vanilla to provide the finishing touches, while the Chardonnay Cuvée Alexandre is a fuller and firmer wine, with toast and nuts more in evidence at first than is the tropical fruit.

Grapes from three areas

The vineyards that provide Casa Lapostolle's grapes are spread over three locations. By far the biggest area, lying close to the winery, is the 240-plus hectares Apalta estate. The level ground here is not irrigated as the subsoil holds sufficient water; drip irrigation is used only for vines on the slopes. José Rabat, joint-owner with 49% of the Casa Lapostolle shares, owns a large house close by, set in a park. Alexandre Marnier-Lapostolle,

> ❝ *Our aim has always been, and will always remain, to produce the best wines Chile can offer* ❞
> ~ *Alexandra Marnier-Lapostolle*

plus consultant winemaker Michel Rolland and other Lapostolle guests, stay here, as do José Rabat and his family. The other Casa Lapostolle vineyards are near Requínoa – which, like Apalta in the Valle de Colchagua, is in the Rapel district – and in the Casablanca valley.

Most vines on the 240-hectare Apalta estate are grown without irrigation.

Environmentally friendly

Since the beginning of 1997 Casa Lapostolle has abandoned the plastic strips it had been using for tying back vine branches, reverting instead to bio-degradable vegetable fibres.

Viña de Larose
Las Casas del Toqui, Viña Anita, Viña Alamosa

Around 1930, the Granella family owned thousands of hectares in and around Totihué, a hamlet between Requínoa and Rengo in the Rapel area, but this vast estate was eroded by inheritance settlements and land reforms. The Granellas did, though, keep their home, an 1870s country house complete with tower, standing in a small park of old trees – but the family fortune was further hit by an earthquake which devastated the winery beside the house.

The tide turned in 1994: Juan Granella was approached by Assurances Générales de France (AGF), which already owned Château Larose-Trintaudon in Bordeaux, to develop a new estate. Granella would provide the land and AGF the capital plus management. Agreement was reached, the vineyard area was enlarged to 100 hectares, and new cellar facilities were built. The joint venture was given the name Viña de Larose.

A special Sémillon

The Viña de Larose winery, with its modern equipment, sells 90 per cent of its production abroad and delivers mouthfilling wines of impeccable quality. The standard Chardonnay is made using oak staves, and combines slight oak plus toast with juicy tropical fruit. Plenty of fruit, especially mango, is to be found in the Chardonnay Grande Réserve, a wine deliberately made not too fat or too heavy. The very noticeable aroma of toast is due to eight months in the casks in which it was fermented.

The Sémillon occupies a special place among the white wines. It comes from vines more than 55 years old. In the last stages of ripening, the leaves are removed from around the the bunches so that the grapes get maximum sun. If this does not happen, an exceptionally herbaceous, unpleasant wine is the result. What characterizes Larose's Sémillon is its roundness, mellow acidity, generous citrus notes, spices and a touch of oak with vanilla (from oak staves).

A trio of Cabernets

The most impressive red wine is the Cabernet Sauvignon Réserve Prestige. This is made from selected grapes which are fermented with

Left: next to the winery stands the striking country house still lived in by the Granella family.

Below: about a quarter of the barrels are renewed each year. Both French and American barrels are used.

Identical quality

The wines sold under the three trade names in use are identical in quality. The inspiration for the name of the main brand, Las Casas del Toqui, was drawn from Chilean native culture: a toqui is a supreme chief.

An area in demand

Totihué, where the humidity level in summer reaches only 40–50 per cent, is a much-favoured wine area. Viña Santa Emiliana and Viña San Pedro both have considerable estates here, and Viña Caliterra buys grapes here under contract.

their skins at relatively high temperature levels (around 30°C; sometimes 32°) and then left to macerate – occasionally for as much as 35 days. French *barriques*, half of them new, are used for maturing this wine for about a year. The wine has a lingering finish, and is distinguished by its noble, well-integrated tannins, its solid, berry fruit and smoky, toasty oak.

Another commendable Cabernet Sauvignon here is the Réserve, which spends a year in used French and American oak barrels. The result is a balanced wine with fruit, oak and concentration. In the estate's basic Cabernet Sauvignon, a hint of cloves can sometimes be tasted besides its jammy fruit.

MONTES

Montes, Montes Alpha, Villa Montes

Facts and figures
▶ Pedro Grand, Aurelio Montes, Douglas Murray, Alfredo Vidaurre, with 10% held by the Estrella Americana Mutual Fund
▶ 1988
▶ 220 ha
▶ 280,000 cases
▶ California 2521, Providencia, Santiago
▶ Tel: (56-2) 274 1703
▶ Fax: (56-2) 225 0174
▶ E-mail: dmurray@monteswines.com

Other brands
Montes has created a number of brands specially for the Dutch, and to a lesser degree the British and Irish, markets. In general these wines are identical to those in the Montes range, but sometimes the quality is just a little lower – the Sauvignon Blanc, for example. In alphabetical order these wines are:
• Don Alfredo
• Don Aurelio
• Los Fresnos
• Pedro Grand
• Montanares
• Nogales
• Palomar Estate
• Los Pumas
• Villa Don Carlos

Important visitors to the Montes winery are nearly always taken first to an old vineyard just south of Curicó. 'Because', the visitor is told, 'this is where it all began for us.' At Montes enormous importance is attached to the quality of the grapes, even at the cost of quantity. In this original vineyard, not far from the Pan-Americana highway, there are vines of between 50 and 100 years old. These gnarled plants still bear grapes in abundance – so many that sometimes fully half of the grape bunches are removed before the actual picking begins. Only then does the wine acquire sufficient concentration. Treatment against mildew and other such afflictions is kept to a minimum, as is irrigation. As in Bordeaux, rose bushes flourish at the ends of the rows of vines – grown not just for their appearance, but as a warning: roses are affected by mildew quicker than grapes.

This vineyard cannot really be worked with any great efficiency as the vines are close together, and capricious in their growth. Ploughing has to be done carefully, with horses, and picking can only be by hand. Yet at Montes they are happy to keep this vineyard as it is; it is not efficiency that counts here, but the standard, the class, the quality of the grapes. Altogether Montes has 220 hectares of vines, at four locations. Three of these are to be found in the Curicó valley; La Finca, the fourth estate, further north in the Colchagua area of Rapel. These supply about 70 per cent of the grapes; the rest are bought in on a contract basis.

Surprised by demand
The firm, which was called Discover Wine until well into the 1990s, began life in 1988 as a boutique winery. The original intention was to produce and sell 50,000 cases a year at most – an amount, they felt, that should be achievable by 1993. However, the success of the Montes wines was so spectacular that 1993 saw 120,000 cases sold: 'we were totally amazed by the international interest in quality wines from Chile.' Montes is now delivering 280,000 cases annually, and 300,000 is in sight.

This leap forward is due above all to an unswerving quality policy on the one hand, and on the other to an almost permanent investment programme, with all earnings being ploughed back into the business. In the beginning some of the partners even worked for a couple of years without drawing a salary, and it was only in 1998, ten years after it was founded, that the firm paid its first modest dividend.

Wide expertise

The four partners who set up Montes – or Discover Wine as it was then known – in 1988 had a great deal of experience in the wine business. The oenologist, Aurelio Montes, had been chief winemaker at Viña Undurraga and Viña San Pedro (he is still adviser to ten or so other producers) and brought with him his own vineyard at Curicó – the one with the old vines. Aurelio was the first in Chile to make white wines with the aid of French oak casks; he was also the first to have stainless-steel fermentation tanks constructed in Chile, using Finnish metal.

Pedro Grand, whose forebears were French, was a winegrower who supplied wine in bulk to Concha y Toro, Viña San Pedro and Viña Santa Rita. His estate just outside Curicó became the basis for the new concern. Alfredo Vidaurre had been dean of the economics faculty at the Roman Catholic University, Santiago, and executive chairman of Viña San Pedro. Finally, Douglas Murray contributed his commercial expertise: he had travelled the world as export director for prestigious Spanish *bodegas* in Penedès, Rioja and the sherry region.

These four remain the biggest shareholders in Montes; to raise capital a minority holding was extended to the Estrella Americana Mutual Fund, the organization with an interest in Viña Los Vascos.

New wines

There are plans for a Syrah and a Pinot Noir. A sweet white wine was added to the collection in the second half of the 1990s: the Montes Vendange Tardive, a Gewürztraminer and Riesling blend. This is not an exaggeratedly sweet or heavy wine, but a stylish one with the aroma of *pourriture noble* splendidly apparent, and with apricot as its fruit.

Attention to detail

Only the very best is good enough for the Montes Alpha M. The wine is not only matured in new casks of French oak, but the bottles come from France, the capsules from Germany, and a special cork was developed in Portugal. Chilean rauli wood is used exclusively for the six-bottle cases.

Aurelio Montes is considered to be one of Chile's most gifted and expert winemakers.

Memorable moments

Alpha honour

Very traditional, super-modern

Since 1988 the cellar facilities at Curicó have undergone a gradual metamorphosis. Alongside the old building, with its ranks of traditional wooden vats, an annexe has been erected that bristles with batteries of stainless-steel tanks and other modern equipment. The difference in age between the wooden vats and these tanks is about a century, but both kinds perform satisfactorily; thus Aurelio Montes still ferments the red wines in the rauli-wood vats. The firm also owns ordinary steel and concrete vats.

Casks are to be seen everywhere – in the fermentation halls and in the *bodega de guarda*, a low-temperature area guarded by the figure of a large wooden angel (this also makes an appearance on some of the labels). Montes has more than 3,000 casks in use, both for the red wines and for some of the whites. Half of these *barricas* are of French oak, half of American.

Winning whites

The first Chilean white wine to win a gold medal at Vinexpo in Bordeaux, the world's biggest wine fair, was a Sauvignon Blanc made by Aurelio Montes. This wine is still in the Montes range; its fairly full, firm taste offers a pleasing amount of fruit – gooseberry, pear, grapefruit. An attractive variant of this is the Fumé Blanc, which has three months' contact with the oak of casks and staves. Its fruit, citrus and melon, is nicely complemented by smoky oak.

Normally, 70 per cent of the Montes Chardonnay is fermented in American oak barrels, and matured in them for five to six months. It is a lively wine in which toast combines splendidly with exotic fruits. The Montes Alpha Chardonnay represents a further step up in quality. This is fermented and aged in French casks – about a third of them new. In contrast to the basic Chardonnay, 40-60 per cent of it undergoes malolactic fermentation. This wine has style, concentration, creaminess, considerable toast, and generous amounts of tropical fruit – passion fruit, for example.

A remarkable Malbec

The Malbec is a remarkable wine, made exclusively from bought-in grapes. Its aroma combines ripe raspberry with plum, berry, cherry and spices; and this supple wine also displays some oak from three months in cask. Berry fruit predominates in the standard Cabernet

Sauvignon, accentuated by a dash of spice and a little toast – this wine spends six months in American oak barrels.

The influence of oak is more marked in the Montes Alpha Cabernet Sauvignon, but not to the extent of overwhelming the blackcurrant and other rich fruit notes. This wine spends a year in cask and can develop beautifully, as was shown in 1997 at a blind tasting organized by the British journal *Wine*. Wines of 1987 were tasted and the Montes Alpha Cabernet Sauvignon 'performed better than any of the Bordeaux except the Lynch-Bages.' A third Cabernet Sauvignon, which in quality comes between the above two, is the very fruity Montes La Finca de Apalta Estate, a wine mainly exported to Britain.

High-standard Merlots

The standard of the Montes Merlots in no way falls below that of the Cabernet Sauvignons. The Merlot Special Cuvée boasts an exuberant character and a supple taste, with elements of generous black fruit, chocolate, oak and spices. This wine generally contains around 85 per cent Merlot and 15 per cent Cabernet Sauvignon. Its time in barrel is limited to between four and five months. The Montes Alpha Merlot comes solely from the grape of this name and goes into French barrels for ten months. It is full of black fruit – including cherry and blackberry – while at the same time this is a wine that charms with a spicy dash of wood and toast.

The best wines
• Montes/Villa Montes Sauvignon Blanc, Curicó Valley
• Montes Fumé Blanc, Curicó Valley
• Montes Chardonnay, Curicó Valley
• Montes Alpha Chardonnay, Curicó Valley
• Montes Vendage Tardive, Valle de Curicó
• Montes Cabernet Sauvignon, Curicó Valley
• Montes La Finca de Apalta Estate Cabernet, Colchagua Valley
• Montes Alpha Cabernet Sauvignon, Curicó Valley
• Montes Merlot Special Cuvée, Curicó Valley
• Montes Alpha Merlot, Curicó Valley
• Montes Alpha M, Santa Cruz
• Montes Malbec, Colchagua Valley

In the vineyard just south of Curicó, vines between 50 and 100 years old still bear such large crops that surplus bunches have to be pruned.

Hundreds of tons of stones

Montes bought La Finca de Apalta in 1990; the estate had belonged to the owner of a hardware store in San Fernando, and had some fruit trees. The ground was so stony that 700 truck-loads had to be removed before a start could be made with planting vines and installing an irrigation system. The vineyard lies partly on a slope – with vines owned by Casa Lapostolle nearby – and Aurelio Montes considered it to have great potential. This was borne out when the first Montes Alpha M was made, for the vines that yielded this great wine were then only seven years old.

The magnificent M

'We took an enormous risk', Douglas Murray, says, speaking retro-spectively about the Montes Alpha M, 'We weren't sitting there with financial backing from the Mondavis or the Rothschilds; besides which our reputation was at stake.' With the Alpha M, the dream that Aurelio Montes and his partners had of creating a super-premium wine, a wine of the highest attainable quality, came true. The grapes chosen were 80 per cent Cabernet Sauvignon, 10 per cent Cabernet Franc and 10 per cent Merlot, all from the Apalta estate. The yield was limited to 56 hectolitres per hectare at most, and the grapes were picked in the very early morning. The vinification was aimed at getting as much extract in the wine as possible, and the 10 or 11 months' ageing was done in new French *barriques*.

The early vintages displayed an elegant and at the same time concen-trated wine, with style and complexity. Ripe blackberry and other fruit,

British illustrator Ralph Steadman made this contribution to the Montes guest book.

together with spices, mint, toast, vanilla, oak and firm yet mel-low tannins – it all added up to a splendid wine, eminently drink-able within two years.

The launch of this very expensive wine immediately banished all its makers' worries, for the entire quantity they had produced – 10,200 bottles of the 1996, and 18,000 of the '97 vintage – sold like snow melting, and the critics were full of praise. Encouraged by this, the Montes team is considering building a dedicated cellar for the Montes Alpha M on the Apalta estate.

Viña MontGras

MontGras

Quality, efficiency and safety: the Viña MontGras bodega was designed according to these tenets. The spacious building is equipped for the minimum possible movement of the wine, for an economical use of energy, for hygienic and ecologically-sound working (all water is recycled, skins and other waste go back into the vineyard), and for the production of clean, high-quality wines.

Viña MontGras has been in business since February 1994. It was set up by Hernán Gras, together with his brother Eduardo and another entrepeneur, Cristián Hartwig. Hernán, whose grandparents came to Chile from Barcelona in 1900, has an impressive curriculum vitae. He gained his diploma in oenology in Santiago and continued his studies, with malolactic fermentation as his special subject, in Bordeaux and in Davis, California. Back in Chile he carried out more research, and subsequently worked as winemaker at Bright Wines, the biggest wine company in Canada, later becoming director general there.

In 1990, with the help of Canadian architects, he started work on plans for a winery of his own. One of the first wines that Hernán made, in 1994, was a Cabernet Sauvignon which the authoritative Guía de Vinos de Chile declared to be the best of that vintage.

Vineyard on a hill

There is more to see at Viña MontGras than the winery. It lies just outside Palmilla, in the Colchagua valley, and a unique vineyard is taking shape close by on the Ninquén hill. Altogether there is room for 200 hectares of vines, both on the slopes and on the undulating, very broken ground at its top. The first 50 hectares have been planted, and harvesting is expected to begin in 2000 or 2001. It has already cost a fortune just to put in an access road up to the top, and to install a drip system for irrigation. In starting this project Viña MontGras has had advice from Californian wine producer Hess, with whom there has been close cooperation on other fronts, too.

A trio of Chardonnays

Besides its correct Sauvignon Blanc, MontGras produces three Chardonnays. The basic one possesses reasonable tropical fruit, a fairly fresh character, and a very slight

Facts and figures
▶ Hernán Gras, Eduardo Gras, Cristián Hartwig
▶ 1992
▶ 435 ha (not yet fully productive)
▶ 220,000 cases, increasing to 450,000
▶ Avenida Eliodoro Yanez 2962, 5° Piso, Providencia, Santiago
▶ Tel: (56-2) 520 4355
▶ Fax: (56-2) 520 4354

The best wines
• Chardonnay
• Chardonnay Ninquén Barrel Select
• Cabernet Sauvignon Reserva
• Merlot Reserva
• Cabernet Ninquén Barrel Select
• Carmenère Reserva

Colchagua Valley is the denominación de origen for these wines.

Rapid growth

At its start in 1994, the MontGras cellar had a capacity of 1.5 million litres, and this has now reached 5 million. The number of casks has increased to 3,400 – 60% of them American oak, 40% French. The temperature of their air-conditioned hall is kept at a constant 15°C.

The lyre system

This system of planting has been chosen for much of the vineyard area from the point of view of both yield and quality. The upper branches are trained into a V-form, so that both leaves and fruit have more of the sun. Developed in France, this is used by MontGras for all the black varieties, and for some of the white grapes too. The firm gets between 70-98 hl per hectare.

New varieties

Besides the familiar varieties, MontGras has planted Cabernet Franc, Malbec, Syrah, Zinfandel, Sémillon and Viognier. There are also experiments under way with Pinot Noir, albeit with limited success so far.

Hernán Gras of Montgras in his climate-controlled barrel cellar.

66 *We try to be as natural as possible, that is our approach to wine* 99
~ *Hernán Gras*

touch of oak and toast – about 17 per cent of this wine goes into cask. The Reserve has more oak, with 30 per cent spending time in barrel, and tastes somewhat creamier. Ripe mango, plenty of toast, smooth acidity and generosity characterize the Chardonnay Ninquén Barrel Select, the best white wine from this producer.

Fruit and oak in balance

One of the most special of the MontGras red wines – which comprise over two-thirds of the output – is the Cabernet/Merlot Ninquén Barrel Select. This is made from equal proportions of Cabernet Sauvignon and Merlot. After macerating for two weeks, 15 months in barrel follows for 94 per cent of the wine: four out of five casks are of French oak. This wine is not filtered, and the result is a very agreeable, substantial, eminently drinkable wine with a sound balance between black fruit and toasty oak.

The range also includes a pure Cabernet Sauvignon and a pure Merlot. The standard versions of these are of extremely reliable quality; Hernán Gras always puts a sixth of their output into American barrels to give these wines an extra dimension.

There is also a Cabernet Sauvignon Reserva: an elegant yet sinewy creation, duly intense and provided with berry fruit and oak from its 12–15 months in American casks, with no filtering. The Merlot Reserva is made in the same way, and often shows even more class. Spicy, generous fruit – cherry, plum, berry – bayleaf, leather and wood give this wine an unmistakable distinction. The Reserva range also boasts a Carmenère: a concentrated, lively wine with elements of green pepper, menthol, pepper and black fruit.

Viña Morandé

Pionero, Nova Terrarum, Vitisterra, Morandé, Dueto, Aventura

Morandé, pioneers of the Valle de Casablanca, is the slogan under which Viña Morandé operates. These words refer to the ground-breaking work that Pablo Morandé carried out in this valley – he was the first to plant vines here, in 1982. At that time Pablo was still technical director at Viña Concha y Toro, the company where he worked for two decades. Thanks to his efforts, Casablanca was developed as a wine-growing area; without him it might still be lying waste. Pablo Morandé still owns 100 hectares in Casablanca himself, but the wine firm that bears his name has only four. What is more, the Viña Morandé cellars are situated 122 kilometres south of Santiago, near Pelequén in the Colchagua valley and not therefore in Casablanca, which lies between the capital and the coast. The founders of Viña Morandé were Pablo himself and two other former Concha y Toro employees; the firm that they established in 1996 has since acquired another two partners.

Viña Morandé was set up on a large scale. In the wholly new winery, sited by the Pan-Americana highway, 7.5 million litres were vinified in the first year and 10 million in the second year, 1998. The grapes come in on three lines and are pressed or crushed according to computer programmes, sometimes after being checked by hand first. All the tanks – for grapeskin contact, fermentation and storage – are of stainless steel. The halls that hold the tanks and the casks are air-conditioned, the bottling line is exceptionally efficient and hygienic. Then there is the nursery: alongside the winery sprawl greenhouses with a combined area of 13,000 square metres. Here millions of young vines are raised each year, both for the firm's own contracted growers and for producers such as San Pedro and Undurraga.

Pionero

This grand scale is also reflected in the wide range of wines, using a number of labels. Pionero is the most important of these, accounting for around 60 per cent of bottles sold. These wines have little or no contact with wood, and

Facts and figures
▶ Pablo Morandé and four partners
▶ 1996
▶ 8 ha plus 430 ha under contract
▶ 1,000,000 cases
▶ Tabancura 1666, Vitacura, Santiago
▶ Tel: (56-2) 217 0542
▶ Fax: (56-2) 217 0543

Pablo Morandé in Viña Morandé's nursery, which supplies young vines to his company and to other wine firms.

Other brands

Viña Morandé's subsidiary Vistamar carries good wines under the brands Vista Sur and Niebla. Vista Andes is the name for wines produced in Argentina.

Aims and objectives

This enterprise has 430 hectares of vineyards under long-term contracts of 15-20 years. The firm wants to increase this area to around 600 hectares. When this has been achieved, 60 per cent of the grapes needed will be harvested under its own control. Originally Viña Morandé supplied 80 per cent of the wine in bulk. However, the aim is to sell all of it in bottle – about a million cases – by the year 2008 at the latest.

are named after a particular grape, but usually contain the legally permitted maximum – 25 per cent – of one or more other varieties. Thus in the substantial, slightly fruity Chardonnay there is also some Sémillon; and a small proportion of this firm-tasting wine is fermented with oak chips. The supple Cabernet Sauvignon tastes of berry fruit, and a quarter of it is Merlot and Carmenère; with this wine the influence of wood is limited to a modest use of oak staves. The Merlot tends to be one of the best red wines here: a juicy, supple creation, with black fruit and some Malbec and Syrah in the blend.

Nova Terrarum

The concept underlying the Nova Terrarum wines is 'one variety from one valley, various vineyards'. In this case the valleys where the grapes come from are Maipo, Maule and Rapel. A proportion of most of these wines spends some time in barrel. The Cabernet Sauvignon from Maipo has the aroma of menthol characteristic of the area: around 80 per cent of this goes into used American barrels for eight months. The full, savoury Merlot from Rapel gets the same spell in oak. The Chardonnay, with a touch of vanilla, fairly rounded and sufficiently fruity, gets less oak.

Vitisterra

Each of the Vitisterra wines comes from a single vineyard, and their cask maturation ranges from five months for the Chardonnay to

Thousands of cuttings in the 13,000 sq m nursery: the vines of the future.

10–14 months for the label's two red wines – a Cabernet Sauvignon from Maipo Valley and a Merlot from Rapel. The effect of the wood is therefore prominent in these two reds. Both wines are generally full-bodied and fruity, with a deep, solid colour. The Cabernet Sauvignon also contains about 10 per cent Merlot grapes; likewise, the Merlot has some 12 per cent of Cabernet in its makeup. Turning to the whites, a

Viña Morandé's complex lies next to the Pan-Americana and is easily recognizable by its large, striking logo.

The best wines
- Chardonnay Pionero, Central Valley
- Chardonnay Nova Terrarum, Valle del Maipo
- Chardonnay Vitisterra, Casablanca Valley
- Chardonnay Dueto, Casablanca Valley
- Sauvignon Blanc Dueto, Casablanca Valley
- Cabernet Sauvignon, Nova Terrarum, Maipo Valley
- Cabernet Sauvignon, Vitisterra, Maipo Valley
- Merlot Pionera, Central Valley
- Merlot Nova Terrarum, Rapel Valley
- Merlot Vitisterra, Rapel Valley
- Merlot Dueto, Casablanca Valley
- Carmenère Aventura, Maipo Valley
- Malbec Aventura, Maipo Valley
- Reserva House of Morandé, Maipo Valley

creamy suppleness, mellow acidity, generous fruit and some toast are the distinguishing hallmarks of the Chardonnay from Casablanca.

Dueto

The 'duet' to which this range refers is that between the Valle de Casablanca, its area of origin, and Pablo Morandé, the winemaker. The grapes are harvested in the oldest part of Pablo's own Casablanca estate. The range includes a slightly floral, fresh and supple Riesling, a quite aromatic Sauvignon Blanc, an exuberant Chardonnay and a colourful, meaty, fresh and accessible Merlot with black fruit notes. Pablo Morandé's own name appears again with the House of Morandé, composed of 75 per cent Cabernet Sauvignon, 15 per cent Merlot and 10 per cent Cabernet Franc. This is a lively wine that has oak as well as fruit and emphatic notes of vanilla, due to its 14 months in new French casks.

Aventura

For adventurous wine-lovers,Viña Morandé has developed a range based on non-traditional grape varieties which it has called Aventura. Some of the wines, such as the Bouchet and César, do not rise above the very simple level of their grapes. However, the dark Carmenère, herbaceous alongside its fruit, is often a success, as is the pleasing Malbec.

VIÑA PORTAL DEL ALTO

*Portal del Alto, Valle San Fernando, Oriente Estates,
El Oriente, Millahue*

Facts and figures

▶ Alejandro
Hernández
▶ 1970
▶ 100 ha
▶ 80,000 cases
▶ Camino El Arpa
199, Alto Jahuel
▶ Tel: (56-2) 821 2059
▶ Fax: (56-2) 821 3371

The best wines
• Cabernet
Sauvignon Reserva,
Maipo Valley
• Merlot Reserva,
Central Valley

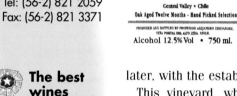

PORTAL DEL ALTO

Reserva
Merlot
1998
Central Valley • Chile
Oak Aged Twelve Months · Hand Picked Selection
PRODUCED AND BOTTLED BY PROFESOR ALEJANDRO HERNANDEZ,
VIÑA PORTAL DEL ALTO LTDA. CHILE.
Alcohol 12.5% Vol • 750 ml.

Few of the Chilean wine estates are run as scientifically as Viña Portal del Alto. Its owner is Alejandro Hernández, the eminent professor of viticulture and oenology at the Catholic University, Santiago. Many of Chile's best-known winemakers have attended his lectures, and Professor Hernández is the author of several books about wine. In 1968 he decided to put his considerable theoretical knowledge into practice by becoming a winegrower himself. The realization of this ambition came two years later, with the establishment of Viña Portal del Alto.

This vineyard, which stands behind its own gateway, covers eight hectares and is situated in Alto Jahuel, near Buin in the Maipo valley, south of the capital. The vines here, exclusively Cabernet Sauvignon, are descended from French plants brought to Chile around 1850. Another piece of land was acquired in San Juan de Pirque, near the Maipo area and at a height of 800 metres. The microclimate is cooler in summer and warmer in winter than other parts of the Valle del Maipo, and the grapes are always picked later here. Both black and white varieties thrive, giving wines that are fine and subtle rather than blatant.

Two vineyards in the south

In San Fernando, 130 kilometres south of Santiago, Viña Portal del Alto has a well-drained vineyard of about 20 hectares. Some of its vines are very old; there are, for example, Merlots with an average age of 60 years, and their yield remains limited to 42 hectolitres per hectare. Near this vineyard, which is planted with black and white varieties, stand the winery buildings where all the Portal del Alto wines are made. Traditional rauli-wood vats are used for the red wines, and stainless-steel tanks for the whites. The wines are bottled at Alto Jahuel, where the firm's offices are also located.

In 1992 Alejandro Hernández inherited from his father a fourth vineyard, El Oriente in the Maule area. This covers more than 60 hectares and was originally planted with simple varieties such as the País. The professor has replaced these with a wide range of superior grapes. At the same time he has experimented on a small scale with Sangiovese, with encouraging results, and with Pinot Noir, Nebbiolo, Syrah and Viognier – the last-named having great potential. All the vines in use at Viña Portal del Alto come from its own nursery.

Restrained oak

Around three-quarters of production consists of red wines, headed by the Cabernet Sauvignon. The basic version generally presents a deep colour, a supple texture, smooth tannins and a lot of fruit, including blackcurrant. The Reserve is more intense, with somewhat more substance, rich fruit – black berry, cherry, raspberry – and with just a modest amount of oak. At Viña Portal del Alto they do not want to 'overlay the fruit and the more complex aromas from the grapes with the taste of oak'. Usually only 40 per cent of the Reserva goes into casks, about 60 per cent of which are new, for between 12 and 14 months. The Reserva spends a further ten months in bottle, for the sake of its balance. Alejandro Hernández and his staff take great care when composing the wine. Various blends are made from the wines at their disposal, which subsequently go into half bottles, and then after a month are tasted for a final assessment.

There are both a standard and a Reserva version of the Merlot. The standard is a clean, pleasant, elegantly firm wine with

All the wines are made at Alto Jahuel, not far south of Santiago. The winery buildings have a rural character.

Hand-picked
The firm does not have a mechanical harvester – all the grapes are picked by hand and collected in 17-kg boxes. As far as possible they are transported by night to the cellar in San Fernando.

Rolling stock
At Alto Jahuel, where the wines are bottled, they are stored temporarily in special horizontal tanks. These were originally on railway wagons – Alejandro Hernández bought them at an auction and they serve their purpose admirably.

Bulk sales
Viña Portal del Alto sells the equivalent of 30,000 cases annually in bulk. A considerable proportion of this goes to Switzerland, where it is bottled under the supervision of Hernández' winemaker.

An authority

Alejandro Hernández is one of Chile's greatest wine authorities. He comes from a family of winegrowers and farmers in the Maule area, and has been involved in many other activities besides his academic work. He has been president of the authoritative Office International de la Vigne et du Vin, which operates worldwide, adviser to Pedro Domecq in Mexico, and to numerous Chilean wine firms as well as to the Ministry of Agriculture. Professor Hernández has many scientific publications to his name, and his books include 'Introducción al Vino de Chile'.

Fully-ripe bunches of Cabernet Sauvignon grapes. The Reserve wine from this variety is delicious.

black fruit, leather and bayleaf. The Merlot Reserva version, which contains 15 per cent Carmenère, tastes meatier, more generous and complete than the standard wine, with more nuances to it. Chocolate, some liquorice, black fruit and oak elements are nicely present in this concentrated wine, which has been made from the 1997 vintage onward. For some markets an attractive Merlot/Cabernet Sauvignon blend is produced.

The white wines

The Sauvignon Blanc from Viña Portal del Alto comes mainly from its own vineyard, which is situated high up in San Juan de Pirque. This is a floral, slightly fruity wine – gooseberry, citrus – with sufficient acidity and a hint of spices. The standard Chardonnay is rounded and creamy, with pear and tropical fruit. The Reserva displays all this, plus smoky oak and some toast. Almost a third of this wine is fermented in casks. The Chardonnay grapes come principally from the southern vineyards, in San Fernando and Maule.

Viña Quebrada de Macul
Domus Aurea

Nuances of ripe red and black berries, a hint of menthol, a slight smokiness, a touch of leather, spice and modest oak: these are the characteristics of the red Domus Aurea. This Cabernet Sauvignon, which also contains a small percentage of Cabernet Franc and Merlot, is the first wine that Ignacio Recabarren created for himself. In 1990 this celebrated winemaker – who had won his spurs at Viña Casablanca and elsewhere, and with the Trio wines from Concha y Toro – became joint owner of Viña Quebrada de Macul, a 36-hectare estate not far from Viña Aquitania.

For many years, the grapes from this estate had been sold to such wineries as Viña Aquitania, Viña Concha y Toro, Viña Santa Rita and Viña Undurraga. However owner Ricardo Peña, a lawyer, decided to invest in his own winemaking equipment after he had talks with Recabarren. Peña even had an underground cellar for casks and bottles excavated beside the vineyard.

Force of gravity

As they come in from the gently sloping vineyard, the bunches of grapes are first tipped on to a conveyor belt so that they can be checked. Fermentation takes place in stainless-steel tanks. As much as possible is done here by making use of the forces of gravity: as Ignacio puts it, 'the less you pump, the better the wine'.

Facts and figures
▶ Ricardo Peña 65%, Ignacio Recabarren 20%, David Williams 15%
▶ 1996
▶ 36 ha
▶ 7,500 to 8,000 cases
▶ Consistorial 5900, Peñalolén
▶ Tel: (56-2) 284 8271
▶ Fax: (56-2) 284 8271

Below: Ignacio Recabarren.Left: the western part of the vineyard.

The best wines
- Chardonnay Domus Aurea
- Cabernet Sauvignon Domus Aurea

The red wine has 10–12 months in *barricas*. These are of French oak – a few of them bought new each year since the 1998 harvest. There is no filtering. The firm also makes a Chardonnay without wood, which has fresh citrus in the taste.

Domus Aurea

The estate first tried to register Dominus as its trade name, but this was already in use. Domus Aurea was then chosen as the name for the best-quality wines. The label, pictured left, shows a watercolour by Benjamín Lira, a Chilean artist living in New York.

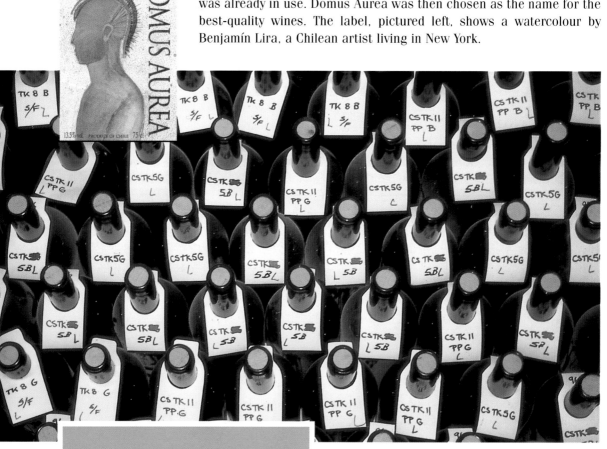

Part of the barrel cellar at Viña Domus Area houses a reference collection of bottled wines, consisting of both earlier vintages and experimental wines. Each bottle is identified by a code number on a tag.

> ❝ *Our red wine is not a sprinter but a marathon runner: it can go on for years* ❞
> ~ *Ignacio Recabarren*

VIÑA LA ROSA

La Palmería, La Palma, Viña La Rosa, Cornellana, Quinta Las Cabras, Casa Leona

Palm trees are often featured on labels and brochures from Viña La Rosa. It may be a picture of a palm branch, or a brand name – La Palmería, La Palma – or it may appear in publicity material. A visit to this winery explains why. Part of its vineyard – the firm uses grapes from its own land only – lies beside an impressive plantation of palm trees, and this is owned by the same family. The plantation is called La Palmería de Cocalán, and is tucked away in one of Rapel's many valleys. You can only reach this valley by way of an unsurfaced, very long, very dusty road. About half of the palm trees are extremely ancient – many more than 1,000 years old. The kind that grows here, the *Jubaea chilensis*, is typical of the country. The coconuts these palms yield are small, and their uses include being made into a special syrup called *miel de palma*, or 'palm honey'.

The name R. Ossa U. is carved in the bark of one of the trees, with the date 1914. This was inscribed by the young Recaredo Ossa Undurraga, whose great-grandfather founded Viña La Rosa in 1824; the Ossa family still own the estate today. The partly sloping vineyard beside La Palmería de Cocalán covers 100 hectares and is relatively new: it dates largely from the 1990s. So far only Cabernet Sauvignon and Merlot vines grow here. Because of the poor soil they yield just 42–56 hectolitres per hectare, about half of what is usual elsewhere in Rapel.

The Cornellana estate

Trees also grow beside the vines at another estate belonging to Viña La Rosa, the equally isolated Hacienda Cornellana. Not palms this time, but Agen plum trees, used for prunes. Viña La Rosa is part of the Sofruco group – the Sociedad Agrícola La Rosa Sofruco – which grows more than a dozen kinds of fruit on 1,800 hectares. Vines were first grown on the Cornellana estate a century ago, but water shortage brought an end to this. This problem allowed Viña La Rosa to buy the land very cheaply in 1990, at an eighth of the price in the nearby Cachapoal valley. Roads were laid with great energy, and a part of La Rosa's water rights was transferred to the new property. Today the serpentine estate in its valley

Facts and figures
▶ Sociedad Agrícola La Rosa Sofruco (the Ossa family)
▶ 1824
▶ 600 ha (increasing to 800)
▶ 500,000 cases (will increase to 800,000–1,000,000)
▶ Huérfanos 979, Of. 819, Santiago
▶ Tel: (56-2) 633 2106
▶ Fax: (56-2) 633 2104
▶ E-mail: vinos@larosa.cl

The best wines
• Sauvignon Blanc
• Chardonnay
• Chardonnay Reserve
• Chardonnay Gran Reserva
• Cabernet Sauvignon
• Cabernet Sauvignon Reserve
• Merlot Cabernet Sauvignon Reserve
• Merlot
• Merlot Reserve
• Merlot Gran Reserva

The denominación de origen for all of these is Rapel

A family business

The founder of Viña La Rosa and the fruit business associated with it was Gregorio Ossa, who at the end of the 18th century made the journey from Spain to Chile, 'the promised land at the end of the world'. The Ossa family have remained the owners to the present day. The sixth generation is now in charge.

Staves versus casks

At Viña La Rosa they believe in a sensible use of oak staves, especially for the Merlots. According to the winemaker, 'you get a better integration of the wood with the wine, without the oak becoming dominant – and this system also works quicker. Using the staves you have in effect casks of 20,000 litres instead of 225 litres'. The staves or planks are applied by placing them vertically in the fermentation tanks.

Above: harvest time.
Right: a vineyard near La Palmería de Cocalán.

setting has some 150 hectares growing grapes, both black and white. The special microclimate of this rocky terrain, with its lowest point 300 metres above sea level, makes for successful grape growing. Here the Chardonnay is usually picked a full two weeks earlier than in the surrounding area. Together with its other vineyards, Viña La Rosa has a total of 600 hectares, and this will increase to 800 hectares in the future.

Total renovation

The company's cellars stand beside the Carretera de la Fruta, or 'Fruit Road', near the small town of Peumo in the Cachapoal valley. Until 1993 the firm was working with completely obsolete equipment, but a year later virtually all had been replaced by modern presses, stainless-steel tanks and other up-to-date items. The ancient equipment has now been housed in a small museum.

La Rosa started to do its own bottling in 1994. In an unbelievably short time it reached a turnover of half a million cases a year, 90 per cent of which is exported; and 800,000 to a million is forecast for the first decade of the new millennium. Part of the turnover is accounted for by own-labels for British chains. The best-known of these brands is Casa Leona, in which the Chileans and Marks & Spencer have equal shares.

Left: palm trees and vines are the symbols of Viña La Rosa. Above: the country house at Peumo.

Memorable moments
The large, low-built country house near the winery has had a number of extensions and is very elegantly furnished. It is enclosed by a fine park and has two courtyards, awash with flowers. I was able to taste the wines in the attractive dining room, and also to enjoy them against the setting of a Sunday lunch. The Chardonnay Reserve proved to be a splendid partner to the free-range chicken with creamed potatoes, avocado and tomato; afterwards the wine went perfectly with the cheese.

Too many roses
Use of the name Viña La Rosa is largely confined to Chile itself as it is difficult to register it in other countries: there are simply too many wine firms with 'rosa' or 'rose' in their names.

Fruit, charm, drinkability

The wines that Viña La Rosa makes today are of an impeccable quality. They are easy to drink and clean-cut, replete with fruit and charm. The standard Chardonnay is full-bodied and fresh – often with passion fruit as its dominant aroma. In the Chardonnay Reserve, both aroma and taste present more mango, as well as a hint of oak and a somewhat creamier texture. Nearly a third of this wine is fermented in new French casks, then matured in them for four months; malolactic fermentation occurs in about a tenth of it.

The Chardonnay Gran Reserva, another delicious wine, offers rather more oak – 30 per cent goes into casks – creaminess and complexity. Like the other wines the Sauvignon Blanc comes from Rapel and in fact tastes just as fresh as a comparable wine from Casablanca. It is fragrant, too, and has some pleasant fruit – in this case gooseberry.

Experiments

The firm is conducting experiments in its own nursery with Syrah (three clones), Malbec, and Mourvèdre grapes.

Extremes

Of the vineyards owned by Viña La Rosa, the one at La Palmería has the biggest temperature fluctuations. In summer it is often 32°C during the day and only 8-10° at night, and usually warmer in summer and colder in winter than in neighbouring vineyard areas. Thicker grapeskins are one result of all this. Only black grapes are grown.

President Alessandri (centre) at La Rosa in the 1920s. Right: steam power from bygone days.

Less wine, more extract

To increase skin contact and thus the extraction process, as much as one-fifth of wines such as the Cabernet Sauvignon Reserve may be run off. This run-off wine is then used for the standard Cabernet.

Comparisons with Pomerol

The standard Cabernet Sauvignon has ripe blackcurrant, a touch of chocolate, some spice and a charming suppleness. The Cabernet Reserve, which is mainly from the La Palmería estate, is quite creamy in style. It has ripe berries; toasty oak from eight months in casks (a third are new), enriches the whole. Intense, juicy black fruit, and the chocolate notes of its aroma, make the meaty Merlot a great charmer. Chocolate, again, in the Merlot Reserve, an attractive, full-bodied wine with toast and vanilla from French oak staves. A considerable proportion of this is Carmenère. The same is true for the Merlot Gran Reserva, an exquisite, generous wine, from a yield of only 28–42 hectolitres per hectare. Its black fruit, its bayleaf, its leather together with its opulence evoke comparisons with a good Pomerol – an impression reinforced by toasty oak from staves.

Viña La Rosa also produces a blended red which is a combination of Merlot and Cabernet Sauvignon. This is a wine with considerable breadth to it, along with elements of bayleaf, black fruit – especially blackcurrant – and chocolate. There is also some oak from the staves used. The blend usually has 60 per cent Merlot.

Viña Rucahue
Rucahue, Casas de Rucahue

If you drive towards the coast from San Javier in the Valle de Maule, you can reach Viña Rucahue by going right at the turning to Cauquenes rather than left. From here the unsurfaced road runs north and leads eventually to a large white building at the foot of a low hill. This is full of fermentation tanks, with gleaming stainless-steel models alongside the 60-year-old concrete ones. This is the home base of Viña Rucahue. The firm itself dates from 1985, but this modern part of the winery has only been operating since the 1993 harvest. Beyond, in a long valley close to the Maule valley, there stretches a 2,000-hectare estate. The plan is for a large part of the property to become a vineyard; so far planting has covered 300 hectares.

Bulk and bottles
Viña Rucahue still supplies mainly wine in bulk, and also makes the Carpe Diem and Condor wines for Agrícola y Vitivinícola Itata further south. The most interesting of its own wines are the reds. These are described as being 'of a Reserva type'. Half the Cabernet Sauvignon spends eight months in casks (half are French, half American). Besides its deep colour, this wine has vanilla, chocolate and some fruit in a fairly full-bodied, supple taste. Black fruit with a hint of herbaceousness and just a little oak characterize the Merlot, an agreeable wine. Some 30–40 per cent of this spends about three months in barrels.

Facts and figures
▶ José Esturillo and Francisco Gillmore
▶ 1985
▶ 300 ha (to be increased)
▶ 250,000 cases (to be increased)
▶ Avenida Vitacura 2909, Of. 806, Santiago
▶ Tel: (56-2) 231 7694
▶ Fax: (56-2) 623 2051

 The best wines
• Cabernet Sauvignon Casas de Rocahue, San Javier
• Merlot Casas de Rocahue, San Javier

Other activities
Joint-owner Francisco Gillmore is also the proprietor of Viña Tabontinaja and supplies wine to Las Viñas de la Calina.

Left: Francisco Gillmore.
Below: not all of the land has yet been planted with vines.

AGRÍCOLA SALVE

Domaine Oriental, Piduco Creek, Casa Donoso

Facts and figures
▶ Les Vignobles
(Robert Wan, Louis
Wane, Julien Siu,
Michel Paoletti)
▶ 1989
▶ 130 ha
▶ 100,000 cases
▶ Fundo La Oriental,
Camino a Palmira 3.5
km, Talca
▶ Tel: 56-71) 242 506
▶ Fax: (56-71) 242 091
▶ E-mail: courrier@
domaineoriental.cl

The best wines
• Chardonnay Clos
Centenaire Domaine
Oriental
• Cabernet Sauvignon
Clos Centenaire
Domaine Oriental
• Merlot Clos
Centenaire Domaine
Oriental
• Donoso Domaine
Oriental

*All the wines have
Maule Valley as their
denominación de
origen.*

The first French vines were planted in the Valle del Maule about a century and a half ago – and this pioneer vineyard was on Rodolfo Donoso's estate, La Oriental. The name of the property refers to its position – it lies just east of Talca. The Donoso family owned this old wine estate for very many generations, but sold the whole of their grape harvests in bulk, mainly to Viña Santa Carolina. A new phase dawned in 1989, when La Oriental, along with its house and cellars, was acquired by a group of Frenchmen living in Tahiti: Robert Wan, Louis Wane, Julien Siu and Michel Paoletti. To the existing vineyard they added a second, La Finca de las Casas de Vaquería, invested in new equipment, and engaged Alvaro Espinoza, a talented winemaker who later moved to Viña Carmen. The reborn concern was given the name Agrícola Salve, and Domaine Oriental was chosen as the main trademark for the wines.

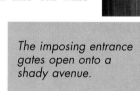

The imposing entrance gates open onto a shady avenue.

Clos Centenaire

In the Domaine Oriental range the Cabernet Sauvignon and the Merlot are good, lively, straightforward wines with attractive amounts of fruit, pleasingly supple and with a deep colour. Greater distinction is offered by the Clos Centenaire selection, which represents a quarter to a third of the total production. Half of the Cabernet Sauvignon Clos Centenaire spends a year in barrel, and about a third of the mainly American oak is new. To complement its dark-red hue, this wine has distinct toast and vanilla, with jammy berry and spices. The Merlot in the range also contains small amounts of Cabernet Sauvignon and Carmenère. With this wine, ageing in cask is kept to a minimum – 10 per cent of the Merlot has three months and the Cabernet component twelve months – so that oak is barely perceptible. The aroma is a blend of green pepper, bayleaf, leather, and black fruit. And in good years the wine has generous extract.

In 1999 a new premium wine was launched: Domaine Oriental Donoso, from the 1997 vintage. Eighty per cent Cabernet Sauvignon and 20 per cent Carmenère, this spent four months in French casks. It is the best wine Agricola Salve has ever made, a lively creation with a seductive amount of berry and black fruit, toast, smoky oak, sinewy strength and depth. It comes from vines some 60 years old, which yield only about 50 hectolitres per hectare.

Domaine Oriental's best white wine is the Chardonnay Clos Centenaire; with a third of it fermented in cask it combines fresh tropical and citrus fruit with restrained notes of oak.

The Piduco Creek wines are very like the Domaine Oriental products, but they are not altogether identical. Unlike the Domaine Orientals, they use some bought-in grapes. The Casa Donoso wines were created for the United States: these are comparable to the best of the Domaine Oriental.

More French oak
The estate intends gradually to increase the proportion of French oak barrels, now just under 30 per cent. About 600 *barricas* shelter behind the thick walls of the cask hall.

Limited irrigation
As a rule, to limit the yield and put the vines under a degree of stress, the estate's own vineyards are irrigated just twice a year.

Estate sales
Exports account for 97 per cent of sales. Most of the bottles sold in Chile itself are bought by visitors to the estate, where they are welcome by appointment from Monday to Friday, between 9am and 6pm, for a guided tour and free wine tasting.

Above: a giant cactus guards the cellar. Left: new oak barrels.

VIÑA SAN MIGUEL DEL HUIQUE

El Huique

The first thing that strikes the visitor to Viña San Miguel del Huique is that grapes grow in the courtyard of the low white winery buildings. These are Cabernet Franc vines, which thrive here thanks to their sheltered surroundings. The grape harvest from these is vinified separately, but the resulting tiny quantity of wine is then blended into the estate's Cabernet Sauvignon, its most important wine. This represents 80–90 per cent of the output.

A severe earthquake partly destroyed the Viña San Miguel del Huique cellar in 1985. With enormous care, the present owner totally restored the building, which dates from 1870-90. Apart from anything else 4,500 square metres of roof had to be re-tiled.

Today, a walk through the shady colonnades surrounding the courtyard would never lead the visitor to suppose that behind the old walls, and the windows shuttered with staves from old vats, some ultra-modern equipment is in place. When this was installed in 1994, no changes were made to the exterior of the century-old property. The new tanks were even assembled and welded inside the building.

Smoky and feral

The winery, which is in the Colchagua valley in Rapel, gets all its grapes from its own land. The property lies north of Peralillo and not far from Viña Caliterra, and its 90 hectares contain both 40-year-old vines and some very young ones. One part of the vineyard lies near the cellar, while two other blocks are a 6-minute and a 45-minute drive away respectively. The latter, to the north-west near Marchihue, is where the firm hopes to do a good deal of planting in the future.

The red wines from Viña San Miguel del Huique can be described as fairly compact and energetic. The Cabernet Sauvignon has a full-bodied core of alcohol, plenty of oak and toast, and fresh berry notes. Its time in cask lasts from six to twelve months. This *bodega* uses French barrels only. The Merlot, which is given no oak, tastes smoky and feral rather than fruity. Its slightly herbaceous quality is due to its 50 per cent or so of Carmenère.

Viña San Pedro

Viña San Pedro, Viña Santa Helena, Las Rocas, Alta Mira

Amazement would be the reaction of anyone who visited Viña San Pedro in 1989, and then not again for ten years: in the intervening decade this wine firm was completely transformed. Until the late 1980s the company was still working with antiquated equipment; most activities were carried on in a confusingly-organized complex at Lontué, and wine was also made and stored at Molina, a little to the south down the Pan-Americana highway, where storage capacity was a tenth that of Lontué.

At Molina today San Pedro has one of South America's largest and most modern wineries. In an area of 14,000 square metres some 30 stainless-steel tanks now stand, each of which can hold 500,000 litres. The firm also invested in horizontal rotating tanks, cooling machines, filters and an all-new, super-efficient bottling line. And the number of oak casks has risen from 2,500 to 5,000: 70 per cent of them French, 30 American.

A man who has really left his mark on the project is international wine-maker Jacques Lurton, of the famous Bordeaux family; he has been a consultant since 1994, before building work began. Thanks to Jacques, the quality of the San Pedro wines has been spectacularly improved. The turnover, too, has risen – especially in exports.

Facts and figures
▶ Compañías Cervecerías Unidas (50.1% of the shares)
▶ 1865
▶ 2,100 ha (370 ha being added)
▶ 4,000,000 cases
▶ La Concepción 351, Providencia, Santiago
▶ Tel: (56-2) 235 2600
▶ Fax: (56-2) 236 3290
▶ E-mail: info@sanpedro.cl

Largest single vineyard
At the same time as the new winery was being built, the vineyard area was considerably enlarged. In

The snow-covered Andes provide water for irrigation for San Pedro, as at many Chilean wine estates.

VIÑA SAN PEDRO

Castillo de
MOLINA

CHILE 1997
LONTUÉ

CABERNET
SAUVIGNON

PRODUCIDO Y EMBOTELLADO POR VIÑA SAN PEDRO S.A.
CAMINO SAN PEDRO S/N LONTUÉ CHILE
IMPORTADO POR TAMAYO & CÍA. S.A. CARACAS - VENEZUELA
VINO TINTO REGISTRADO EN EL M.S.A.S. BAJO N.º E-1341

CONTENIDO NETO 0.75 L.   GRADO ALCOHÓLICO 13 G.L.

The best wines
- Sauvignon Blanc Gato Blanco
- Sauvignon Blanc 35 Sur
- Chardonnay Gato Blanco
- Chardonnay Siglo de Oro, Santa Helena
- Chardonnay 35 Sur
- Chardonnay Castillo de Molina
- Cabernet Sauvignon Gato Negro
- Cabernet Sauvignon 35 Sur
- Cabernet Sauvignon Castillo de Molina
- Cabernet Sauvignon Cabo de Hornos
- Cabernet Merlot Gato Negro
- Merlot Gato Negro
- Merlot Santa Helena
- Merlot Siglo de Oro, Santa Helena
- Merlot Castillo de Molina
- Merlot Selección del Directorio, Santa Helena

All are denominación de origen Lontué Valley

1989 vines covered 1,000 hectares, compared with 2,100 hectares today – and there are a further 450 hectares to be planted. When all this area is productive San Pedro will be getting three-quarters of its grapes from its own vineyards. That land is at five locations, from Maipo to Maule.

By far the most important source of the firm's grapes is the Molina vineyard, which lies around the modernized winery there. At 1,200 hectares, this is the largest single vineyard block in Chile. The part flat, part undulating terrain has alluvial soil, with lots of gravel and stones. Both gravity-flow and drip irrigation are used. The training of the vines varies, according to grape variety, from the traditional pergola method to the relatively recent lyre system. Despite its vast extent, the Molina vineyard is cared for with a great feeling for detail: each individual plot gets attention. Just before the harvest three or four people go round the vineyard testing the grapes for flavour, ripeness and tannins.

The company also takes pains over ecological matters. In cooperation with the University of Valparaiso, ground-up grapeskins and stalks provide a natural fertilizer for the vines. As far as possible the firm works with purified water, and water from the winery is recycled after use.

Gato Blanco and Negro

The new complex was built primarily for the Gato range – labelled Gato Negro for the reds, Gato Blanco the whites. These are competitively-priced wines; clean, fruity and pleasantly drinkable. Sales have already

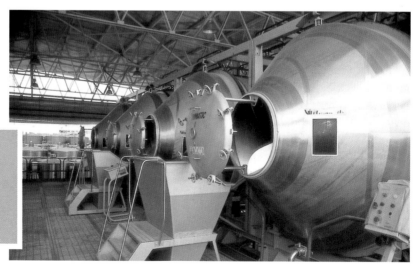

These rotating fermentation tanks give red wines more colour and extract. The winery also has a battery of regular vertical tanks.

Shafts of sun highlight new oak barrels ranged against the whitewashed cellar walls.

Additions

The Gato Blanco Sémillon is a recent addition to the collection. Pinot Noir and Syrah wines can be expected in the future. A sweet Late Harvest is sometimes made from Riesling grapes.

Experimental plot

Near the cellar in Molina, tests are being carried out with various kinds of grapes and systems of planting. There is also a small weather station.

Propellers

Huge propellers have been erected in the vineyards to move cold air and avert the danger of frost. Each of these can protect some seven hectares.

reached a million cases a year, which amounts to about a quarter of Viña San Pedro's total production.

The Gato Blanco Sauvignon Blanc is the basic white. This is fermented at low temperature with the aid of selected yeast cells, and generally offers exemplary value for money with its freshness, considerable fruit – gooseberry, pear, tropical – and a certain grace. There is also a charming Chardonnay, with citrus and exotic fruit in nose and taste, combined with a stimulating acidity.

The Cabernet Sauvignon accounts for the biggest proportion of the Gato Negro wines. It comes across as smooth and supple, with jammy fruit: blackcurrant in particular is clearly in evidence. The Gato Negro Merlot combines roundness with blackberry, plum and cherry, while the Cabernet/Merlot is a most pleasing 60:40 blend of these two grape varieties. It is both firm-tasting and fruity, with berry and black fruits.

During the harvest, tractors work constantly in Chile's largest single vineyard.

The 35 Sur range

Quality and price rise somewhat with the 35 Sur wines. For this range, the Sauvignon Blanc has eight hours' skin contact before its fermentation begins. After fermentation is complete, the wine is left for four months in contact with the lees to 'soften the sensation in your mouth'. Notes such as asparagus can be tasted in this very clean wine, as well as hints of fruits such as fresh figs. The Chardonnay is more buttery – about 30 per cent of it undergoes malolactic fermentation – and it offers flavours of both citrus and exotic fruits. The Cabernet Sauvignon 35 Sur is opaque in colour, the taste decently intense, the berry fruit inviting. You also find some vanilla, as the wine has been in contact with oak chips and staves. The Merlot too sees oak, acquiring comparable nuances to complement its spices, black fruit and leather.

Castillo de Molina

The name Castillo de Molina was devised as a label for the Reservas. As with the 35 Sur, all the grapes come from the Molina vineyard – in this case, though, they are mostly picked by hand. Half of the Chardonnay is fermented in *barricas*, two-thirds of them of French oak, the rest of American. Seven months in cask follow. Fruit such as mango and oak nuances are nicely in balance in this wine.

The Cabernet Sauvignon goes into cask for a full year, during which time it develops a sturdy constitution, a lot of toast and oak, some tobacco, berry fruit and sometimes a slightly bitter note. It is a wine that generally calls for a few years' patience before it fully unfolds. It matures in barrels of which usually 20 per cent are new; 70 per cent of these are of French oak. This also holds good for the Merlot Castillo de Molina, a cherry-like wine with a herbaceous touch.

The Cabo de Hornos, a Cabernet Sauvignon, is at the top of the San Pedro range. This unfiltered wine is indulged with 18 months' maturation in French casks. Its substantial taste contains nuances of various fruits, with blackcurrant to the fore, a touch of mint and aniseed, vanilla, oak, toast and spices. This is truly a wine for laying down, classic in character and impressive in quality.

Viña Santa Helena

Viña Santa Helena operates under the Viña San Pedro umbrella. It was originally a separate firm, established in 1942; today, though, its grapes come from the same sources as those for the San Pedro. They are processed at the same winery by the same winemaker, and some of the wines show a great resemblance to the Viña San Pedros, although sometimes in a rather smoother, milder form. This is noticeable if – for example – you taste the Sauvignon Blanc next to the 35 Sur version. The creamy, round Siglo de Oro is a successful Chardonnay which has a slight oakiness along with pineapple and peach. Half of it is given malolactic fermentation. A tenth then goes into cask, and a further fifth comes into contact with oak staves.

Among the Santa Helena red wines the Merlots generally produce the highest quality: this goes both for the standard Merlot and the rather superior Siglo de Oro, as well as for the Selección del Directorio, which is aged in cask. About half a million cases of Viña Santa Helena are sold a year. The aim is to give the wines with this label more of a character of their own in future, partly by using grapes from separate vineyards.

Parallels with the past

The expansion of Viña San Pedro, an enterprise which is quoted on the Chilean stock exchange, came about through the dynamic management of the biggest shareholder, Compañías Cervecerías Unidas. This is Chile's most important brewer and distributor of beer. Until 1941 the firm was the owned by the Correa family, its founders back in 1865. In that year the brothers Bonifacio and José Gregorio Correa combined their own and inherited estates and had them replanted with classic grape varieties, importing the vines from France. Interestingly, there are parallels with today to be found in the firm's early history. The owners a century ago also engaged a French oenologist who – like Jacques Lurton – had a progressive approach: in 1907 a cooling system was installed in the Viña San Pedro winery that was the first of its kind in the world.

Differences

Oak chips and staves are used for the Gato wines, never casks.

At 13–14 tons per hectare, the plots used for the 35 Sur are lower-yielding than those for Gato. With the Castillo de Molina wines the yield drops further, to 8–10 tons/ha; these wines spend time in wood, and some of the Chardonnay is fermented in cask. The reds undergo a long, Bordeaux-style fermentation and maceration of at least 21 days.

The fruit for the Cabo de Hornos comes from two small plots and is fermented in half-filled oak vats: this gives a high degree of extraction. The yield per hectare is only five tons, and no more than 2,000–3,000 cases a year are produced.

VIÑA SANTA ALICIA
Santa Alicia

The best wines
• Sauvignon Blanc
• Chardonnay Reserve
• Chardonnay Gran Reserva
• Cabernet Sauvignon Reserve
• Cabernet Sauvignon Gran Reserva
• Merlot Reserve
• Merlot Gran Reserva

All wines are from Maipo Valley.

About half a century ago the winery that today serves as the headquarters for Viña Santa Alicia was built in a remote spot in Pirque, 700 metres up at the foot of the Andes. The builder was Máximo Valdes, who owned 1,850 hectares of land, 400 of them planted with vines. For the four decades before, the whole harvest from this vineyard had been sold to large wine firms. But to Valdés, making his own grapes into his own wine seemed a much more attractive business proposition. He called his winery Viña Las Casas de Pirque, and used Casas de Pirque and As de Oro as trade names.

Máximo Valdés died at the end of the 1960s, and it was to be 1994 before his estate began once more to make a name for itself. On New Year's Day of that year it not only acquired six new owners, but a new name as well – Viña Santa Alicia. This name came from Máximo's granddaughter, who was also the wife of Andrés Pérez, one of the six new proprietors and chairman of the board. Alicia, moreover, proved to be one of Chile's few 'Santa' names as yet unregistered.

Affordable quality

The relaunch went well. Viña Santa Alicia now sells 200,000 cases a year, all to foreign customers. According to Andrés Pérez, the strength of the firm lies in 'affordable wines of good quality'. The basis of the range is wines from single grape varieties, such as the juicy Sauvignon Blanc with its citrus, pear and dash of spices. The Chardonnay is a generous mouthful, with tropical fruit, hints of hazelnut and honey. Berry and spices are to be found in the Cabernet Sauvignon; feral and woodland scents, with prune and black fruit, in the Merlot.

The Reserve range

The wines sold as Reserves have all had contact with wood to a greater or lesser degree. The Chardonnay Reserve derives its modest oak and toast aroma from oak chips and staves. For the rest it is a well-balanced, slightly buttery wine, with a good amount of tropical fruit. In the

Right: founder Máximo Valdes. Above: the Santa Alicia cellars are in the lower right corner of this dramatic view towards the

Cabernet Sauvignon Reserve there are black-berry and spices – especially aniseed – to be tasted, along with oak. This long, lingering wine acquires its oak from casks, plus staves and chips. Depth, length, backbone, black fruit and bayleaf are recognizable qualities of the Merlot Reserve. This, too, gets its oak from the same mixture of sources as does the Cabernet.

The Gran Reservas

The best wines are selected for the Gran Reservas. The Chardonnay Gran Reserva comes exclusively from the El Cipres vineyard, and it is fermented in French barrels. Spicy oak, butter, pineapple, banana and toast generally define its aroma, and this is a wine that goes particu-larly well with white meat and poultry. The grapes for the Cabernet

Designed with care

Many Chilean wineries are purely functional; but here at Viña Santa Alicia great care has been given to visual detail. The interior walls of the winery at Pirque have been painted in shades of yellow ochre, there is a spacious, sunken reception area for visitors with decorated walls, and for small groups of visitors an unusual tasting-room has been created by joining two vast old vats together.

Soil, grapes from old vines and sheltering slopes: the raw material for Santa Alicia's Gran Reserva reds.

Sauvignon Gran Reserva come from the Los Maitenes vineyard. Toast, cherry, plum, berries and spices are among the nuances of this powerful wine, which has a year in *barricas* of French oak. The Merlot, similarly treated, is generous in character, with its integrated oak, black fruit, chocolate and a hint of liquorice.

Of the roughly 650 casks here, half are of French oak, half of American; besides these barrels, the firm has 4.5 million litres of storage capacity available. Santa Alicia is able to source some 70 per cent of its grape needs from its own vineyards.

VIÑA SANTA AMALIA
Chateau Los Boldos, Santa Amalia

French as well as Spanish is spoken in the tiny village of Santa Amalia, just south of Requínoa in the Rapel area. A number of French people have been here since 1990: they all work for Viña Santa Amalia, which belongs to a Frenchman, and the most important range from this producer bears a Franco-Chilean name, Chateau Los Boldos.

The owner is Dominique Massenez, whose family make fruit distillates and liqueurs in Alsace. For about a century before Massenez took over this winery it had been a cooperative. The buildings stand around a large courtyard; one is reserved for the making of a pear distillate, destined for chocolate manufacturers; Massenez produces 80,000 litres a year of this. The wine production is more than 1.6 million litres.

Cooled by the night air

Both stainless-steel tanks and the traditional oak vats are used for fermenting. These were totally renovated after Massenez took over, and give very good results – particularly with the Cabernet Sauvignon. The Frenchmen speak of 'excellent extraction', because in these wide vessels the contact between the wine and the grapeskins is relatively intense. The casks, about 400 of them, are all of French oak and are stacked in a ground-level cellar with thick walls. To keep the temperature down in the summer, night air at a consistently cool 6–8°C is blown in. As the walls give good insulation, this keeps the cellar cool through the day.

Viña Santa Amalia is a self-contained operation in that only grapes from its own 250-hectare property are used. Most of the vineyards lie in the former bed of the Cachapoal river, which explains why the soil is full of pebbles. Massenez runs his vineyard on almost wholly organic lines; the only remedial treatment applied is against mildew.

There are many old vines in the vineyard here; the Sauvignon Blanc comes from a 12-hectare plot planted in 1936. This is a very aromatic wine, with citrus, gooseberry, fresh-mown grass, apple and also a brisk acidity. The Chardonnay Vieilles Vignes comes from much younger vines, dating from 1975: the term 'old vines' in its name is an indication of quality rather than age. Like the Sauvignon Blanc, this Chardonnay is lively in

Facts and figures
▶ Dominique Massenez
▶ 1850 (in French ownership since 1990)
▶ 250 ha (not yet fully productive)
▶ 180,000 (will be increased)
▶ Camino Los Boldos s/n, Requínoa
▶ Tel: (56-72) 551 230
▶ Fax:(56-72) 551 202

The best wines
• Sauvignon Blanc
• Chardonnay Château Los Boldos Vieilles Vignes
• Cabernet Sauvignon
• Cabernet Sauvignon Chateau Los Boldos Vieilles Vignes
• Merlot
• Merlot Chateau Los Boldos Vieilles Vignes
• Chateau Los Boldos Grand Cru

Requínoa, a sub-district of Rapel, is given as the denominación de origen.

Two labels

Around 70% of the wines are sold as Chateau Los Boldos, the rest as Santa Amalia. Originally the Santa Amalia name was not available to Dominique Massenez, which led him to devise Chateau Los Boldos de Santa Amalia; the 'Santa Amalia' was later dropped from this. The Vieilles Vignes and Grand Cru qualities carry the Chateau Los Boldos name only, whereas the basic wines may be sold under either label. Some 80% of production consists of red wine, 20% of white.

Whole bunches

As with Champagne, for example, bunches of grapes are pressed whole for the white wines. Half of all the fruit at Viña Santa Amalia is picked by hand, particularly from the older vines.

character. Its taste is not too heavy or tedious, and it has mango fruit as well as vanilla, smoky oak and toast. It gets six months in casks of new French oak, and 20-30 per cent of it undergoes malolactic fermentation.

The standard Cabernet Sauvignon is a wine of considerable merit, with reasonable substance, spicy blackcurrant fruit, an elegant firmness and smooth tannins. The Vieilles Vignes (in this case from 1948 vines), boasts greater concentration and more nuances. As well as fine fruit – black fruits, berries – there is spicy oak: the wine has been matured in *barricas* for a year. There are also two variants of the Merlot. The basic one is now 100 per cent Merlot: leather, liquorice, bayleaf, blackberry and cherry define its aroma, and its taste usually displays an attractive vitality. The Merlot Vieilles Vignes has the same liveliness, and similar nuances – here in more pronounced form, supplemented by oak from a year in barrel. The all-Merlot vines were planted in 1960.

The Grand Cru

The best, rarest and most expensive wine has been given the name Chateau Los Boldos Grand Cru. It has been made since 1998 from vines at least 40 years old. The blend is generally around 80 per cent Cabernet Sauvignon and 20 per cent Merlot. Its time in oak lasts from 12–18 months, and about a third of the *barricas* are new. This wine is distinguished by a solid, deep colour and a complex bouquet with a good deal of black fruit, toast, bayleaf, and forest scents. The meaty, stylish taste offers similar impressions – and the finish lasts long minutes. Only 3,000 cases a year of this exceptional wine are available, which in part explains why it costs some $50 to $60 per bottle.

The view across the Santa Amalia vineyards from the tower that guards them.

VIÑA SANTA CAROLINA
Santa Carolina, Ochagavía, Miraflores, Planella

In 1875, wealthy mine-owner Luis Pereira commissioned Germain Bachelet to find him the best possible location for a vineyard. The French consultant chose him a property, which was duly planted with French vines, six kilometres from Santiago's Plaza de Armas. At that time the site lay well outside the city, but the intervening years have seen it lost to urban sprawl, and where once grapes grew is now the industrial district of San Miguel. What survives is the winery built for Pereira – by another Frenchman, Emile Doyère. The buildings, partly underground, are near the national stadium, and over the years the complex has been extended with warehouses, offices, and an attractive tasting room. Going down into the cellar today brings the visitor to a cool, vaulted area with brick walls, pillars and arches. Some of Viña Santa Carolina's 5,000 barrels are stored here. Casks both large and small are also to be seen above ground: soft, filtered light, a wood floor and a dark wood ceiling give this hall a special ambience. The whole structure has been declared an historic monument.

Better quality than ever

Today Santa Carolina's vineyard area is mainly composed of two large properties, one at Santa Rosa del Peral in Maipo, and another at San Fernando in the Valle de Colchagua, Rapel. The firm's own vineyards have a total area of 580 hectares – not including the 60 hectares of its Viña Casablanca subsidiary (which see). These vineyards, though, yield only one-seventh of the fruit required. The rest is bought in – always as grapes, and often on the basis of long-term contracts.

The firm has four centres for winemaking at its disposal. These have been partly modernized during the 1990s – the one at Molina, for example, beside a railway crossing and close to Viña Echeverría. The average quality of Santa Carolina wines has improved considerably, in part due to this modernization, and is better than ever

Facts and figures
▶ Fernando Larrain (main shareholder)
▶ 1875
▶ 580 hectares
▶ 3,000,000 cases
▶ Til Til 2228, Macul, Santiago
▶ Tel: (56-2) 450 3000
▶ Fax: (56-2) 238 0307
▶ E-mail: beckdor@santacarolina.cl

 The best wines
• Sauvignon Blanc Reservado, Maipo Valley
• Gewürztraminer, Lontué Valley
• Chardonnay Reservado, Maipo Valley
• Chardonnay Gran Reserva, Maipo Valley
• Chardonnay Reserva de Familia, Maipo Valley
• Late Harvest, Lonfué Valley
• Cabernet Sauvignon Reservado, Maipo Valley
• Cabernet Sauvignon Gran Reserva, Maipo Valley
• Cabernet Reserva de Familia, Maipo Valley
• Merlot Reservado, San Fernando Valley
• Merlot Gran Reserva, San Fernando Valley
• Malbec, Maipo Valley

Visiting the cellars

Anyone visiting the Viña Santa Carolina cellars in Santiago has to wear special white clothing, which the porter provides. The house beside the old cellar was the home of the founder, Luis Pereira, and was built in 1875. It now contains offices and reception areas. Visits are by appointment only: tel (56-2) 450 3084.

Argentina connection

Viña Santa Carolina owns 60% of Santa Ana, an Argentine wine firm. This does well in its home market.

Macération carbonique

María del Pilar Gonzalez, who has been making the wine at Viña Santa Carolina since the late 1970s, says of the macération carbonique that it gives the red wines a deeper colour, different aromas ('more marmalade'), more fruit and greater complexity.

before. At the same time the quantity has also been increasing greatly: in 1993 the firm exported 315,000 cases, and six years later had reached nearly 1.8 million.

White specialities

Besides the basic single grape-variety white wines, which are very reliable, Viña Santa Carolina produces a number of wines made from specially selected grapes. One such is the Sauvignon Blanc Reservado, for which the vines are 60 years old. This wine has an extremely pleasing fruitiness (including passion fruit), and is just a little fat, but nevertheless tastes fresh. The Chardonnay Reservado is made by pressing whole bunches, after which half of the juice is fermented and kept in used French and American barrels for seven months. One-seventh of it undergoes malolactic fermentation. The wine is lively, its oak aromas in balance, with sometimes a touch of cinnamon or other spices, and always considerable fruit – mango, pineapple, banana and more.

A Chardonnay Gran Reserva is also produced. Half of this undergoes malolactic fermentation; and for the half fermented in cask only French oak barrels are used, and about a third of these are new. The wine is firmer, creamier, more generous than the Reservado, with generous exotic fruit and an impeccable balance.

The Chardonnay Reserva de Familia offers yet more concentration: you taste the real essence of the grape. Vines 80–100 years old, and very low-yielding at 35 hectolitres per hectare, are used for this wine. Practically the whole of it is fermented in *barricas* of French oak, half of them new; 70 per cent has malolactic fermentation, and ageing in cask lasts eleven months. Totally different in style is the Gewürztraminer, produced since 1998, a firm wine with a warm spiciness, a scent of roses and a generous character.

Viña Santa Carolina sometimes makes a little Late Harvest from Sémillon and Sauvignon Blanc, fermented in new casks of French oak. The grapes, from vines about half a century old, are often not picked until the end of May, some three months after many other whites. Noble rot means that this wine displays great class, and a delicious fruitiness that tends towards apricots.

Class in the cabernets

The best-selling red wine is the Cabernet Sauvignon Reservado, recognizable on the Chilean market by the three stars on its label, and thus known as Tres Estrellas. Every year 1.8 million litres are made, and even this is not enough to meet demand. The grapes are from vines 30–70 years old, and around a third of the wine has contact with oak barrels or staves. In addition the winemakers give it a small measure of *macération carbonique*. This mode of fermentation inside the skins is aimed at making the wine extra-rich in colour, more complex and fruity. Features of the Reservado Tres Estrellas are a lively, generous dose of fruit – berry, blackcurrant – a mouth-filling structure, a hint of vanilla and a pleasant suppleness. Quality and concentration increase with the

The Santa Rosa del Peral estate in the Maipo Valley is one of the two vineyard properties that Viña Santa Carolina owns.

Ochagavía

One of the subsidiary lines is Ochagavía. This is not an invented name: Viña Ochagavía was one of Chile's very first wine concerns, founded in 1851 by Silvestre Ochagavía. Part of the Viña Santa Carolina vineyard in Santa Rosa del Peral, Maipo, is the original Viña Ochagavía. There is no difference between the Santa Carolina and the Ochagavía wines.

Cabernet Sauvignon Gran Reserva. This fruity wine also has more oak, as 60 per cent of it spends around eight months in French barrels. The Cabernet Sauvignon Reserva de Familia, from vines in some cases 100 years old, is a traditional, high-quality Maipo Cabernet: toast, spicy oak, a touch of menthol and berry fruit are discernible in this special wine, of which two-thirds usually goes into all-new, French oak casks for a year.

Other good buys

Viña Santa Carolina makes a couple of pleasing wines by blending Cabernet Sauvignon and Merlot. The Merlot 60 per cent/Cabernet Sauvignon 40 per cent came into being at the request of an American importer, and tastes rather velvety, with a reasonable amount of black fruit. Also pleasant, with a little more freshness, is the very accessible Cabernet Sauvignon 75 per cent/Merlot 25 per cent. Both wines come from the San Fernando valley.

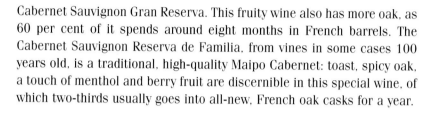

Fairly long maceration (sometimes 20 days or more), use of all the press wine, fermentation by way of *macération carbonique* for a fifth of it, and a modest eight months of cask-ageing for 20 per cent, make the Merlot Reservado into a supple, charming wine in which the black fruit is stylishly framed by oak. The Merlot Gran Reserva can be recognized by its generosity, vitality, concentration, fruit and a deep colour. It has 15 per cent *macération carbonique* and it spends a year in French barrels.

A Syrah from Maule has recently appeared in the Santa Carolina collection. The first vintage, 1997, was of striking quality though the vines were still young. As they mature this wine will gain depth. About one-tenth Cabernet Sauvignon is added, and it gets ten months or so in barrel.

Above: chief winemaker María del Pilar Gonzalez. Left: part of her domain.

The firm also makes limited amounts of a meaty Malbec, characterized by smoky black fruit. A fifth of this goes into cask.

Viña Santa Ema

Santa Ema, La Playa, Maison du Lac, Marqués de los Andes

There are two aspects to Viña Santa Ema. The winery in Isla de Maipo is a model of efficiency, with its warehouses, air-conditioned storage, modern bottling line, its laboratory and functionally-furnished offices. Further south, however, the Funda Rosaria farm in the Rapel district has a wholly rural ambience. Behind and to the side of the white house there are whitewashed cellars, barns and stables, and around them part of the 300 hectares of vineyard owned by this producer. The reason for Viña Santa Ema's winery being divided between two sites is that the price of land in Isla de Maipo became too expensive, and during the 1960s the search was on for more affordable locations in the south. Pedro Pavone, with his son Félix, established Viña Santa Ema in 1955. He had come to Chile from Piedmont in 1917, and by 1931 he had bought a vineyard in Isla de Maipo which supplied large wine firms with grapes. Today, the Pavone family are still the owners of Viña Santa Ema. The greater part of its wine is sold in bulk, but the turnover in bottled wines is growing steadily, especially in the American market so important to this firm.

Cosmopolitan reds

The fact that so much of the wine is exported to the United States, under four different labels, means that the style of some of the lines is geared to American tastes. Thus the Sauvignon Blanc usually contains five grams of residual sugar, and the ordinary Chardonnay as much as eight. The red wines have a more cosmopolitan personality. The standard Cabernet Sauvignon offers a fairly lively taste, with a good amount of fruit, a certain herbaceous quality, a little chocolate, and a modest measure of toast. One-seventh of it spends eight months in used casks. More substance, more black

The Funda Rosario house at Peumo.

Facts and figures
▶ Vinos Santa Ema (the Pavone family)
▶ 1955
▶ 300 ha
▶ 350,000 cases
▶ Izaga 1096, Isla de Maipo
▶ Tel: (56-2) 819 2996
▶ Fax: (56-2) 819 2811

The best wines
• Cabernet Sauvignon, Maipo Valley
• Cabernet Sauvignon Reserve, Maipo Valley
• Cabernet Sauvignon/Merlot Barrel Select, Maipo Valley
• Merlot Reserva, Maipo Valley
• Catalina, Rapel Valley

Memorable moments

*Turkey with
green asparagus,
tomato from the Isla de
Maipo, chicory,
courgette salad,
potatoes and fresh
bread, plus a glass of
Chardonnay: that was a
lunch outdoors in the
garden behind the wine
cellars in the Isla de
Maipo that I still recall
with great pleasure.*

*Young vines
planted in
experimental
plots next to
existing
vineyards in
the Rapel
district.*

fruit, more oak is offered by the Cabernet Sauvignon
Reserve. This matures for ten months in barrels of
French wood, a third of them new.

The Cabernet Sauvignon/Merlot Barrel Select is a
beautiful wine: a broad, supple mouth-filler. What is
also striking about this wine, which is 60 per cent Cabernet with the rest
Merlot, is the generous fruit, including black cherry and berry, while oak
aspects provide additional nuances. Half of it goes into barrels, a quarter of them new, for around eight months. Besides the velvety standard
Merlot there is a Reserva. This has a robust core, and the charred, toasty
aromas of oak, alongside ripe black fruit, form its most important
impressions. It usually spends some 11 months in oak: American barrels
are used exclusively, a third of them new.

Catalina

The name Catalina was chosen for the top red wine. This is a blend of
50 per cent Merlot, 25 per cent Cabernet Sauvignon, and 25 per cent
Cabernet Franc. All of the Catalina goes into new French casks to
mature for a year. The resulting wine has solid colour, a nuanced
bouquet, and an expansive taste that has elements of black fruit,
bayleaf, chocolate and toast. So far the amount of Catalina made has
remained limited to around 1,000 cases a year.

VIÑA SANTA EMILIANA
Santa Emiliana, Andes Peaks, Walnut Crest, Santa Isabel

Santa Emiliana was originally a brand belonging to Viña Concha y Toro. In the second half of the 1980s, when many Chilean wines were still being kept in wooden casks to give them some oxidation, the Concha y Toro shareholders decided to introduce a new line of wines that would be named for their grapes, and would be particularly fresh and fruity. To this end, 300 hectares of vineyards and three wineries were hived off from Concha y Toro and a subsidiary firm was set up, christened Viña Santa Emiliana and quoted on the Chilean stock exchange.

The new company's wines had an enthusiastic reception at home and abroad. Viña Santa Emiliana's annual sales have in the interim reached 1.6 million cases, three-quarters of which is exported: the most important market is the United States, where the Walnut Crest brand enjoys great success. The area of vineyards owned or leased has grown to 1,400 hectares, and the number of wineries to four, which have all been modernized. The firm also has a large wine storage area. Casks are not used at Viña Santa Emiliana: the oak aromas that some of the wines acquire are from the use of oak staves.

Chardonnays from Casablanca

The Sauvignon Blanc comes from three areas, Casablanca, Bío-Bío and Rapel, and tastes fresh with some pleasing gooseberryish fruit. The Chardonnay from the Casablanca valley is just as attractive. Viña

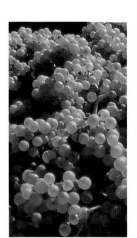

Santa Emiliana presses its grapes on the spot, right where they are grown, bringing in presses from Santiago. The must is then transferred in refrigerator trucks to one of the wineries. Grapes are picked round the clock by machine in the Casablanca valley. The Chardonnay gets neither oak nor malolactic fermentation, and is characterized by fresh tropical fruit. Walnut Crest, the American-market version of both the Sauvignon Blanc and the Chardonnay, contains rather more residual sugar.

In 1995 the firm launched a few wines from individual estates, described as 'oak aged'. At first the names Acacia Estate, Cordillera Estate

Facts and figures
▶ Guilisasti family (biggest shareholders)
▶ 1986
▶ 1,400 ha
▶ 1,600,000 cases
▶ Avenida Nueva Tajamar 481, Torre Sur, Of. 701, Las Condes Santiago
▶ Tel: (56-2) 353 9130
▶ Fax: (56-2) 205 6936

 The best wines
• Chardonnay, Casablanca Valley
• Chardonnay Palmeras Estate, Casablanca Valley
• Cabernet Sauvignon Palmeras Estate, Nancagua
• Merlot, Rapel
• Merlot Palmeras Estate, Maipo Valley

The philosophy

A spokesman for Viña Santa Emiliana describes the company philosophy as 'supplying good quantities of consistently good wines that give good value for money'.

The first Emiliana

The name Santa Emiliana comes from the wife of Melchior Concha y Toro, who founded Viña Concha y Toro in 1883.

and Palmeras Estate were used for these; however, problems with brands and marketing meant that from 1999 they now all appear under the single name Palmeras Estate. The Chardonnay has plenty of toast and vanilla in both aroma and taste, as 40 per cent of it is fermented with oak staves; alongside the oak it has elements of mango, passion fruit and peach with, too, a hint of honey and some butteriness from its malolactic fermentation.

Cabernets and Merlots

The Cabernet Sauvignon from Rapel is simply a good, clean wine with suppleness, berry fruit, a touch of plum, and just slightly herbaceous. In the Palmeras Estate version of this variety there is somewhat more depth to discover, as well as fruit (black and other berries) and oak notes; a juicier, livelier wine. The standard Merlot, from Rapel, offers a good measure of cherry, blackberry and blackcurrant, with a dash of green pepper, all contained in an almost velvety texture. In the Merlot Palmeras Estate, from Maipo valley, these aspects are enriched by chocolate, oak and toast.

Santa Emiliana use this house amid the vineyards of the Casablanca Valley for receptions

Viña Santa Ines

Santa Ines, De Martino

Within walking distance of the Viña Santa Ines cellars, in the verdant town of Isla de Maipo, you will find the various homes of the De Martino family. Their siting symbolizes the very close involvement the members of this family have with their wine firm: all the adults occupy key positions in it.

Pietro De Martino started the company in 1934, after emigrating here from Vignanello, a village near Rome. Pietro began by producing inexpensive bulk wine, based on simple grape varieties such as País. Then, in 1959, he acquired the greater part of the present 300-hectare vineyard, and this was gradually planted with superior classic French varieties. Viña Santa Ines began bottling and exporting its wines in 1990, and since that year a great deal has been invested in both cellars and vineyards. Some 85 per cent of the wine can now be fermented and kept in stainless-steel tanks in the very efficient winery buildings, and bottling is done by gravity.

Top consultants

The gifted Aurelio Montes (see Montes) acts as consultant winemaker, coming here nearly every week. And in the planting of new vines the de Martinos have been advised by the Australian Richard Smart, a well-known specialist in canopy management and like areas. The vineyard, situated not far from the winery, has sandy and clayey soil, with gravel in most of it. Some plots are carpeted with larger stones: the Maipo river once flowed here. Artificial fertilizer is not used, just chicken manure. Viña Santa Ines tries to keep the yield to at most 70 hectolitres per hectare – and since the De Martino family also owns a factory which makes concentrated grape juice, any grapes not required for wine can be most satisfactorily converted.

The Carmenères

Carmenère has a special place among the varieties here, for Viña Santa Ines was the first Chilean wine producer to register this grape officially, with a view to possible export to the European Union. In the late 1990s Santa Ines had 20 hectares growing Carmenère, an area that is set to increase after 2000.

Facts and figures
▶ Sociedad Agrícola Santa Teresa (the de Martino family)
▶ 1934
▶ 300 ha
▶ 300,000 cases
▶ Manuel Rodriguez 229, Isla de Maipo
▶ Tel: (56-2) 819 2959
▶ Fax: (56-2) 819 2986
▶ E-mail office@demartino.cl

Earthquake
The fermentation tanks acquired in 1996 have been mounted on concrete bases as a precaution against earthquakes.

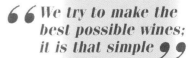

" We try to make the best possible wines; it is that simple "
~ *Paulo V. de Martino, export and marketing director*

The best wines

These all have the denominación de origen Maipo Valley, except a Chardonnay from the Casablanca Valley (the De Martino Reserva de Familia, from bought-in grapes).

• Sauvignon Blanc Reserve
• Chardonnay Legado de Armida, Santa Ines
• Chardonnay Reserva de Familia, De Martino, Casablanca Valley
• Late Harvest
• Cabernet Sauvignon Reserve
• Merlot Reserve
• Carmenère
• Carmenère Reserve
• Carmenère Las Pierras, De Martino
• Malbec Reserve

Reserves in the Santa Ines range are usually sold as Legado de Armida; those in the De Martino range as Prima Reserve or Reserva de Familia.

Various Carmenère-based wines are made here. The most common one, which also contains 15 per cent Cabernet Sauvignon, is given no wood and has an agreeable, almost creamy taste with elements of green pepper, plum and liquorice. The Reserve, with 20 per cent Cabernet Sauvignon, goes into cask for six months: it has a forest aroma, black fruit, vanilla and some toast, and is smoothly rounded. In the Santa Ines range this wine is labelled Legado de Armida, and Prima Reserve when it carries the De Martino label. Similar distinctions of nomenclature also occur with other wines. The wines of the two brands differ only slightly.

Las Piedras, a pure Carmenère, provides good concentration, plenty of colour, nice doses of fruit, and a slightly herbaceous quality. This wine spends five to six months in barrel. Around 60 per cent of Santa Ines' 2,000 casks are American oak, the rest French.

Fine Reserve wines

The Cabernet Sauvignon is made entirely from that grape, and the Cabernet/Merlot has a large proportion of it; these are good wines. More exciting, complex and substantial is the Cabernet Reserva de Familia De Martino (or Legado de Familia when it is a Santa Ines). This spends 14–18 months in new French casks, and is a seductive wine with its ripe fruit, its mint, its toast, its vanilla, its spice and its smooth yet firm tannins. The range also includes successful Merlots, the regular and the Reserve, as well as two versions of Malbec, both of which are good examples of their type.

Three white varieties

The basic Sauvignon Blanc is a pleasing wine. In the Reserve version the style is somewhat more serious, with half being fermented and then matured in cask. It can be recognized by white fruit, a silky texture, and plenty of vanilla plus other oak elements. The basic Chardonnay is rounded and smooth, creamy (40 per cent undergoes malolactic fermentation) and with slightly spiced

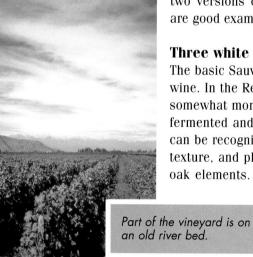

Part of the vineyard is on an old river bed.

Left to right:
Giorgio, Marco,
Paula, Reno and
Pietro De Martino
amid their vines.
Together they run
the company.

tropical fruit. The Chardonnay Reserve is some notches higher in quality: an elegant, balanced wine with notes of fresh tropical fruit, nuts, butter, generous vanilla and toast. This wine, generally sold under the Santa Ines Legado de Armida label, is fermented and matured in barrel. Around 60 per cent of the casks – all American – are new, and maturing lasts six months.

While this wine comes from Maipo, grapes from Casablanca are the rule for the Chardonnay Reserva de Familia De Martino. Here contact with oak lasts 11 months, and in this case 70 per cent of the barrels are new. A splendid bottle, it is copiously endowed with exotic fruit such as mango, the best possible oak, plus toast and kindred aromas, and great generosity. This pale gold, top-class wine was first produced in 1997.

Another white wine in the range is the agreeable Sémillon/Sauvignon, fresh, citrus-like and balanced. Nor should the Late Harvest be omitted here. In this the two latter grapes are supplemented by the Chardonnay, giving a wine with a fairly rich, sweet taste, often having 80 grams of sugar per litre, and with a quite gracious character.

Isla de Maipo

The Isla de Maipo, with 15,000–20,000 inhabitants, acquired its name because it lay between two river channels. One, however, has dried up, so it is an island no longer. As a rule Viña Santa Ines does not use water from the river for irrigation, but from three springs below the vineyard. This is of drinking water quality.

VIÑA SANTA LAURA
Laura Hartwig

The Hartwig family lived in Canada for ten years, from 1971–1981. It was from there that they started on the creation of a winery, when the wife of Alejandro Hartwig senior inherited part of the Santa Laura estate in Santa Cruz, in the Colchagua valley.

This land had been bought by her grandfather in 1928, and then used mainly for raising cattle. The much-travelled Alejandro senior was a wine lover: he had visited very many wine regions, and saw a great potential for winegrowing on the Chilean estate. After first doubling the total area, he began to plant superior grape varieties. These included Chardonnay, in 1981, and Merlot – Hartwig was one of the first in the region with this variety. The wine project, given the name Viña Santa Laura, was meant at first to be 'a retirement hobby', but it straight away developed into something more than a mere pastime. After they started to export their wines in 1997, the demand was so great that the Hartwigs had to double production after just one year, from 5,000 to 10,000 cases. This meant that they also had to extend their cellar facilities, and new buildings went up for casks and for wine-tasting. For the time being the firm does not want to grow beyond 14,000 cases a year, 'for only then can we remain personally involved in all stages of the wine process'.

Stringent selection

This personal involvement is apparent, for example, in the stringent policy of selection to ensure top quality. Only the best grapes from the firm's own 80 hectares are used – the rest go to other producers. Thus it was not until the third harvest that the Merlot was considered good enough for selling under their own Laura Hartwig name. The Hartwigs, father and son, also took great care over the choice of cask. After the first Chardonnay vintage had been fermented and aged in both new French and new American casks, samples from the various types used were then tasted blind. The wines from the casks of French oak proved to be the better. Alejandro junior believes that the French wood blends better with the fruit, is more delicate and 'adds an agreeable nutty taste'. As a result of this tasting they decided to use chiefly French oak, for the Chardonnay at least.

Elegance

The Chardonnays of later vintages show a sound balance between restrained oak aromas and fruit – spicy citrus, pear and apple. Firmness and elegance are splendidly combined in these wines, which are also slightly creamy and nutty. About 40 per cent of each harvest is fermented in cask, followed by six months' maturing, also in barrel.

In the Cabernet Sauvignon – deep red in colour, with a lively character – there are nuances of berry, black cherry, spices and oak, which combine to produce an outstanding wine. Some 50–60 per cent of it goes into cask for a year. The first Merlot vintage was the 1998: a solidly-coloured wine characterized by creamy toast, bayleaf, blackberry and other fruit. It normally spends seven to eight months in barrel.

Three varieties

Viña Santa Laura also makes Gran Reserva, a wine which is a combination of grape varieties. The leading role in this goes to Cabernet Sauvignon, with a 75 per cent presence; the two other varieties involved are Carmenère and Merlot, with 12.5 per cent each. The wine is given a whole year in used barrels, and tastes full-bodied and velvety, with plenty of black fruit and a peppery spiciness. Its structure displays a firm elegance, and its finish lingers long.

> **" Our range shows that wines can be well-made and friendly at the same time "**
> *~ Alejandro Hartwig Jr*

Below: Alejandro Hartwig senior's home. Bottom: grapes on their way to the winery.

VIÑA SANTA MÓNICA

Santa Mónica, de Solminihac

Facts and figures
▶ Emilio and Mónica de Solminihac
▶ 1976
▶ 93 ha
▶ 80,000 cases, plus over twice that in bulk
▶ Las Lilas 625, Rancagua
▶ Tel: (56-72) 231 444
▶ Fax: (56-72) 225 167
▶ E-mail: vsmonica@ctcreuna.cl

 The best wines
• Chardonnay Tierra del Sol
• Riesling
• Cabernet Sauvignon Tierra del Sol
• Merlot
• Merlot Tierra del Sol

The wines have Rancagua and Rapel as their denominación de origen.

Exports since 1983
In 1983, seven years after founding the firm, Emilio de Solminihac began exporting. At first it was solely wine in bulk, but from 1989 wine in bottle as well. Delhaize, the Belgian supermarket, is an important customer for the bulk wine.

In 1976, when Emilio de Solminihac bought the Purísima estate at Rangacua, in the Rapel region, paying $1,000 a hectare for it, some said he was mad. At that time wine grapes were often sold at below cost, and there was much more uprooting of vines than planting.

De Solminihac, however, was convinced that better times would come for the Chilean wine industry; what is more, he had discovered that in Rancagua, with its late-autumn rains, the grapes ripen superbly, giving wines with at least 12–12.5 per cent natural alcohol. Emilio, a qualified oenologist who had studied in Bordeaux as well as in Santiago, was running a wine laboratory in Rancagua at the time. Besides this, he had worked as a consultant for various winemakers. He therefore had extensive knowledge of the craft, and was extremely well-informed about all aspects of Chilean winegrowing.

Considerable investment

At first Emilio made only wines in bulk at his own firm, which he named after his wife Mónica. Viña Santa Mónica still produces more bulk than bottled wine, but even so 80,000 cases of bottles a year are already being sold, mainly abroad.

With modern equipment, Emilio has gradually extended the original old-fashioned rauli-wood vat cellar. Between 1989 and 1999 the winery underwent continuous enlargement and modernization. More than half the wine can now be stored in stainless-steel tanks, a big new platform has been built for receiving the grapes, good wine presses have been bought as well as cooling plant, and the number of maturing casks has risen from 150 to 650 – all of French oak.

Emilio has also been able to acquire the neighbouring *hacienda*. This low-built house, covering no less than 2,000 square metres, had stood empty for years. It is now used as the reception area and office.

Restrained character

All the grapes for wines to be bottled come from the firm's own land. Viña Santa Mónica has 85 hectares next to the cellar, with another eight hectares close by. The character of the wines can best be summed up as restrained. The collection includes a pleasant, slightly herbaceous, rather spicy, smooth and fresh Sémillon. And there is a gracious

Riesling: floral, fresh-tasting, with flinty, grapefruity notes. One of the most attractive white wines from the more usual grape varieties is the Chardonnay Tierra del Sol. This is fermented in barrels, half of them new, then matured in them for five months. The wine tends to have more toast than fruit, a structure that is neither too light nor too heavy, and a pleasing degree of juice.

Attractive reds

The Cabernet Sauvignon Tierra del Sol is generally an attractive red wine, its elegance of taste displaying toast, oak and a good amount of berry. It is put into casks (a third of them new) for a year. The Cabernet Sauvignon Envejecido en Bodega is matured for some years, first in large barrels and then in concrete vats. This appeals especially to lovers of traditional, if not old-fashioned, wines. The standard Merlot offers a smooth suppleness and a dark-toned flavour, with some black fruit too. The Tierra del Sol version is often Viña Santa Mónica's best red wine, thanks to a reasonable firmness, some toast – it has six months in new casks – and blackberry, cherry, a touch of bayleaf and a good balance.

> ❝ Why do I make Riesling? Not because I sell a lot of it, but because I like it ❞
> ~ Emilio de Solminihac

Top the ever-affable Emilio de Solminihac. Right: visitors are received at this handsome renovated hacienda.

Memorable moments
Viña Santa Mónica was the first Chilean wine firm I ever visited, in 1989. After tasting the wine I dined with Emilio, his daughter Mónica – who has since studied oenology at Bordeaux – and three of her friends. We ate freshly-made empanadas (hot rolls with fillings that included minced meat, onion and olives), grilled beef, sausages, potatoes and vegetables. The Sauvignon Blanc and Cabernet Tierra del Sol went deliciously with the food, complementing the very Chilean character of the meal.

VIÑA SANTA RITA

Santa Rita

Facts and figures
▶ Ricardo Claro
▶ 1880
▶ 2,000 ha (not all productive yet)
▶ 1,400,000 cases
▶ Apoquindo 3669, Of. 701, Las Condes, Santiago
▶ Tel: (56-2) 362 2000
▶ Fax: (56-2) 228 6335
▶ E-mail:
www.santarita.com

Other interests
Ricardo Claro, proprietor of Viña Santa Rita, also owns Viña Carmen, and has a 40 per cent minority holding in Viña Los Vascos.

Coming soon
New wines can be expected in the near future, including the varieties Gewürztraminer, Riesling, Viognier, Cabernet Franc, Malbec, Sangiovese and Tempranillo.

More than 30 hectares of trees, shrubs, flowers and lakes are tucked away behind the Viña Santa Rita winery buildings in Buin. This partly-walled parkland dates from the second half of the 19th century, and belongs to the firm. Standing amidst all the greenery and flower-beds is a brilliantly restored country mansion, in colonial style. Splendidly refurbished, it has been functioning as a luxury hotel since 1997. Beside it there stands a chapel – also renovated – with a steeple and a richly-painted ceiling: the bishop who was to become Pope Pius IX once celebrated mass here, and from time to time there are concerts – by I Musici, for example.

Both villa and chapel figure on the label of Viña Santa Rita's most prestigious red wine, Casa Real, which is also the name of the mansion. This wine producer has provided for gastronomic enjoyment as well: an excellent restaurant is run in an extension of the main buildings. Everything bears witness to a great sense of style and good taste – the most positive association a wine firm could wish for itself.

Cellars with a history

The story of Viña Santa Rita begins in 1880, when the senator and banker Domingo Fernandez Concha built a mansion and planted a vine-yard with French vines at Buin, not far south of Santiago. He also built his winery on the French model, next to cellars already on the site. In 1814 one of these, still standing today, had served as a hiding place for Bernardo O'Higgins, the general who achieved independence for Chile. The commander and 120 of his men were in flight after being defeated by the Spanish at Rancagua. Santa Rita's most important range has been called '120' in homage to these patriots. The second owner of the wine estate was Vicente García Huidobro, Marqués de Casa Real. He was the son-in-law of the founder and held many receptions, often attended by artists of the day, in the big house.

Exactly a century after its foundation Viña Santa Rita passed in part into the hands of the successful entrepreneur and lawyer Ricardo Claro, who eight years later acquired the remaining shares. Claro, who also runs Chile's

The hotel has its own restaurant. Below: winemaker Cecilia Torres.

glass factory and other concerns, has modernized and expanded Viña Santa Rita in a remarkable way, while at the same time more than doubling the area of the vineyards to the present 2,000 hectares. Claro was also behind the restoration of the overgrown, run-down house, the dilapidated chapel, and the less than presentable park.

Rigorous quality control

A commercial milestone was passed on December 15 1998, for on that day Viña Santa Rita exported its millionth case of wine within one year. This also signalled a complete turn-around since the early 1980s, when this producer was still mainly supplying the home market. Today foreign countries take two to three times as much of the wine as Chile.

The international trade has grown so greatly chiefly because of the extraordinarily reliable, good to very good quality of the wines. The winemakers are fond of talking about a 'consistent excellence' and a 'rigorous rejection of wine that is not wholly acceptable'. That so much has been invested in new vineyard land under Claro's direction has to do with the desire for total control of grape quality. At present their own land produces 50–60 per cent of the fruit; the rest of the grapes are bought from contracted growers. These receive bonuses if they limit their yield.

The Viña Santa Rita vineyards are spread across locations in Maipo, Rapel, Curicó, Maule and Casablanca. An increasing slice of the firm's own land is being cultivated organically – about one-fifth at present.

The best wines

• Sauvignon Blanc '120', Valle de Lontué
• Sauvignon Blanc Reserva, Valle del Maule
• Chardonnay '120', Valle del Maule
• Chardonnay Reserva, Valle del Maipo
• Chardonnay Medalla Real, Valle de Casablanca
• Late Harvest Sémillon, Valle del Maipo
• Late Harvest Sémillon Viognier, Valle del Maipo
• Cabernet Sauvignon '120', Valle del Maipo
• Cabernet Sauvignon Reserva, Valle del Maipo
• Cabernet Sauvignon Medalla Real, Maipo
• Cabernet Sauvignon Casa Real, Valle del Maipo
• Merlot Reserva, Maipo
• Merlot Medalla Real, Valle de Casablanca
• Merlot Medalla Real, Valle de Maipo
• Merlot Cabernet Sauvignon, Maipo
• Carmenère, Valle del Maipo
• Carmenère Reserva, Valle del Maipo
• Petite Syrah Merlot Reserva, Valle Central
• Pinot Noir Reserva, Valle de Casablanca
• Syrah Medalla Real, Valle del Maipo
• Syrah Cabernet Sauvignon Carmenère, Valle del Maipo
• Triple C, Valle del Maipo

Replacement of casks

Around 30 per cent of the 7,500 casks are replaced for each vintage. American oak barrels are in the majority: 60 per cent of the total.

Argentine vineyards

Viña Santa Rita has more than 700 hectares of vineyards in the Mendoza area in Argentina. The winery there is called Viña Doña Paula.

Besides its original winery at Buin the firm has some other winemaking centres, such as the relatively new one in the Rapel region.

Santa Rita '120'

The very great care Viña Santa Rita takes with its wines is clear from the products in its basic '120' range. These are most acceptable wines at altogether reasonable prices, and are produced in large quantities into the bargain. The Sauvignon Blanc crackles with freshness, its fruit often gooseberry and citrus. The Chardonnay '120' evokes a morning in the tropics: there's a freshness to the taste, alongside the bountiful tropical fruit. At least 100,000 cases a year are made of this wine alone. The Cabernet Sauvignon '120' is a supple wine that offers vanilla, berry, spices and some mint. The vanilla is due to the use of oak chips. The aroma and taste of the Merlot '120' can be described as dark-toned, with leather, bayleaf, spices and black fruit. A

Behind the cellars is a splendid park dating from the second half of the 19th century. Within the park is Santa Rita's hotel.

wine on the same quality level as the '120s' is the Cabernet Sauvignon Doña Paula rosé, popular in Belgium, Canada and Denmark. It tastes just slightly sweet and somewhat herbaceous.

Santa Rita Reserva

Grapes for wines with the Reserva designation are more stringently selected. Their yield per hectare is generally much lower, typically 12 tons per hectare for the '120' and 7 tons for the Reserva. Additionally, most of the Reserva wines have some contact with oak. The Sauvignon Blanc Reserva is rather fuller and richer, more rounded than the '120' version, with a smoother fruitiness. With the comparable Chardonnay 40 per cent goes into cask for seven months. This wine has a fine but not exaggerated toast element, along with mango and pineapple.

Abundant ripe blackcurrant is there to be tasted in the Cabernet Sauvignon Reserva, and this quite full-bodied wine has oak aromas, as 90 per cent of it spends about seven months in American barrels. Smoky toast, meatiness and a red fruit undertone are to be found in the Pinot Noir Reserva. This Casablanca wine has an almost identical time in cask to the Cabernet Sauvignon. With the Merlot, on the other hand, only about a third has contact with wood. Coffee, cocoa, spices and generous amounts of juicy black fruit typify this very good wine. The Petite Syrah/Merlot – the ratio is 70/30 – has elements of plum, chocolate, spices, oak and tannin. The Merlot percentage is fermented in barrel.

Medalla Real

The Santa Rita Medalla Real is a series with, again, a rather higher quality. Its Chardonnay is furnished with the best possible oak and a lot of toast, from its fermenting and seven months' maturation in French casks. It has a smooth roundness and creaminess after its complete malolactic fermentation, tropical fruit – mango, banana, melon – and is even more generous than the Reserva. The opaque Cabernet Sauvignon Medalla Real is apt to be very concentrated, with a long finish. Its ripe berry fruit, a touch of mint

Hotel Casa Real

The hotel in the park here at Buin has 14 rooms and suites, which cost $200–$300 a night. It is not open to ordinary travellers and tourists: reservations can only be made through Viña Santa Rita, telephone (56-2) 362 2000.

Early recognition

At a 'Wine Olympiad' organized in 1987 by the French monthly Gault-Millau, Viña Santa Rita won the first prize for red wines with a Cabernet Sauvignon Medalla Real 1984. The firm had only started exporting the year before. It was on the initiative of the winemaker at that time, Ignacio Recabarren, that Viña Santa Rita had bought its first French barriques for the 1984 vintage.

Left: Sauvignon Blanc as apéritif. Above: the famous '120' cellar.

Memorable moments

I have had the pleasure of lunching several times at Viña Santa Rita. In the restaurant, where you can eat on a balcony over a courtyard full of flowers, I enjoyed fresh congrio (a typical Chilean fish, at least as good as sole) with a juicy, fruity Chardonnay '120'. At dinner in the hotel there were hot cheese puffs and Sauvignon Blanc '120', followed by tender beefsteak with mustard sauce and Cabernet Sauvignon Casa Real.

66 *All the taste of the fresh grape should be present in the wine* 99
~ *Cecilia Torres, winemaker at Viña Santa Rita*

and its attractive oak give it an unmistakable distinction. It spends 15 months in French barrels, a third of them new. One of the other wines produced as a Medalla Real is a Syrah, spicy and fruity, and matured in *barricas* of French oak. Since the 1966 vintage there has also been a Merlot Medalla Real: a generously fruity, aromatic, dark-hued wine from Casablanca.

Casa Real

The Casa Real, a pure Cabernet Sauvignon, comes outside the regular range. It is intense in colour, aroma and taste, its fruit is black cherry and berry. It has a considerable degree of extract, a firm core and noble oak – from a year in French casks, all of them new.

Even more complexity is to be found in the scarce, prestigious Triple C, an impressive, exceptional blend of Cabernet Sauvignon, Cabernet Franc and Carmenère. Viña Santa Rita's collection also includes a lively, typical Carmenère, a powerful unoaked Carmenère Reserva, a balanced Late Harvest Sémillon, and a rather more complex Late Harvest Sémillon/Viognier.

Viña Segú Ollé

Viña Segú Ollé, Calibro, Doña Consuelo, Los Caminos

In the south of the Maule river basin, about halfway between Talca and Linares, lies the hamlet of Melozal. Four centuries ago Spanish colonists planted the first vines here, and by 1915 Melozal was exporting wine. The terrain round about is a broad valley with low hills on three sides, where the days are warm, dew forms at night and water comes from the nearby Río Loncomilla. Various kinds of soil are found in the valley, and very many hectares are planted with vines. Some plots need irrigating only twice a year, others need watering eight times. The biggest landowner is Viña Segú Ollé, a firm with a cellar complex here in which 4.5 million litres of wine can be stored.

From beer to wine

The firm dates from 1924. Its founders were three Catalans from Lérida in Spain who had gone first to Argentina. In 1910 they arrived at the village of Nueva Imperial, just west of Temuco, in the cool south of Chile. There they bought themselves a brewery, and also began local distribution of wine from the Valle del Maule. After acquiring land for themselves in this region, these enterprising Catalans started producing wine here. Jaime Segú, Antonio Segú and José Ollé (whose mother was a Segú) gave the business their family names. Vina Segú Ollé still belongs to two branches of the Segú family.

The move to quality

At first the Viña Segú Ollé land was planted solely with País and Moscatel, and the firm supplied simple, everyday wines to the Chilean home market. In 1981, however, the enterprise made a start with replacing these traditional grapes with classic varieties. Chardonnay, Gewürztraminer and Sauvignon Blanc vines were brought from the United States, and Cabernet Sauvignon and Merlot were sourced in the region. Later Riesling was planted and a nursery, which has become extensive, was begun: this includes such varieties as Carmenère, Malbec, Pinot Noir and Syrah. When the whole 240-hectare estate is productive, 70 per cent of vines will be black varieties, and 70 per

Facts and figures

▶ The Segú Amoros and Segú Segú families
▶ 1924
▶ 240 ha
▶ 80,000 cases (still increasing)
▶ Yumbel 383, Casilla 72, Linares
▶ Tel: (56-73) 210 078
▶ Fax: (56-73) 214 607

 The best wines
• Sauvignon Blanc
• Cabernet Sauvignon
• Cabernet Sauvignon Reserva
• Cabernet Sauvignon Reserva Especial
• Merlot

The denominaciónes de origen used are Valle del Maule or Maule Valley.

French oak
The few dozen casks the firm uses are all of French oak.

No difference
The different brands of wines are of identical quality.

Over-capacity

Melozal can store more than four times as much wine as Viña Segú Ollé produces, so there is considerable surplus capacity. This is used by family members who make simple wines from País, Muscatel and other such grapes. The equipment here consist 80% resin-coated concrete tanks, 10% oak barrels, 10% stainless-steel tanks.

Above: the Segú family pictured in Spain around 1900. Below: director Jorge Segú Amoros (left) and manager Justo Segú Segú.

cent of these will be Cabernet Sauvignon – Viña Segú Ollé's particular speciality.

Almost black

Cultivated yeast cells are used for the Cabernet Sauvignon, as for the other wines, and the fermentation temperature is allowed to rise to a maximum 28°C. A dark, almost black colour characterizes the red wines from this corner of Maule, and this is a noticeable feature of the three types of Cabernet Sauvignon made by Viña Segú Ollé. The regular Cabernet Sauvignon, which has 8-12 months in cask, is full of juicy, rather spicy berry fruit, tastes supple and has considerable weight. A touch of mint is sometimes perceptible. Before this charming wine goes on to the market it is given a year's bottle ageing. The Cabernet Sauvignon Reserva receives similar treatment, although its grapes are specially selected. The wine is therefore more generous and concentrated, with more nuances to it as well. Besides its fruit – berries – chocolate, cocoa and tobacco can often be tasted.

With only about 8,000 bottles a year, the Cabernet Sauvignon Reserva Especial is a fairly rare wine. It is made from only the very best grapes, it generally spends a full year maturing in barrel, and it also undergoes malolactic fermentation in cask. Among the impressions coveyed by the Reserva Especial are oak, toast, vanilla, spices and black fruit. What is striking about all the Cabernets, and the other Viña Segú Ollé wines, is their controlled alcohol content: it nearly always remains below 13 per cent. This can be credited to the microclimate of the Melozal valley.

Surprising Sauvignon Blanc

The standard Segú Ollé Merlot perhaps does not have the depth of the equivalent Cabernet Sauvignon, but it is generally a really good-tasting wine all the same, rounded and with plenty of black fruit and some bayleaf. Also in the range there is a pleasing, fruity and accessible Cabernet Sauvignon/Merlot blend.

The Sauvignon Blanc from here is a surprisingly good white wine of its kind. Partly because of its restrained alcohol content of 12–12.5 per cent, this wine has a refreshing character, is fragrant, and has plenty of fruit – gooseberry in this case. Among the other whites, the standard Chardonnay is very correct. The likeable Chardonnay Reserva, which goes into cask, offers smoky toast, smooth spices and some tropical fruit. And the Chardonnay Reserva Especial, which is fermented with oak chips and has eight months in cask, is characterized by more mild spices than the Reserva, in combination with toast and some chocolate.

Visitors welcome

Although the cellars – Bodega Mirador is the official name – are fairly isolated and can only be reached by an unsurfaced road, a reception and tasting area has nevertheless been fitted out. Visitors are always welcome, without prior appointment.

The entrance to the hospitable tasting room is marked by this sign.

SEÑA
Seña

Facts and figures
▶ Viña Errázuriz
(50%) and the Robert
Mondavi Winery (50%)
▶ 1995
▶ None (grapes are
from the Viña Errázuriz
estate)
▶ 6,000–7,000 cases
▶ Avenida Nueva
Tajamar 481, Torre Sur,
Of. 503, Las Condes,
Santiago
▶ Tel: (56-2) 203 6900
▶ Fax: (56-2) 203 6346
▶ E-mail:
jmasot@caliterra.cl

**The best
wine**
•Seña

'With Seña we wanted to get the utmost out of our joint venture', explains cellarmaster and oenologist Edward Flaherty, describing the genesis of Chile's first ultra-premium wine. Seña, a very expensive red, was created through the combined enthusiasm and exertions of the Errázuriz and Mondavi families, close collaborators in Chile.

In 1991, when legendary Californian wine producer Robert Mondavi made his first journey around Chile, he had as his guide Eduardo Chadwick, owner and director of both Viña Errázuriz and Viña Caliterra. Acquaintance led to closer contacts, and the two families not only decided to become partners in Viña Caliterra, but also to collaborate in the creation of a truly great, world-class red wine. Its basis would be grapes from the best of the Viña Errázuriz plots, and vinification and ageing would also take place there. Robert's son Tim was appointed chief wine-maker and Edward Flaherty, who worked at Errázuriz, became his right-hand man. The project was begun in 1995, and codenamed Chile 1. Later the name Seña was coined; this stands for a variety of concepts, among them 'signature', 'distinguishing feature', 'sign' and 'signal'.

Selecting and eliminating

Seña comes mainly from plots in the Aconcagua area, although fruit from Maipo is sometimes added. The vineyards at Aconcagua are often the same as those that yield Don Maximiano Founder's Reserve, the top-ranking red wine of Errázuriz (which see). As a rule, Flaherty ferments the grapes a plot at a time, resulting in hundreds of separate parcels of wine. These are tasted one by one, 'preferably from used casks, as we want to sample the wine without a lot of influence from the wood'.

The Chilean team puts together a top group of samples, and this is then tasted blind by all involved, including Tim Mondavi. The selection process lasts three days, and Mondavi has the last word. Some 60 wine samples can appear on the table on the first day, of which about two-thirds are eliminated. The second day is spent determining possible basic blends, and the final day is devoted to the definitive composition. During this process Tim Mondavi usually adds some smooth, juicy wine, as he wants the Seña style to be clearly distinct from that of the Don Maximiano: more rounded, richer, with a somewhat less heavy structure; also rather less oak. The Don Maximiano Founder's Reserve gets 16–18 months in

Seña matures in partly new, but exclusively French, barrels.

cask, the Seña a more modest 14. For both wines the barrels are French, but for Seña the proportion of new ones is a little higher (40 per cent rather than 33). At first as many as half the Seña barrels were new, but the winemakers soon found this too much and reduced the percentage.

> **The alliance of two families in which the essence of Chile, the soil and our passion for excellence are embraced**
> ~ *Eduardo Chadwick and Robert Mondavi on the Seña project*

Ageing potential and drinkability

Where the style of the Don Maximiano has been fixed (which means that this wine nearly always contains 85 per cent Cabernet Sauvignon grapes), Seña's is seen as 'developing'. The composition can therefore vary with the vintage: with or without a proportion of Carmenère or Merlot, for example. The basic grape is Cabernet Sauvignon, with nearly always a very small amount of Cabernet Franc. The proportion of Cabernet Sauvignon was around 70 per cent in the first vintages.

Seña is a wine with potential for keeping, but is also very drinkable young. In blind tastings in the USA and Germany, Seña 1995 was ranked with celebrated Bordeaux stars like Châteaux Margaux and Lafite-Rothschild; all agreed that Seña was the most drinkable wine at that moment. Supported by a solid core of often 13.5 per cent alcohol, Seña offers a taste full of style, with aspects of coffee, generous vanilla, some toast, ripe berry fruit (bilberry, blackcurrant), mint, cherry and prune; similar impressions are conveyed by its bouquet. As Eduardo Chadwick and Robert Mondavi put it, 'with Seña our dream became a reality.'

VIÑA CASA SILVA

Viña Casa Silva

Facts and figures
▶ The Silva family
▶ 1892
▶ 780 ha (only partly in production)
▶ 300,000–400,000 cases (and production is still rising)
▶ Hijuela Norte Angostura, Casilla 97, San Fernando
▶ Tel: (56-72) 716 519
▶ Fax: (56-72) 716 519
▶ E-mail: casasilva@entelchile.net

The best wines
• Sauvignon Gris
• Chardonnay Reserva
• Cabernet Sauvignon Reserva
• Merlot Reserva

All are denominación de origen Colchagua Valley

More varieties
In their new vineyards the Silva family have planted Malbec, Petit Verdot, Pinot Noir, Sangiovese, Syrah and Viognier. In total they now have the original 300 ha at Angostura, the 100-ha Santa Domingo de los Linges estate, north of San Fernando, and the 380-ha Culenco farm near Lolol, between San Fernando and the coast.

White is the predominant colour at Viña Casa Silva. Most of the walls are whitewashed, many floors have white tiles, and the concrete fermentation tanks still used here hold white wines. White has been chosen deliberately to keep a check on whether everything is spotlessly clean, for they like to be hygienic at this winery at Angostura, just north of San Fernando. Here and there on fermentation tanks you come across names such as Viña Angostura or Bouchon Hermanos, for this concern had other titles over the years. It is only since 1997, when the company started doing its own bottling, that it has been called Viña Casa Silva.

The firm's earliest history runs parallel with that of Viñedos J. Bouchon y Compañía (which see), for the two enterprises were combined for several generations. The founder, Guillaume Bouchon, travelled from Saint-Emilion to Chile in 1892, where he called himself Emilio.

In the mid-1970s, the wine estate that he founded passed into the hands of Mario Silva, on Silva's marriage to Maria Teresa Bouchon. At first Mario combined his own profession of dentist with that of wine-grower. In 1979, however, he decided to devote himself wholly to the growing of grapes and the making of wine. And enthusiastically: since then there have been vast investments, both in the cellars and in the vineyards. The area of land the firm owns has more than doubled, from 300 hectares to 780, in three locations. The day-to-day management now rests with Mario's three sons.

Remarkable Sauvignon Gris

Straight away, in its very first year, Viña Casa Silva achieved sales of 300,000 cases. That success was due in particular to the attractive price the Silva family were asking for good-quality wines. Casa Silva wines do not aim at the stratosphere, but rather at the broad middle section of the market. The emphasis is very much on reds, and these make up 80 per cent of the production. The standard Cabernet

Sauvignon is a somewhat slender wine with adequate fruit and sub-stance; the Cabernet Sauvignon Reserva offers more depth and body, as well as oak nuances.

Similar differences are to be found between the Merlot and the Merlot Reserva, and likewise between the Chardonnay and its Reserva version. This white Reserva is fermented in new barrels – half of them of French oak, half of American – and 40 per cent of the wine usually undergoes malolactic fermentation. Toast and kindred oak aromas are dominant at first.

The most remarkable wine in the Viña Casa Silva range, however, is the Sauvignon Gris. This variety was identified in 1997 by a Chilean grape expert, and since then it has been processed separately. Picking, more-over, takes place earlier than with the related Sauvignon Blanc. The wine – 10,000 litres annually in half-litre bottles – has a special aroma that evokes associations with ripe and juicy plums, together with a slight smoky quality. This is a most charming wine that comes from vines half a century old.

Character plus technology

Major modernisation of the winery took place in 1997. Since then fermentation has mainly been carried out in new stainless-steel tanks. The alterations were painstakingly done so as not to lose the character of the buildings. 'What we wanted', explains managing director Mario Pablo Silva, 'was to combine the atmosphere of yesterday with the technology of today.'

Right: white is the dominant colour here. Below: the main facade.

VIÑA TABONTINAJA

Gillmore

Facts and figures
▶ Francisco Gillmore
▶ 1990
▶ 60 ha
▶ 10,000 cases
▶ Alonso de Cordova 4281, Santiago
Tel: (56-2) 245 6500
Fax: (56-2) 242 9028
▶ E-mail:
tabontin@cepri.cl

The best wine
• Cabernet Franc, Maule Valley

Experiments with casks
Francisco Gillmore, who is also joint-owner of Viña Rucahue (which see), experiments with every possible kind of maturing cask, including steel ones with oak ends. Of the more conventional barrels, Viña Tabontinaja has around 250 in use. About one in seven of these is replaced every year. Some 60 per cent of the *barricas* are made of American oak, the rest of French.

Although the present Viña Tabontinaja cellars date from 1990, the origins of this wine estate go back three centuries. Late in the 17th century the Spanish governor of the time asked the crown for permission to plant grapes to the south of the Maule valley. So it was that between San Javier and the coast an estate emerged, at which the wine was fermented in large earthenware jars – called *tinajas*. The estate was christened Viña Tabontinaja, a name that has continued to this day – but for making the wine the jars have been replaced by stainless steel tanks and other rather more modern equipment.

Limited production
The owner, Francisco Gillmore, uses only grapes from his own land, a stretch which follows the base of a line of hills. The total area is 60 hectares; about a third of this provides grapes for Gillmore's wines, while the rest are sold to Las Viñas de la Calina (which see). Gillmore has close connections with this American firm, as can be seen from the Calina cellars sited directly behind those of Viña Tabontinaja.

The 1993 was the first vintage that Gillmore bottled, and he gave the new brand his own surname. Production has so far remained limited to 10,000 cases a year.

Excellent Cabernet Franc
Beside the Viña Tabontinaja vinification and maturing buildings, there is a fine colonial country house with a tiled underground cellar that also serves as a tasting room. The wine that Francisco Gillmore serves with most pride here is his Cabernet Franc. This wine, kept for a year in American and French wood casks, is of a high quality – as well as scarce in Chile. It has a firm yet elegant constitution, and on both the aroma and taste it evokes impressions of blackcurrant, strawberry, vanilla, and a touch of menthol.

French barrels only are used for the firm's Cabernet Sauvignon. This is generally a fairly concentrated wine with distinct elements of oak and toast, against a background of ripe berry fruit. Of the other wines made here, the pleasant, smooth Carignan is worth mentioning.

VIÑA TARAPACÁ EX ZALAVA

Viña Tarapacá, Rosario Estate, Santa Cecilia, Terra Nova, Baco

Facts and figures
▶ Compañía Chilena de Fósforos
▶ 1874
▶ 600 ha
▶ 1,000,000 cases
▶ Avenida Los Conquistodores 1700, Piso 15, Santiago
▶ Tel: (56-2) 707 6288
▶ Fax: (56-2) 233 3162
▶ E-mail: ccilveti.tarapaca@ chilnet.cl

The best wines
• Chardonnay Reserva
• Cabernet Sauvignon
• Cabernet Reserva
• Merlot Reserva
• Milenium

The wines are labelled Maipo Valley or Valle del Maipo as their denominación de origen.

Californian contact
Viña Tarapacá works closely with the Californian producer Beringer; two or three Beringer winemakers are usually present during the vintage. In Chile itself there is also a connection with Vitivinícola del Maipo.

Tarapacá's winery is classical in appearance, but the equipment inside is ultra-modern.

A bout halfway between Isla de Maipo and Talagante, you cross the Maipo river by a narrow bridge. An equally narrow road then winds up to a brick archway with a huge wrought-iron gate – the entrance to Viña Tarapacá Ex Zavala. Anyone with permission to drive through encounters one surprise after another.

The property covers a total of 2,600 hectares, and forms a little world in itself. Some 15 families, around 70 people, live here, with their own small school and a church. And here you find a large, brick-built winery – of classical appearance on the outside, but inside all state-of-the-art fermentation tanks, air-conditioned halls and an underground cellar for cask and bottle storage.

There is a small museum on site, which can be visited; and for special receptions or for accommodating business visitors a delightful 1920s country house is available in the middle of a park. Vines are in sight all the way from the entrance gates to the winery buildings. Most of them grow in an idyllic basin-shaped valley watered by the Maipo river and cooled by sea breezes. Ancient palms and other trees shade the cellars and the employees' dwellings, adding to the appeal of the place.

Wine club

Roughly one-third of the million cases a year that Viña Tarapacá produces is sold on the home market. The company is very active here with, for example, an exclusive Tarapacá wine club for private individuals, and a national football competition for restaurant waiters.

Gran Reserva

For those who like their wines traditional, with oak strongly predominant, there are the bottles with the Gran Reserva designation – Chardonnay, Cabernet Sauvignon and Merlot. Besides the usual grape varieties, in the vineyards there are Carmenère (plantings of which were quadrupled in 1999), Malbec, Petit Verdot and Syrah (used in Milenium).

Wine sans frontières

As well as its French and American casks, Viña Tarapacá uses German presses, South African de-stalkers and Italian cooling installations, filters and bottling equipment.

Unprecedented investment

It is hard now to imagine that until the early 1990s this wine valley was largely desolate and uncultivated; but so it was. Viña Tarapacá Ex Zavala only acquired this virgin land near the Isla de Maipo in 1992, after the firm had been taken over by the Chilean consortium Fósforos. Before this it had just 110 hectares of vineyard south-east of Santiago, and had led a somewhat sleepy existence.

Fósforos, a major concern whose agricultural interests include asparagus-growing, forestry, timber and more, had the financial muscle to inject no less that $50 million into Tarapacá. This huge amount, unprecedented in Chile, was spent over four years on buying the land near the Isla de Maipo, reclaiming and planting part of it (about 550 hectares at present), and building a new winery complex. Then there was the purchase of 6,000 casks – 75 per cent of them French, 25 per cent American, and a quarter of them replaced each year – among many other items. No detail was overlooked. The guest house for business visitors was tastefully furnished and decorated, with not only antique furniture but also modern works of art on the theme of wine. The bedrooms were given the names of grape varieties.

Milenium

For the resurrected Viña Tarapacá, November 28 1998 was a great day: in the presence of hundreds of guests the premium wine Milenium (the spelling is Spanish) was launched. This was born after the management asked winemaker Sergio Correa what he needed 'to create the wine of his dreams'. All his requests were granted, and not until long after the first vintage, the 1996, had been bottled did Tarapacá's owners breathe a word about the scale of the investment.

The wine is 52 per cent Cabernet Sauvignon, 30 per cent Merlot, and 18 per cent Syrah, all from carefully-selected plots. Maceration for 25 days follows the completion of alcoholic fermentation. Malolactic fermentation takes place, like the 18 months' maturing, in new French barrels. Finally the wine is given a year in bottle. In the glass, Milenium offers a deep colour, plentifull aromas of oak and of toast, ripe fruit – blackcurrant, cherry, fresh fig, red fruits – herbs including bay, a slight spiciness and a hint of menthol. Smoothness, intensity and balance are other characteristics of this long, lingering Maipo wine.

What's in a name?

In 1874 Francisco de Rojas y Salamanca planted French vines here and called his estate Viña Rojas. A later owner, Antonio Zavala, changed the name to Viña Zavala. But problems arose after Antonio Zavala and his wife separated. Eventually the president of the republic himself intervened. This statesman, Arturo Alessandri, was nicknamed 'the lion of Tarapacá'. The estate therefore acquired the name Tarapacá, with Ex Zavala added as a compromise for the two feuding parties.

66 With Milenium we want to convey our passion for excellence 99
~ René Araneda, managing director

Rooms open onto a covered central courtyard at Tarapacá's country house on the estate.

With and without oak

At a rather simpler level, less expensive wines are made from Cabernet Sauvignon alone. The ordinary version, which has no oak contact, is accessible in style with juicy berry fruit and a good structure. The Viña Tarapacá Reserva, called Gran Tarapacá on the home market, combines ripe blackcurrant with black cherry, generous vanilla, toast, and often a totally opaque colour. After the Milenium, this is probably the best red wine in the range. The Reserva is given six months in barrels, half of French, half of American oak. The Merlot Reserva benefits from similar treatment, and is dark in hue and taste – chocolate, toast, bayleaf, leather – with black fruit. As the Merlot vines age this wine will undoubtedly gain in depth and length, as will the good basic Merlot.

The Sauvignon Blanc is a clean and correct wine, with adequate fruit. Two versions exist of the Chardonnay: a slightly sweet one designed for

Some of the company's many wine awards and diplomas line a wall leading to the cellar with its 6,000 barrels.

the American market, with more than five per cent of residual sugar, and a rather drier one for the rest of the world. In both, mango and other tropical fruits are discernible, along with toast. About a fifth of the Chardonnay is aged in cask, and nearly a third undergoes malolactic fermentation. The Chardonnay Reserva is fermented in its entirety in *barricas* (some of them new), and malolactic fermentation is also total. The wine comes across as creamy, with generous fruit – both ripe pear and exotic kinds. Along with these there is plenty of toast, vanilla and spicy oak to be tasted.

VIÑA TERRA ANDINA

Terra Andina, Alto de Terra Andina

In 1995 Pernod Ricard, the French drinks group which operates world-wide, began preparations for producing wine in Chile. Unlike other players in the field of Chilean wine, however, the group opted neither to invest in vineyards of its own, nor to take over or build a winemaking facility. Instead, they went for a policy of sub-contracting. To obtain grapes, Pernod Ricard made agreements with growers for three- to five-year periods; for the winemaking, they turned to producers who would make wines for them on contract – initially seven firms. A key role in this was assigned to the Cooperativa Agrícola Vitivinícola de Curicó (which see). This cooperative, which had considerable excess capacity, was chosen not only to vinify a percentage of the wine, but also to do all the storing, ageing, blending and bottling.

Pernod Ricard also brought in the Australian winemaker Robin Day as supervisor of the project. As their international wine development director, he had already created successful wines for his French employers in Argentina, Australia, California, Hungary, South Africa and elsewhere. As Day could only get to Chile twice a year, talented French and Chilean oenologists were also engaged to oversee the day-to-day management. By 1996 this Chilean subsidiary was a fact, and was given the name Viña Terra Andina.

Terra Andina uses only bought-in grapes from the various valleys.

Facts and figures

▶ Pernod Ricard
▶ 1996
▶ None
▶ 100,000 cases (and rising)
▶ Las Urbinas 81, Of. 1a, Providencia, Santiago
▶ Tel: (56-2) 333 0735
▶ Fax: (56-2) 333 0648
▶ E-mail: prchile@entelchile.net

The best wines

• Sémillon Terra Andina, Central Valley
• Chardonnay Alto de Terra Andina, Casablanca Valley
• Cabernet Sauvignon Terra Andina, Central Valley
• Cabernet Sauvignon Alto de Terra Andina, Cachapoal Valley

1997
TERRA ANDINA
SEMILLON
CENTRAL VALLEY
PRODUCT OF CHILE

13.0% vol. 75cl.

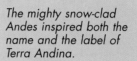

The mighty snow-clad Andes inspired both the name and the label of Terra Andina.

Sémillon a speciality

Despite a diversity of vine-yards, scattered here and there over various wine sub-regions – Casablanca, Bío-Bío, Curicó, Maipo, Maule, Rapel – the team of winemakers was at first not satisfied with the quality of what was being offered as Sauvignon Blanc. Robin Day, however, came across old Sémillon vines in Curicó and Maule, and also in Rancagua, in the somewhat cooler Rapel Valley. The growers concerned rather looked down on Sémillon – it was, after all, meant mainly for simple home-market wines.

But Day, who knew Sémillon well from both Australia and Bordeaux, believed in the poten-tial of the variety. He persuaded the growers to limit the yield to a maximum 14 tons per hectare – which still represented around 98 hectolitres – and to pick only when the fruit was fully ripe. If Sémillon grapes are not prop-erly ripe the wine will be unpleasantly grassy and herbaceous.

Thus, from grapevines 20–30 years old, a wine emerged that is marked by spicy citrus and tropical fruit: a well-balanced creation which combines a generous, smoothly rounded quality with an appetizing acidity. The wine was so well received that right from the start Viña Terra Andina sold more of it than of the Chardonnays.

The range grows

The Terra Andina range has been gradually extended since that first year. Besides the single-variety wines with which the company began, there are easy-to-enjoy blends like Sémillon/Chardonnay and Cabernet/Merlot.

> **We do not aim to make château wines, but products of a consistently high quality, in more than small amounts** *99*
> ~ *José Luis Martin Bouquillard, general manager*

Some Reserva-level wines were launched, and the French company also developed a Sauvignon Blanc and a Carmenère. Without being particularly exciting, the standard versions display a quality that is at minimum correct to good. Among the whites the Sémillon is still the front-runner, and with the reds the best to date is the Cabernet Sauvignon, a fairly supple, very enjoyable wine with blackcurrant notes. This usually contains a small percentage of Merlot, 'to heighten its elegance and complexity'. Likewise, to give the Merlot extra backbone and depth it has some Cabernet Sauvignon added.

A Cabernet Sauvignon called Alto de Terra Andina was first produced in 1997. The grapes for this did not come from a number of areas, as with the ordinary Cabernet, but solely from Requínoa, in Rapel's Cachapoal Valley: here a vineyard with low-yielding vines – eight tons per hectare – had been found. The resulting deep-red wine is striking for its powerful structure, its smooth, ripe tannins, its fine, fruity aroma (berry and prune especially). Oak and toast are also to the fore, from its 12 months in French barrels – mostly used casks

Manager José Luis Martin Bouquillard, winemaker Adriana Ceron and advisor Robin Day (right).

imported from Bordeaux, planed to give a 'new-wood' effect. The white Alto de Terra Andina is a Chardonnay, the grapes for which are harvested in Casablanca. It is fermented in *barricas*, 80 per cent of them being new, and 70 per cent French, and then ages in wood for ten months. Smooth tropical fruit, such as mango, and generous vanilla and toast generally mark this firm, pale-golden wine.

TERRAMATER

*TerraMater, Alma TerraMater, Altum TerraMater,
Casa Las Loicas*

Facts and figures
▶ Antonieta, Edda and
Gilda Canepa
▶ 1996
▶ 417 ha
▶ 300,000 cases
▶ Luis Thayer Ojeda
236, 6° Piso,
Providencia, Santiago
▶ Tel: (56-2) 233 1311
▶ Fax: (56-2) 231 6391

 **The best
wines**
• Chardonnay
Altum TerraMater,
Maipo
• Cabernet Sauvignon
Altum TerraMater,
Curicó
• Malbec TerraMater,
Curicó

It was exciting, but I would never want to go through it again, was the heartfelt comment of general manager Alfredo Schiappacase on the 1997 harvest. That year, grapes from more than 400 hectares had to be processed while a new wimery was still under construction. Complete equipment was not yet available: TerraMater had only just been established. Its birth in September 1996 after a splitting of the family estate among the Canepas. One branch kept the Viña Canepa winery, the vineyard around it, and all the brands. The other branch – the sisters Antonieta, Edda and Gilda – had the remaining vineyards.

TerraMater was founded on the basis of the sisters' inheritance, but winery buildings had to be designed and constructed fast – ahead of the coming grape harvest. A site just outside the Isla de Maipo was chosen, alongside the new firm's own 200 hectares there. The whole complex was very modern, efficient, and on a big scale. The gleaming stainless-steel tanks have a capacity of no less than 6.3 million litres – 'therefore, our mission is to grow.'

Chardonnay stands out

The basic range, consisting of single-variety wines, is sold under the trade names TerraMater and Alma TerraMater. The Sauvignon Blanc generally tastes slightly herbaceous, with juicy white fruit. A fresh, sweet version, the Late Picked, is made from this same grape. A certain generosity and a correct fruitiness characterize the Chardonnay.

The standard rises considerably with the Altum Terramater Chardonnay, a wine fermented in French barrels and then matured in them for 12 months at most. It also undergoes full malolactic fermentation. This lavish wine usually has plenty of toast and other oak aromas such as caramel and toffee, and ample ripe exotic fruit.

Fruity Malbec

Next, the reds. Because oak chips are used during malolactic fermentation, the supple Cabernet Sauvignon, along with its berry and its touch of herbaceousness, has a hint of vanilla. This is also noticeable in the Merlot, with its slight notes of bayleaf and liquorice. The Malbec can be considered one of the TerraMater specialities. It is a fairly fruity wine, not overly heavy or substantial, and with a smooth freshness to it. High in alcohol – more than 14 per cent as a rule – the Zinfandel Shiraz is a spicy, fruity wine with a deep-red colour.

Grapes from vines about 40 years old are used for the Cabernet Sauvignon in the Altum TerraMater range. These grow at the 75-hectare Hacienda San Jorge, south-east of the town of Curicó. The wine is given 12–14 months in French and American barrels. Old vines and oak combine to produce a decently concentrated and substantial Cabernet, in which there are aspects of smoky oak, black fruit and berry. This is a wine that benefits from a few years in bottle.

In 1994, not long before the division of the estate, the Canepa family had bought and planted the Hacienda San Clemente property in the Maule Valley. This is where the grapes for the Altum TerraMater Merlot come from. Because the vines here are relatively young, this wine does not yet have great depth; at the moment its aroma and taste are dominated by oak and toast from a year in French casks. The slightly herbaceous element in the taste is due to a good dose of Carmenère.

Fruit and olives
The same three sisters also own the Hacienda El Condor (which see); they grow fruit as well – particularly apples – and produce olive oil.

A quarter replaced
Of some 400 casks (80:20 French:American) around 100 are replaced with new every year.

More bottled wine
At present the greater part of the wine is sold in bulk (to Viña Terra Andina, for example – which see), but in the 21st century the firm hopes to be selling 100,000 or more cases of bottled wine annually.

Grapes that come from vines around 40 years old are used for the Cabernet Sauvignon in the Altum TerraMater range.

TerraMater S.A.
Fundo Caperana
Av. Balmaceda 4900

VIÑEDOS TERRANOBLE

TerraNoble, Valle Andino

Facts and figures
▶ Jorge Elgueta, Jorge Icaza, Pablo Prato, Patricio de Solminihac
▶ 1993
▶ 120 ha
▶ 75,000 cases (to increase to 120,000)
▶ Avenida Andrés Bello 2777, Of. 901, Las Condes, Santiago
▶ Tel: (56-2) 203 3360
▶ Fax: (56-2) 203 3361
▶ E-mail: terranob@ctcreuna.cl

 The best wines
San Clemente-Maule is TerraNoble's denominación de origen

• Sauvignon Blanc TerraNoble
• Cabernet Sauvignon Oak Aged TerraNoble
• Merlot TerraNoble
• Merlot Oak Aged TerraNoble

The Reserva line is very promising; its first wine was a Carmenère.

Wines for Calina
At Viñedos Terranoble a large amount of wine is also vinified and bottled for the American firm of Las Viñas de la Calina, which supplies bought-in grapes for this.

The six Chilean businessmen who at the beginning of the 1990s set out to start a wine business were taking no chances. First they defined the project very precisely, and then they travelled around the Chilean wine regions, looking for sites that met their requirements. In this they were advised by Henri Marionnet, a well-known French wine-grower from the Touraine district of the Loire.

The search produced three suitable properties. Their final choice fell on a 120-hectare estate, halfway between Talca and San Clemente, in the Valle del Maule east of the town of Maule; the sale went through in September 1993. In the following month the new owners, who gave their enterprise the name Viñedos Terranoble, started not only with planting the land – then lying fallow – but also with building a modern *bodega*. The design was by a firm from Stellenbosch, South Africa.

Oats among the vines
Before their own vines were mature Viñedos Terranoble used bought-in grapes. The estate now provides 70 per cent of the fruit it needs, and with an additional 40 hectares planted in 1999, this percentage will grow even greater. 'We start to make the wine while it's on the vine' is the Terranoble philosophy. Accordingly, enormous attention is given to the management of the vineyard. Chemicals are used sparingly, weed-killers never. Oats are grown between the rows of vines. This cereal crop regulates the moisture and the vines' growth rate, and at the same time inhibits weeds. The vines are only irrigated while they are still young – that is to say in the first three years. The yield is kept down to 52–78 hectolitres per hectare, at least for the top wine TerraNoble; a rather higher yield is allowed for the somewhat simpler Valle Andino wines, which represent about a third of the total quantity.

A Merlot with charm
Gamay fermented by *macération carbonique* – fermentation of whole, uncrushed grapes – is one of Henri Marionnet's specialities. The Frenchman wanted to try out this technique, which gives very fruity wines, in Chile. However, with no Gamay grapes he had to choose another variety. He chose Merlot, and the result was a great success. The Merlot TerraNoble, made with uncrushed grapes, is generously

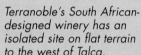

> 66 We make wines for enjoying – and always look for fruit 99
> ~ Pablo Prato, general director

Terranoble's South African-designed winery has an isolated site on flat terrain to the west of Talca.

rounded, with a meaty taste, some spiciness and plenty of black fruit – especially prune. It is an exceptionally charming wine.

The unfiltered Merlot Oak-Aged is more classic in character; it is fermented in the usual way, and 60 per cent of it goes into cask for six months. The Merlot Valle Andino contains 60 per cent Carmenère, which explains why this supple wine has green pepper on the aroma. Its slight hint of vanilla comes from oak staves and chips.

Intense berry aroma

There is, too, a Cabernet Sauvignon Oak-Aged. Between 30–80 per cent of this goes into cask, and four out of ten of the Terranoble *barricas* are of French wood. The wine spends seven to eight months in them. The features of this Cabernet are its dark colour, its backbone, and an intense aroma of spicy berry fruit, nicely supported by toast, oak and vanilla; the description 'noble' is not out of place.

Frequent contact is kept up with Henri Marionnet, and he is always in Chile for the harvest. Besides his Gamay from Touraine, the Loire winemaker has a second speciality, Sauvignon Blanc. With his help an extremely good Sauvignon Blanc has been created for the TerraNoble line. This has a floral perfume, with hints of gooseberry and asparagus too. Its lively, fresh, fairly firm taste fulfills the promise of the aroma, and there are additional notes of grapefruit and other citrus fruit.

CHILEAN RED WINE

TerraNoble

M E R L O T
1 9 9 7

SAN CLEMENTE-MAULE

PRODUCED & BOTTLED BY
MIS EN BOUTEILLE AU DOMAINE PAR
VIÑEDOS TERRANOBLE S.A., TALCA, CHILE
13 % ALC./VOL - 750 ML

PRODUCE OF CHILE - PRODUIT DU CHILI

Reserva range
Halfway through 1999 Viñedos Terranoble launched the first wine of a Reserva series, a Carmenère.

Viñedos Torreón de Paredes

Torreón de Paredes

Facts and figures
▶ The Paredes family
▶ 1997
▶ 150 ha (a further 200 ha to come)
▶ 100,000 cases (eventually to be more than doubled)
▶ Avenida Apoquindo 5500, Las Condes, Santiago
▶ Tel: (56-2) 211 5323
▶ Fax: (56-2) 246 2684
▶ E-mail: torreon@torreon.cl

The best wines
• Fumé Blanc Reserve
• Chardonnay
• Chardonnay Private Reserve
• Cabernet Sauvignon
• Merlot
• Merlot Reserve
• Don Amado Reserva Especial

The denominación de origen is Rengo.

Three late-eighteenth century watchtowers, or *torreónes*, used to stand in and around Rengo, a town of some 50,000 inhabitants. One was in the town itself, one near a Benedictine monastery, and one on an estate just south-east of Rengo, close to the Río Claro. The earthquake of 1985 left little of these bastions unscathed, but the one on the estate was soon rebuilt in its original style. There were two reasons for this: first, one of its owners was an architect with a great sense of history, and second, the tower served as an emblem and trademark for Torreón de Paredes, the wine firm based here.

A family concern

It is not known who first made wine on the site. Wine was certainly being produced here when Amado Paredes bought the property, then called El Peruano, in 1979. The new owner had left the large south-Chilean island of Chiloé in his youth, and had made his fortune in metallurgy; then, at the age of 70, he decided to become a winegrower. This came as a surprise to his seven sons, who had all followed other callings. Two of them, the lawyer Javier and the architect Alvaro, gave up their careers to bring Torreón de Paredes to prosperity. In this they succeeded in exemplary fashion. From its own land alone the firm now produces some 100,000 cases a year of high-quality wine, 80 per cent of which goes abroad.

Vineyard in the wilderness

At present Torreón de Paredes has 150 hectares of vineyard around the winery itself, though future plans are for a further 200 hectares else-where to be added in the future. The vineyard was created with the help of consultants – one from as far away as South Africa – specializing in irrigation, weed control, soil quality and canopy management. The Paredes family has also started their own vine nursery, the first plants for which came from France. But the most impressive of their projects was the development and planting of 35 hectares of stony wasteland,

A flair for design is apparent from the gateway onwards.

so desert-like that a viticulture professor at Montpellier University, the great centre of wine studies in southern France, published a study of it – with the title *How to plant a vineyard on the moon*. It took no less than five years, until 1992, to get this area under cultivatation, with 90 per cent of the vines Cabernet Sauvignons. The drip irrigation system alone that they had to install demanded ten kilometres of pipes. Fertilizer was not used anywhere, for the firm wanted to keep the average annual yield below nine tons per hectare (this equals about 60 hectolitres per hectare).

Bigger barrels

There are some concrete vats in the rectangular cellars, but stainless-steel tanks are used mainly, along with other modern equipment. There is also a cask cellar dating from the end of the 18th century, thick-walled and full of atmosphere. For visitors it is lit by candles. The 550–600 barrels it holds are of French oak, and have a capacity of 300 litres instead of the usual 220. With this larger size the influence of the wood is somewhat reduced, and there is a modest financial advantage in using bigger casks. Next to this cellar there stands a fine, colonial-style house, set in its park. This is used solely for receptions and wine tastings.

The white wines

Whites are in the minority at Torreón de Paredes, representing only a quarter of the total production. The standard Sauvignon Blanc is a fresh-tasting wine, and has mainly citrus fruit in its aroma, including some

A little support

In the basic Cabernet Sauvignon there is always some 5 per cent of Merlot, and 2–5 per cent Cabernet Sauvignon in the Merlot. This 'hidden help' gives the wines just that little bit extra.

Viña Las Nieves

In 1997 the brothers Javier and Alvaro Paredes set up a subsidiary, which began to come on stream in 1999. Sited in Chanqueahue just north-east of Rengo, Viña Las Nieves is expected to be producing half a million cases a year before 2005. The firm works both with grapes from its own 100 or so hectares and with bought-in fruit.

Bottling

To get impeccably bottled wines all the bottles are washed in purified water, and then corking is done under vacuum 'to boost the life of the wine and the cork'.

Clear water

The water available to Torreón de Paredes is very pure and clear. The Río Claro, which flows nearby, is certainly well-named, and the source for one of Chile's best-known brands of mineral water is in the Rengo area. Besides its wine, this narrow part of the Valle Central is known for its peaches, tomatoes and almonds.

grapefruit. The Fumé Blanc Reserve offers greater depth and more nuances – not only because a quarter of it is fermented in cask and then matured in them for at least five months, but also thanks to some 20 per cent of Sémillon with which the Sauvignon Blanc is augmented. This wine has power, slight nuances of oak, toast and vanilla, juicy white fruit and balanced acidity.

A lively character, fresh tropical fruit and a dash of spices make the basic Chardonnay a very attractive wine. There is, too, a flinty-fruity Chardonnay Reserve characterized by oak and given four to six months in cask. The top of the range is the Chardonnay Private Reserve, a frequent prize-winner with toast noticeably present in both its bouquet and its firm taste. Some of it is fermented in casks (40 per cent new) and kept in them for five months. In addition, malolactic fermentation occurs in about a seventh of the volume.

Torreón de Paredes also sells a Late Harvest wine: this is made from roughly equal amounts of Riesling, Gewürztraminer and Sémillon. A fairly rich yet at the same time elegant creation, it is not overly sweet and has fine nuances.

Jammy fruit

The standard Cabernet Sauvignon is a striking wine, with its firm structure and its almost jammy fruit – ripe blackcurrant and black cherry. Often this meaty wine also offers small doses of mint, herbs, spices, tobacco and oak – a quarter of it goes into used casks for a year – and its tannins are smooth and fine rather than aggressive. This is the wine

Cornucopia in the winery's courtyard.

that Torreón de Paredes makes most of, and it has perhaps greater appeal than the more traditionally-styled Reserve and Private Collection Cabernets. In the standard Merlot, black fruit, leather, bayleaf and a smoky quality can be discerned, together with some hints of green pepper – perhaps from one-fifth of it being Carmenère. The Merlot Reserve comes from vines of around 20 years old, and matures for six months in cask. This wine has an expansive, mouth-filling taste with ample fruit, including cherry, blackcurrant and blackberry, with of course oak.

Don Amado Reserva Especial

A small amount of Don Amado Reserva Especial – some 1,000 cases – is produced in very good years only: so not in 1995, for example. The first selection takes place in the vineyard, and a second is carried out after the malolactic fermentation is complete. What is remarkable about this wine is that the blend of varieties used can vary greatly from year to year. Thus for the 1996 vintage 75 per cent Cabernet Sauvignon and 25 per cent Merlot was used, and for the 1997 around 85 per cent Merlot, 10 per cent Carmenère and 5 per cent Cabernet Sauvignon. And ageing – always in new wood – can vary from a year to 16 months. Blends with the most Merlot are matured for the shortest period, which is perhaps one reason why they are the best. This 1997 wine offers a lot of toasted bread and black fruits, splendid concentration, a velvety generosity.

Above: 'Torreón' refers to this ancient, restored watchtower.
Left: entrance to the atmospheric barrel cellar.

Vintage celebration

Every year the Paredes family organizes a vintage party for all the estate's employees, from the grape-pickers to the office staff. It includes a barbecue, and there is much dancing of the traditional Cueca.

66 *Fine wine can only be made from fine grapes* 99
~ *the brothers Javier and Alvaro Paredes*

Sociedad Vinícola Miguel Torres

Miguel Torres

Facts and figures
▶ Miguel Torres
▶ 1979
▶ 345 ha (not all in production yet)
▶ 165,000 cases (and increasing)
▶ Pan-Americana Sur Km 195, Curicó
▶ Tel: (56-75) 310 455
▶ Fax: (56-75) 312 355
▶ E-mail: mtorres@entelchile.net

 The best wines
• Sauvignon Blanc Santa Digna
• Sauvignon Blanc Bellaterra
• Sauvignon Blanc Bellaterra
• Chardonnay Reserve Santa Digna
• Riesling Late Harvest/Cosecha Tardía
• Cabernet Sauvignon Santa Digna
• Cabernet Sauvignon Manso de Velasco
• Cordillera, Valle del Maule
• Miguel Torres Brut Nature

When a denominación de origen is used, this is generally Curicó.

Within two decades Miguel Torres has managed to increase the area of his Chilean vineyard three-fold.

In the autumn of 1995 the Spaniard Miguel A. Torres received the high Chilean honour of Gran Oficial de la Orden Bernardo O'Higgins. This award, seldom given to foreigners, was intended as a tribute from the government 'to a person who had distinguished himself at world level' with 'great humane and enterprising qualities'. This is the most important among the many honours and tributes that Torres has been given in Chile. A typical accolade came in a dedication from restaurateur Jorge 'Coco' Pancheco: 'To Miguel, the winegrowing father of our country'. This refers to the way in which Miguel Torres revolutionized the Chilean wine industry, introducing previously unheard-of techniques, single-handed. He was the first to ferment white wines at low temperatures in stainless-steel tanks, and also the first to import American casks.

Journey of exploration

Torres' decision to go and have a look at the country in the first place was partly due to the Chilean oenologist Alejandro Parot, a fellow student of his from Dijon. Alejandro had made a number of visits to Miguel at his very successful wine enterprise in Vilafranca del Penedès, in Catalonia, and had told him a lot about Chile. At the end of March 1978 Miguel explored the South American country for the first time. He remembers how light the traffic was then, the old American cars, the hotels with no air-conditioning, the rural poverty, and the old-fashioned equipment in the wineries. He was, however, struck by the impressive scenery, by the exceptional climate, the good soils and the plentiful presence of excellent European grape varieties. Along with Alejandro he travelled to the southern town of Concepción and back again.

It was in Curicó that they came upon a wine estate belonging to the old aristocratic Ahrex family, who had financial problems at the time. Alejandro advised Miguel Torres to buy at least part of their estate, as otherwise this would just go to the bank. After consulting with his father, who also visited Chile a few times, the deal was struck. This was in January 1979; Miguel immediately set about modernizing the estate. The equipment needed was not then available in Chile, so everything had to be imported from Spain: presses, tanks, cooling system. Even the welders who put it all together were Spanish.

Vive la différence

For Torres it was a great adventure. He saw that it was very important to make different wines from the other producers, 'otherwise I might

Constant experiment

As in Catalonia, the firm is continually experimenting – with grape varieties, cloning, irrigation methods, density of planting and various types of maturing casks.

Sweet wine for Chile

The Miguel Torres Late Harvest/Cosecha Tardía, made from Riesling grapes, is available only in Chile. The wine comes from grapes affected by noble rot, has an almost golden hue, and nuances that include apricot and honey. It is sold in half-bottles.

Early picking

In the Torres vineyards, which supply 90 per cent of the grapes required, all picking is by hand. This normally takes place from 7am to 1pm. The grapes are then kept in a cool place until they are processed.

Visitors welcome
*A billboard beside the
Pan-Americana tells
travellers that they can
visit the estate. So far
some 2,000 people a
year have accepted
the invitation.*

**Festival in the
square**
*Miguel Torres is the
initiator of an annual
wine festival held on
the Plaza de Armas in
Curicó. Lasting for
three days, the event
consists of various
contests (treading
grapes, racing with
bottles on a serving
tray), the election of a
wine queen – who is
given her weight in
wine – an exhibition of
wine-related art, and
the reciting of poetry
on wine. At the
conclusion there is a
paella lunch in the
Torres cellars for a few
hundred guests. Other
wine producers now
take part, including the
local cooperative and
La Fortuna.*

just as well take my wine to Concha y Toro, for example. I would rather make bad wines that everyone talks about than wines like everyone else's.' Bad wines, however, are not what Torres' Chilean establishment was, and is, all about. They made such an impression that the country's whole industry was jolted awake. Other wine firms emulated Torres and bought stainless-steel tanks and cooling equipment; and now that the potential of such grape varieties as Chardonnay and Sauvignon Blanc had finally been grasped, these were planted more often.

More land, more production

Miguel Torres' original investment totalled $200,000, but since then many times this amount has been spent. To the 102-hectare vineyard in Curicó, the Fundo Maquehua, two others were added: the Fundo San Francisco Norte in the Lontué Valley in 1984, and the Fundo Cordillera in the valley of the Río Claro in 1991. These acquisitions brought the total land area to 345 hectares, of which about 300 hectares will have been planted by the beginning of the 21st century.

Since then Torres has bought land near San Clemente and Linares expressly for black varieties – not just French but Catalan as well. The winery in Curicó, situated close to the Pan-Americana highway, was also

enlarged. A battery of tanks with all their fittings stands outside the building under a lean-to roof, while the bottles and around a thousand 300-litre casks are accommodated in air-conditioned halls. A chalet-type tasting and sales building was constructed, and an office in the same style. For himself, his family and guests Miguel had a comfortable *casita* built on the edge of a vineyard, where he stays two or three times a year.

Improvement in quality

The quality of Torres' Chilean wines has improved alongside the quantity. The Santa Digna Sauvignon Blanc is today a fairly full-bodied wine, characterized in particular by tropical fruit with, too, a hint of fennel. Bellaterra is the name of a Sauvignon Blanc partly – 60 per cent – fermented in barrel, with elements of toast, vanilla, exotic and citrus fruits, and gooseberry. The casks are new and American, and the ageing period is around six months. Oak, as well as toast and roasted almonds, are also found in the Santa

Digna Chardonnay: 90 per cent of this wine is fermented in new French *barriques*, and it then spends seven months in them. Ripe pear and juicy tropical fruit can be tasted in this quite generous wine, about a third of which is given malolactic fermentation.

The Don Miguel is popular in Britain and Sweden, among other countries. It is a slightly sweet white wine based on equal parts of Riesling and Gewürztraminer. The first gives it freshness and a flowery quality, the second spiciness and a touch of orange.

Sparkling wine

There is a special niche in the range for the Miguel Torres Brut Nature, a sparkling wine that is among Chile's best. It carries a vintage date, and is composed of Chardonnay and Pinot Noir, the percentages varying by vintage. The proportion of the white grape can range from 60 to 75 per cent – it was even 90 per cent in the early years. Brut Nature is made by the Champagne method – i.e., with a second fermentation in the bottle. The wine then rests on its lees. Its characteristics are a correct mousse and a quite high degree of acidity, which is balanced by its creaminess, yeasty aromas and citrus fruit. The annual production is around 6,000 cases.

The Santa Digna Rosé is another speciality, made exclusively from Cabernet Sauvignon. The wine displays a little sweetness (with some eight grams of residual sugar, about 13 per cent alcohol), flavours of red fruits such as strawberry, and a slight herbaceous quality. It is a great success in Spain, and Miguel himself recommends it with Oriental dishes.

Varietal and blended wines

'Friendly' is a good term to describe the Santa Digna Cabernet Sauvignon, a supple wine containing a lot of blackcurrant and some

The best grapes are always picked by hand.

Above: some of the 1,000 300-litre casks at Torres. Right: Miguel Torres on receiving his Chilean order.

Culture and wine

In 1999 Miguel Torres opened the Centro Culturel del Vino in Santiago at Roger de Flor 2900, Las Condes. Tel (56-2) 245 1101, fax (56-2) 245 1219.

plum, with oak and vanilla as well. It is left to mature for about seven months in casks. The Cabernet Sauvignon Manso de Velasco comes from vines in the Fundo San Francisco Norte vineyard which are at least a century old. This wine, named after the founder of Curicó, spends 18 months in barrels – 45 per cent of them new – and combines a dark colour with muscular strength, concentration, ripe berries, smooth oak notes, and a certain refinement.

Since the harvest of 1998 Miguel Torres has made a remarkable blended red wine, the Cordillera. This is a generous-tasting *assemblage* made from 60 per cent Cariñena grapes from old, dry-farmed vines, supplemented by 30 per cent Syrah and 10 per cent Merlot (in the future the Merlot will probably be replaced by Garnacha). It comes across with red and black fruit and a hint of liquorice, smoky oak and plenty of vanilla. It is kept for 10-12 months in barrels, mostly of French wood, of which a quarter are new, and in which malolactic fermentation also takes place.

> **Chile is a paradise for winemakers**
> ~ Miguel A. Torres

VIÑA UNDURRAGA
Undurraga

Some 25,000 people a year visit Viña Undurraga, attracted not just by the wine and the cellars, but by the park as well. This was laid out at the end of the 19th century in classical French style by the Paris-trained Pierre Dubois. Huge eucalyptus trees, palms, brightly coloured bougainvillaea, feathery pampas grass and oleander grow around lawns and lakes. In the centre of the park there stands a modest bust of Chile's liberator Bernardo O'Higgins; as far as is known this is the only sculpture of him in civilian clothes.

Beside the park there is a house in Basque style, with a lot of dark wood and old furniture; Francisco Undurraga, founder of this wine firm, came from a Spanish Basque family. The year of its foundation was 1885, but Francisco had bought the necessary land, 34 kilometres south-west of Santiago in the Valle del Maipo, three years earlier.

He called the estate Santa Ana, after his wife; the couple are portrayed almost lifesize in a painting in one of the offices. There they both sit, on a bench with the park and a water tower as background; he in a straw hat, she with a folded parasol. This portrait, dated 1895, was by Francisco himself, for besides being a winegrower he was a politician, lawyer, writer and painter.

Investment in land

Francisco Undurraga obtained the vines for his estate directly from France and Germany. To preserve them on the long sea voyage – and to check their growth – he had them packed in lead and kept cool. By 1903 the first exports of Undurraga wines, to the United States, were already being made; today Viña Undurraga exports about 60 per cent of its total annual production of 1.5 million cases to more than 50 countries.

Under succeeding generations – the firm is still run by Francisco's descendants – the area of the Undurraga vineyards has grown. At present the estate covers nearly 1,000 hectares, divided over four properties – two each in the Maipo and Colchagua valleys. About half of the grapes that the firm uses for its wines come from these holdings; the rest are bought in.

Facts and figures
▶ Undurraga family and Inversiones Hampton Chile
▶ 1885
▶ 995 ha
▶ 1,500,000 cases
▶ Lota 2305, Providencia, Santiago
▶ Tel: (56-2) 372 2900
▶ Fax: (56-2) 372 2901
▶ E-mail: info@undurraga.cl

 The best wines
• Sauvignon Blanc, Lontué Valley
• Chardonnay, Colchagua Valley
• Chardonnay Reserva, Maipo Valley
• Chardonnay Winemaker's Reserve, Maipo Valley
• Cabernet Sauvignon Colchagua Valley
• Cabernet Sauvignon Reserva, Maipo Valley
• Cabernet Sauvignon Bodega de Familia, Maipo
• Merlot Reserva, Maipo Valley
• Carmenère Reserva, Colchagua Valley
• Pinot Noir, Maipo Valley

VIP visitors

Many heads of state, other dignitaries and distinguished visitors have been entertained at Viña Undurraga. Among them have been the King and Queen of Belgium, the Duke of York (later George VI of Great Britain), the Queen of Denmark, the King of Norway, presidents and prime ministers from around the world and of course Chile, and Nobel literature prizewinner Gabriel García Márquez.

Ambience and efficiency

The original cellars, dating from 1885, still exist, protected by their thick white walls, and partly underground. They have atmosphere in plenty, but today are used only to a limited extent for storing wine; the splendid big, old casks there are now filled with water. Since 1996 Viña Undurraga has boasted an ultra-modern, functional complex tucked away behind the handsome old cellars. This state-of-the-art winery is fully equipped with stainless-steel fermentation tanks, with pneumatic presses that move on rails, with various kinds of filters, and with cooling apparatus. A number of the 3,000 or so barrels (two-thirds of them French, one third American) are also housed in the new buildings.

White wines for export

In Chile itself most of the Undurraga wines can easily be recognized by their flat, squat bottles, the shape of which calls to mind Germany's traditional *Bocksbeutel* from Franconia. These simple wines for local consumption bear such names as Roble, Rhin, Cabernet Pinot and Merlot. The export qualities, though, are shipped in the normal Bordeaux- and Burgundy-style bottles. Among them is the Sauvignon Blanc, a floral, fresh wine with citrus and a very slightly spicy touch. The standard-quality Chardonnay, made from Colchagua grapes, is a friendly, very supple, reasonably generous wine with just a little fat and some tropical fruit notes. For the Chardonnay Reserva, grapes from Santa Ana,

Three thousand barrels are in use for maturing the wine here, the majority of them French.

Undurraga's handsome old cellars, full of atmosphere, are today mainly for show rather than for use.

Memorable moments

One of my visits to Viña Undurraga concluded with lunch in the Basque-style house. Pedro Undurraga – later to be an ambassador – had some fascinating stories to tell. A splendid, fresh and fruity Chardonnay accompanied smoked Chilean salmon served with thick green asparagus: a harmonious pairing of delicacies.

the original estate in Maipo, are used. The juice from these grapes is fermented and matured in French casks; a little of it undergoes malolactic fermentation. Toast, fruit and freshness are equally balanced in the resulting wine.

The Late Harvest, made from Sémillon, is altogether different in composition. It is not exuberant, but is gold-coloured and sweet, with quite a lot of oak in aroma and taste. The generous, slightly spicy and full-bodied Gewürztraminer is a wine of a very different character again.

Splendid Cabernet

Among the red wines the standard Cabernet Sauvignon is notable for its tempting jammy fruitiness – with a lot of blackcurrant – and at the same time it is nicely mouth-filling, with some creaminess and a hint of mint. The Cabernet Reserva, aged for a year in cask, generally sports a deep colour and a supple taste with nuances of smooth berry and spicy oak, which together add up to a delightful whole.

The characteristic aromas of black fruit (especially cherry), spiced with bayleaf, are to be discovered in the sound basic Merlot. The Merlot Reserva adds oak to this, as 85 per cent of it spends six months in French wood casks. The Carmenère Reserva is related to this Merlot, and is a model of its kind with hints of green pepper, black fruit and chocolate. This charming wine with its rounded taste does not see wood.

Food for dinosaurs

In the park there stands a tree-sized shrub called the ombu. This also grows a lot in Patagonia – and would once have served as a 'vegetable' for dinosaurs. Pierre Dubois, who laid out the Undurraga park, designed others in Chile, including the Parque Forestal in Santiago.

Visiting Undurraga

The Viña Undurraga premises and park can only be visited by appointment. Tel: (56-2) 372 2932. The estate lies between Malloco and Talagante.

Beautifully integrated

The Pinot Noir is Burgundian in style, strongly expressive of its grape, smoothly fruity and well-structured. To give it more backbone and colour, the press wine is usually blended in. The Reserva version tastes rather more mature and also offers some wood, from its eight months in used casks. The top red wine of the Undurraga range is called Bodega de Familia, and it is a pure Cabernet Sauvignon. Its grapes come from old vines, and macerate with their skins for about 20 days. Its year-long maturing takes place in new French barrels. This method produces a solidly-coloured wine, very substantial, tremendously fruity – blackcurrant and prune – and with toasty, smoky, beautifully integrated oak.

Other wines

The 1998 vintage saw the first appearance of the Chardonnay Winemaker's Reserve, a generous, creamy wine, 80 per cent of which undergoes malolactic fermentation. Other, as yet unnamed, wines in the range are a somewhat earthy, simple sparkling wine, 60-40 Chardonnay and Pinot Noir, which undergoes its secondary fermentation in tank, and a rosé. Then there is the firm's brandy, made from Sémillon grapes, called Peruetxea (Basque for 'Peter's house').

Self-portrait of the company's founder, Francisco Undurraga, with his wife Ana.

Viña Valdivieso
Valdivieso, Stonelake, Saint Morillon, Mitjans

Facts and figures
▶ The Mitjans family
▶ 1879
▶ 200 ha
▶ 500,000 cases of still wines, 400,000 sparkling
▶ Juan Mitjans 200, Macul, Santiago
▶ Tel: (56-2) 381 9269
▶ Fax: (56-2) 238 2383
▶ E-mail: valdivie@ctcreuna.cl

The music sounded as if old Bach had secretly been a Chilean all along. And as I listened I had a vision. It was of a champagne, as good as the fine Clicquot that Doña Camila served that evening, but from Chile, not from France. And this would show the world the burning fire in our souls that makes us Chileans!

So wrote Alberto Valdivieso in his diary on February 10, 1876, after he had attended a piano recital at the house of Camila Aldunate. Until that day Alberto had led a carefree existence. Four years earlier he had come back from France after completing studies there; life since then had consisted mainly of attending parties and musical performances, enjoying his champagne the while. But the idea of making a Chilean version of champagne changed Alberto overnight from hedonistic loafer to passionate entrepreneur.

He travelled to Champagne and studied the technology there, hired experts, and had the first Chardonnay and Pinot Noir vines imported into Chile. These were planted at the Santa Elena estate near Santiago, which he acquired in 1879 and named after his wife. French engineers also helped him with the building of a partly underground winery complex, and with the installation of all the necessary winemaking equipment. Finally, in 1887, Alberto opened his first bottle of Brut and his vision of eleven years before had become a triumphant reality.

The best wines
• Chardonnay Reserva, Lontué
• Cabernet Sauvignon Reserva, Lontué
• Merlot Reserve, Lontué
• Pinot Noir, Central Valley
• Pinot Noir Reserve, Lontué
• Malbec, Central Valley
• Malbec Reserve, Lontué
• Cabernet Franc Reserve, Lontué
• Caballo Loco, Lontué

The term Reserve is sometimes replaced by Reserva or the letter V, and The Primavera Vineyard may be named on Stonelake labels.

Presidential encouragement
Valdivieso's sparkling wines had an enthusiatic reception: they were not only served in all the better restaurants and hotels in Santiago, but also in all of Chile's government ministries, all the embassies, and in the presidential palace. Success was his – but eventually Alberto found himself left with a small surplus of Chardonnay grapes. He decided to use them for still wine, at first just for his family. However, after the president of the republic had had supper at the Valdiviesos' and drunk Chardonnay 1908 there, he insisted on having the wine to serve in his palace and summer residence. On 19th September 1912 Alberto wrote,

Many brands

Viña Valdivieso supplies a great deal of wine for private labels, and its products are therefore in circulation under many brand names – Los Catadores is one example. Of the firm's own brands, Stonelake is generally a little cheaper than the comparable types with Valdivieso's own label, partly because more American wood casks are used for it. The simplest range, with just the basic wines (and no Reserves) is the Saint Morillon. This line was created initially for the United States.

Early picking

The first grapes – for the sparkling wines – are generally picked early, between January 20–25, and at the point when the Chardonnay and Sémillon have enough sugar to give around 10 per cent alcohol. The 200 hectares of vineyard owned by Viña Valdivieso yields sufficient grapes for 30 per cent of its production. The rest of the grapes are bought in, mostly on the basis of 5–15 year contracts.

'I found it impossible to refuse. And now the decision has been taken, I note that I am excited about the possibilities.' So it was that a second range, of still wines this time, came into being.

Large-scale investment

Less than 15 years after Alberto Valdivieso's death in 1935, Viña Valdivieso was taken over by the family firm of Mitjans. Founded in 1903 by Juan Mitjans, of Spanish origin, it produces not only wines but every kind of distilled drink and liqueur. This energetically-run business was the first in Chile to develop cold storage for grapes, and during the 1990s in particular it invested in modern cellar equipment on a large scale. This can be seen most clearly in the winemaking centre at Lontué, where all the firm's own or bought-in grapes are processed. Until about 1994 some three million litres were still being kept there in old wooden casks, but today stainless steel gleams practically everywhere.

The Alberto Valdivieso tradition of making sparkling wine has been carried on by the Mitjans family. Viña Valdivieso produces 400,000 cases of it a year. The greater part of this is sold in Chile: Valdivieso is the leader in the sparkling wine sector there. More than half of the production consists of wines made by the Charmat method, with secondary fermentation in closed tanks, but the champagne technique introduced by Alberto Valdivieso is still used as well. Measured by international norms even the wines sold as Brut or Extra Brut are on the sweet side: 12–13 grams of sugar per litre is customary.

Where 90 per cent of the sparkling wines remain in Chile, exactly 90 per cent of the still wines are exported. The latter are quite clearly of international standard. And nine out of ten bottles contain red wine.

Unusual reds

As a proportion of Pinot Noir had long been used for the better sparkling wines, it followed that Valdivieso would also make still wines from the same grape. The basic version is distinctly supple, with plummy fruit. The quality rises with the Pinot Noir Reserve: the grapes for this come from the firm's own vineyard of La Primavera, in the Sagrada Familia district not far from Lontué. It is a sturdily-built wine with ripe fruit – cherry, plum and berry – supplemented by toast and smooth, spicy oak. Some of this appealing, well-balanced wine is fermented in cask and, like all the Reserves, it is also given between 12 and 14 months' maturation in *barricas*, about a third of which are new.

Another noteworthy varietal here is the Malbec. This generally ample wine also boasts plenty of black fruit. The Malbec Reserve tastes more voluptuous and intense: a wine that along with its generous fruit – blackberry, blackcurrant, and sometimes red fruits – has an attractive undertone of toast and vanilla. When the well-known Argentine wine-maker Nicolas Catena tasted this wine from the cask he paid it a back-handed compliment: 'This is unfair! After all, we Argentinians are the Malbec specialists.' A third remarkable red varietal is the Cabernet Franc. The vines for this wine, which is generally sold as a Reserve, are

During the 1990s Valdivieso invested heavily both in new winemaking equipment and in oak barrels.

Thousands of casks

In 1994 there were 500 casks in the cellars at Lontué; five years later there were 5,000. About 30 per cent of these are new each year; the ratio of French to American oak is 75:25.

Historic cellars

The cellars in Lontué date from the beginning of the 19th century, and were acquired in 1850 by the wealthy Correa Errázuriz family – who at one stage supplied half the wine in Chile. The wine, in those days usually of ordinary quality, was carried by train to Santiago. The Mitjans family bought the winery not long after World War II. The brand name F. J. Correa Errázuriz is still used by the cooperative at Curicó.

nearly a century old. It is distinguished by a deep colour and a some-what liquorice note, with ripe fruit, some chocolate, a hint of vanilla and integrated oak. Mention must also be made of Valdivieso's substantial Carignan Reserve, characterized by toast.

Cabernets and Merlots

Staves or chips are used as a rule to give the basic single-variety reds a slight touch of oak – as with the Cabernet Sauvignon, a wine of correct quality, rich in colour with reasonable body and berry fruit. The Cabernet Sauvignon Reserve, a wine with around 14 per cent alcohol, offers more colour, more fruit, more breadth, more length and more oak. There is often even more alcohol in the Merlot Reserve: this wine comes from low-yielding vines – eight tons per hectare – and is redolent of sun-drenched black fruit, raisins and oak. The standard Merlot is less over-whelming: a readily drinkable wine that in fact also contains Carmenère.

Caballo Loco

Since the amount of wine needed to fill a given number of 12-bottle cases does not always correspond exactly with what is available in the barrels, there are always some casks of Reserve quality left over. On the initiative of Viña Valdivieso's winemaker, it was decided to blend these small 'remnants'. This was how Caballo Loco was created, an *assemblage* put together from different types of wine left in the cask, and from two successive harvests. This remarkable wine therefore differs in character with each bottling, but toast, oak, vanilla and chocolate are nearly always to the fore, with varying fruit notes and a firm constitution. Its production is kept to around 800 cases a year.

Whites in a minority

Although still white wines are very much in the minority here, these can be thoroughly charming in the glass. They are led in quality by the Chardonnay Reserva, a wine mainly fermented in cask and dominated by creaminess and tropical fruit. It undergoes malolactic fermentation in its entirety, and spends seven months in wood. The grapes come exclusively from the La Primavera estate.

The fairly generous basic Chardonnay is not so complex or expressive. Depending on the market it is meant for, the standard Sauvignon Blanc can be either reasonably dry, fruity and a little grassy, or more neutral and slightly sweet, with about six grams of residual sugar.

VIÑA LOS VASCOS

Los Vascos

The office is in traditional style.

Facts and figures
▶ Domaines Barons de Rothschild (51 per cent), Viña Santa Rita (40 per cent), Estrella Americana Mutual Fund (9 per cent)
▶ 1975
▶ 500 ha (about 300 ha in production)
▶ 300,000 cases (and rising)
▶ Benjamin 2944, Of. 31, Las Condes, Santiago
▶ Tel: (56-2) 232 6633
▶ Fax: (56-2) 3214373

The best wines
• Cabernet Sauvignon, Colchagua
• Cabernet Sauvignon Grande Réserve, Colchagua

When Domaines Barons de Rothschild, the controlling company of Château Lafite Rothschild among others, decided to extend its activities to Chile, technical director Gilbert Rokvam travelled over to investigate. His first step was a tasting of 167 wines, assisted by a French oenologist. In the top group there was a wine from a family estate that worked only with grapes from its own land. This concept appealed greatly to the Rothschilds, not least because that was exactly how they operated at their own châteaux in Bordeaux.

Baron Eric de Rothschild accordingly went to Chile himself, and spent a few days at the property in question. It was called Viña Los Vascos, and it so happened that its owners, Jorge Eyzaguirre and his wife María Ignacia, were looking for a foreign investor. 'I cast my line', Jorge told an Associated Press journalist afterwards, 'but I never expected to catch the biggest fish of all.'

The two families reached an agreement, and the French became partners, with a 50 per cent holding. The first investments came directly afterwards: the deal was reached in November 1988, and within three months Viña Los Vascos had at its disposal stainless-steel fermentation

Centuries of history

Viña Los Vascos dates back to the mid-18th century when Basque army captain Miguel Echenique planted the first vines at Peralillo. About 225 years later, when the Rothschilds came to call, the Echenique family still owned the estate – through Jorge Eyzaguirre's wife, María Ignacia Echenique. During the 1960s land reforms meant the loss of the vineyard, but Jorge and Maria Ignacia managed to buy back the original property, plus some neighbouring plots. It was they who devised the name Viña Los Vascos. Formerly the estate had borne such names as Viña San Miguel and Viña Canetes de Puquillay. The first French vines were planted here in the mid-19th century, by Pedro Gregorio Echenique and Bonifacio Correa.

tanks with a capacity of 12,000 hectolitres. The Rothschilds have gone on investing since then, not only in winemaking equipment but also in the vineyard. In mid-1995 the Chilean partners sold most of their shares to Viña Santa Rita.

Early vendange

Any professional who wishes to look around Viña Los Vascos – ordinary wine-lovers are not welcomed – must drive from San Fernando in Rapel towards the coast, as far as Peralillo. Just past this village, which is also known for its cheese, an unsurfaced road leads off to the left over a wooden bridge. The route takes you past poplars, bramble thickets, small houses and low hills, eventually reaching a large, fan-shaped valley. Here, grapevines spread across the valley floor and some of the slopes. A large gateway forms the entrance to the wine estate.

Driving from plot to plot, it is clear to see that this extensive property has various types of soil, with sandy loam the most prevalent. The microclimate is characterized by an invigorating sea breeze in the afternoons (the Pacific Ocean is 40 kilometres away), by frost-free winters, and by a higher average temperature than the more central areas. The grape harvest at Los Vascos therefore takes place earlier than elsewhere. Everything is done by hand, by some 350 pickers. Various systems are used for irrigation – which is not necessary over the whole estate. The water needed here, far from the Andes, comes from four reservoirs and from springs deep underground. In total 500 hectares are suitable for winegrowing, and 300 of these have now been planted.

Winemaking à la Bordelaise

Wines are made according to the French model, Bordeaux-fashion. This means that after they have fermented, the grapes macerate for a long time – about 20 days. When Gilbert Rokvam introduced this system, the Chilean winemaker handed in his notice because 'he didn't want to be the father of a baby like this'. In practice the Bordeaux method proved highly satisfactory – better in fact than Rokvam had expected. Many other producers have subsequently followed suit.

Although Merlot gives excellent wines elsewhere in the Rapel region, this does not seem to hold good for the greater part of Los Vascos, so this grape is little grown here. Plantings now consist of 95 per cent Cabernet Sauvignon; Chardonnay is the only white grape. Originally a Sauvignon Blanc was also produced, but no longer. Viña Los Vascos now deliberately confines itself to two types of wine – Cabernet Sauvignon and Chardonnay. Whether or not others will be added depends on small-scale experiments with varieties such as Malbec and Syrah.

With and without oak

The basic Cabernet Sauvignon contains 4–5 per cent Merlot, and has no contact with wood. Its taste has a firm elegance, juicy black fruit – berries and more – and a pinch of spice. The Grande Réserve is a Cabernet Sauvignon that does go into cask. It spends nearly a year in *barriques* from the Lafite cooper's workshop; a fifth to a quarter of these are new. The wine has a dark, sometimes slightly earthy aroma with aspects of ripe blackberry, plum and spicy oak.

The Chardonnay is not matured in cask, nor does it have malolactic fermentation. Its fruit tends to the tropical in a restrained way, and it is somewhat spicy. About five grams of residual sugar add a touch of generosity to the whole, and the best vintages are those where the alcohol level remains limited to 12.5–13.5 per cent. At a higher level – the 1996, for example, had 14 per cent – the wine gets out of balance and drinking it becomes rather wearisome.

Steel, concrete, oak

Stainless-steel tanks are used for fermenting the wines, but concrete ones for storing them. Then there are 600 casks of French oak in the cellar – the Cabernet Sauvignon Grande Réserve matures in these. The beams for this building were old telephone poles from the Chilean government.

Immediately after becoming partners the Rothschilds installed stainless-steel fermentation tanks.

VERAMONTE
Veramonte

Facts and figures
▶ Alto de Casablanca
(a joint venture
between Augustín
Huneeus, who owns all
the land, and German
partners)
▶ 1991
▶ 450 ha (about 350
planted)
▶ 150,000 cases (and
rising)
▶ Casilla 122,
Casablanca
▶ Tel: (56-32) 742 421
▶ Fax: (56-32) 742 420
▶ E-mail:
marcel@franciscan.com

The best wines
• Sauvignon
Blanc, Casablanca
Valley
• Chardonnay,
Casablanca Valley
• Cabernet Sauvignon,
Valle Central
• Merlot Primus,
Casablanca Valley

*On many labels Alto de
Casablanca appears,
along with Veramonte.*

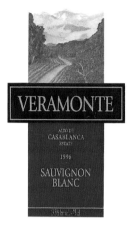

*French allure on
a Californian
scale.*

From Santiago, you reach the Casablanca
Valley by way of the road to Valparaiso and
the Zapata tunnel. Once you are through this,
the valley comes into view – and at practically the same time one of
Chile's most striking wineries, the Veramonte complex. The building
stands just before the turnpike and to the right of the road, and combines the grand manner of a French château with the design and scale
of a Californian winery.

The hospitality, too, strikes one as American. On the ground floor
there is a tasting room where visitors are welcome seven days a week
to sample and to buy the wines. That Veramonte as a firm should have
an international character is not really so surprising. This winery,
opened in October 1998 with fanfares and Cuban dance music, is the
brainchild of Augustín Huneeus. He is a Chilean who has not only been
very much involved in Chilean wine firms such as Concha y Toro and
Caliterra, but went to California in 1974 and there made a success of
the once nearly-bankrupt Franciscan Vineyards.

Casablanca pioneer
Huneeus, advised by the Bordeaux oenologist Jacques Boissenot, was
one of the very first to see the potential of Casablanca. This Chilean
subregión reminded him of the cool Carneros in California, and in 1990
he bought 3,000 hectares of land here. Of this, nearly 350 hectares of

the planned 450 vineyard hectares have been planted. The estate is well to the east in the valley: the highest part of Casablanca. As a result the temperature there is at least two or three degrees higher than down in the lower parts nearer the coast, which allows black grapes like Carmenère and Merlot to ripen fully. Sauvignon Blanc and Chardonnay are grown too: both thrive everywhere in the Valle de Casablanca.

Because of the problems California is having with the phylloxera louse, all vines are being grafted on to resistant rootstocks as a precaution. Huneeus has chosen high-density planting on the California model. Harvesting the grapes is done partly by machine, and also at night. The first vintage was the 1995; at first Veramonte did not have a bottling line – up to and including the 1997, all the wine was bottled in California. This was justifiable financially, since around 80 per cent of Veramonte's total production is sold in the United States.

The Sauvignon Blanc grapes arrive at the winery in the morning, at a temperature of around 16°C. The must ferments at low temperature, and malolactic fermentation is avoided; the wine does, though, spend three to four months in contact with its lees. The result is a wine distinguished by its stimulating character, a firm core of alcohol, and slightly spicy notes of citrus fruit plus asparagus.

After the 1997 vintage there was a change of style for the Chardonnay. The 1997 was too strongly dominated by oak: a quarter of it was fermented in new casks, then the whole vintage spent six months in barrel. Since 1998 only a quarter of the wood has been new, with much more pleasing and more balanced results. The wine now shows a lively, firm taste with both toast and fruit, especially pineapple.

The red range

The Merlot from the firm's own land is called Primus, and is probably largely Carmenère-based. The vintages tasted had an opaque colour, a slightly herbaceous quality; an aroma with a lot of toast, coffee and bayleaf; a sinewy, meaty, decently concentrated and supple taste, and soft tannins. After fermentation the must spends about 20 days macerating with the skins, and then has a year in used French and American casks, after which comes a further 12 months in bottle. Veramonte has also produced an agreeable Merlot made from bought-in grapes, with Valle Central as its *denominación de origen*, as well as a similar Cabernet Sauvignon. This Cabernet – which usually also contains some Merlot – as a rule combines juicy berry fruit with a mellow spiciness.

Memorable moments

After first tasting the Merlot Primus analytically, I then discovered how good it is at table. At a meal in the spacious Veramonte dining room, women in blue and white costume served the wine with lamb cutlets and mushrooms: a delightful combination.

Visiting times

Visitors are welcome Monday–Saturday, 10 am–5 pm, and on Sunday, 10–12 noon. Winelovers wanting a guided tour should telephone (56-32) 742 421. Veramonte hopes that the Valle de Casablanca will, like the Napa Valley, develop into a wine region attractive to tourists, with good restaurants as well as wineries to visit.

VILLARD FINE WINES

Villard Estate

Facts and figures

▶ Thierry Villard (67%) and Viña Santa Emiliana (33%)
▶ 1989
▶ 18 ha
▶ 25,000 cases (and rising)
▶ La Concepción 165, Of. 507, Providencia, Santiago
▶ Tel: (56-2) 235 7857
▶ Fax: (56-2) 235 7671
▶ E-mail: villardl@ctcreuna.cl

 The best wines
• Sauvignon Blanc, Casablanca Valley
• Chardonnay, Casablanca Valley
• Chardonnay Premium Reserve, Casablanca Valley
• Cabernet Sauvignon (Reserve), Central Valley or Maipo Valley
• Merlot Reserve, Maipo Valley
• Pinot Noir Casablanca Valley

CASABLANCA VALLEY
SAUVIGNON BLANC
1 9 9 8
PRODUCT OF CHILE

In 1989, after many years of selling wines on the international market for a big Australian firm, the Frenchman Thierry Villard moved to the homeland of his Chilean wife. He went to work for Viña Santa Emiliana, again on the export side – but at the same time he set up a company of his own, Villard Fine Wines. Partly through connections with some local growers, this was established in the Valle de Casablanca. Here Thierry bought land on which, in 1996, the first phase of a modern winery complex was built: it was ready in time for the 1997 vintage.

The grapes arrive here in 400-kilogram boxes, which are tipped on to a conveyor belt: two to four people then remove anything that should not be there. Fermentation takes place in stainless-steel tanks of various designs, at strictly controlled temperatures. Some of the tanks are suitable for skin contact to be applied in making white wines, while others are used only for Pinot Noir: these are the type of tank in which regular immersion of the grapeskins, which give colour and extract to the wine, can be precisely pre-programmed.

The vinification building – always spotlessly clean – is kept at about 17°C all year round. Presses and other machines are all on wheels, so that they can be trundled indoors after the harvest season, and thus protected from the effects of the weather. The planning of this *bodega* has been well thought through, in immense detail.

Power and aroma

Thierry Villard, whose ambition is eventually to make 60,000 cases of good wine a year, has the grapes in Casablanca picked only in the first half of the morning. This includes the Sauvignon Blanc, which produces a quite rich, powerful wine with a lively character, that offers substance, moderate acidity, and aromas of passion fruit and melon.

Half of the basic Chardonnay, also from Casablanca, is fermented and stored in casks for ten months. This explains why this wine is generously provided with toasty notes, along with the tropical fruit that is just as clearly present. There is also a Chardonnay Premium Reserve, all of it fermented in barrels, a fifth of them new. For most of this wine, alcoholic fermentation is followed by malolactic. It spends 10–11 months in cask. Creaminess, mango, toast, adequate acidity and a substantial dose of alcohol – often around 14 per cent – characterize this wine.

The helicopter's task is to blow
moisture off the vines.
Right: Thierry Villard.

Ever-improving Pinot

In 1996 Villard Fine Wines
made its first Pinot Noir from
Casablanca. Since then various
techniques have been tried out:
satisfactory results came from
the aforementioned plunge tanks, first used in 1998. Today a silky finish, a good structure, plenty of red fruit and restrained oak – only about
a third goes into cask – are the hallmarks of this Burgundy-style wine.

Thierry describes his Merlot Reserve, which is made from bought-in
Maipo grapes, as 'easily drinkable, yet with character'. This is an aromatic creation with a hint of green pepper, notes of cedarwood, pepper,
bayleaf and black fruit; 11 months in French oak barrels endow the
whole with some toast and vanilla.

The Cabernet Sauvignon Reserve comes from the Valle del Maipo, with
sometimes a small percentage from Rapel. Its colour is generally deep,
its taste full of spicy oak and warm, mellow, ripe fruit. Just a slight
herbaceous note and tobacco may also be present, while oak is never
lacking after 11 months in cask.

Strict selection

To find the very best
wines for the
Chardonnay Premium
Reserve, Thierry Villard
and his winemaker
taste the wines from
some 250 barrels.
Villard Fine Wines has
around 350 300-litre
barrels, 98% of them
French. A fifth are
replaced yearly.
Thierry Villard has a
joint venture with the
coopers Nadalié, of
Ludon, Bordeaux.
Thierry's son
Sebastien manages
this Chilean firm.

Deep well

Villard's own vineyard
has a drip irrigation
system. To supply this, a
well 80 metres deep
had to be sunk.

VIU MANENT

Viu Manent, San Carlos

Facts and figures
▶ The Viu family
▶ About 1850
▶ 200 ha (not all in production yet)
▶ 150,000 cases (and rising)
▶ Antonio Varas 2740, Santiago
▶ Tel: (56-2) 225 2653
▶ Fax: (56-2) 341 6436
▶ E-mail:
internationalsales@
        viumanent.cl

The best wines
• Fumé Blanc Reserve
• Chardonnay Reserve
• Cabernet Sauvignon
• Cabernet Sauvignon Reserve
• Malbec
• Malbec Reserve
• Merlot

All wines carry the denominación de origen Colchagua Valley.

The *hacienda* San Carlos de Cunacó lies between Santa Cruz and Cunacó, in the valley of the Río Tinguiririca in the Rapel region. It has been a wine estate since the mid-19th century, which makes it one of Chile's oldest. The white, nicely-renovated *casa patronal*, where by tradition the owner lives, stands in its park close to the road. Its cellars and other winery buildings are a few hundred metres further on. The finest building is the reddish-brown *llavería*, where in the Spanish period the keeper of the estate's keys lived. Today it serves as an office and a reception area plus wine-tasting centre for visitors.

Since 1966 the whole estate has belonged to the Viu family. The buyer was Miguel Viu Manent, descendant of a Catalan family. At first producing only wines in bulk, in 1990 the firm turned its attention to doing its own bottling, particularly for export. The name Viña San Carlos can still be seen on wrought-iron gates here, and for some markets San Carlos is kept as a trademark; otherwise the firm uses the family name, Viu Manent. In quite a few countries San Carlos could not be used as a trademark because similar names were already registered.

No outside grapes

Viu Manent uses only grapes from its own vineyards. Of the 200 available hectares here, about 160 are in production. The largest vineyard – the one that lies around the winery itself – covers 150 hectares: Chardonnay, Sauvignon Blanc, Sémillon, Cabernet Sauvignon and Malbec are grown here. At Peralillo, some 30 kilometres away towards the sea, Chardonnay, Cabernet Sauvignon, Carmenère and Merlot are cultivated in the La Capilla vineyard. White grapes are mostly picked at night, some by machine; the black by day.

To ferment the basic white varietal wines, cultivated yeast cells from France, Australia and the United States are used; about three weeks after this, the sugar present is converted at 14°

or 15°C into alcohol (and carbon dioxide). This takes place in stainless-steel tanks – unlike the white Reserves: these start fermenting in tanks, but the wines are then transferred to American casks, some of which are new, where the process is completed. The Reserves mature in barrel too, for periods varying from two to six months. The grapes for the Reserves are carefully selected on the basis of plot, soil, yield and quality – the final, definitive phase always being the tasting of the fruit.

Red wines are made in the Bordeaux way, so that after their alcoholic fermentation, which lasts about six days, the must is left for 21 days with the skins. Press wines are then drawn off and malolactic fermentation takes place in the tank – including for the Reserves, later to be matured in *barricas*. At least eight months are allowed for this ageing. Some of the barrels used for the red Reserves are French, some American; these will have been used once for the white Reserves. The Reserve qualities make up about one-seventh of the total production, 60 per cent of which is of red wines, 40 per cent of white.

Barrels
There are around 700 barrels in the cellars, all for use for the Reserve wines. A fifth of these are replaced every year. French barrels predominate, at 60 per cent.

Former brands
At Viu Manent bottles can still be seen with brand names that are seldom, or never, used now, such as San Carlos de Cunaco and Hacienda Cunaco. Some importers make up their own blends at Viu Manent.

The largest vineyard the firm owns lies around the winery near Cunaco.

Fine Malbec

There are not many wineries in Chile that
make a pure Malbec, but Viu Manent is
one of them. There are in fact two
versions. The standard Malbec has personality, vitality, a good finish; and for its
fruit blackberry, cherry and plum. The
Malbec Reserve tastes more complex and
intense: an absolutely delicious wine with
ripe fruit – blackberry, blackcurrant and other
berries – sometimes some bayleaf, masses of toast
and vanilla and a generous roundness.

The standard Merlot is fairly appetizing in character. This firm wine
has a taste in which the leathery, earthy and black-fruit elements are
pleasingly balanced – sometimes with hints of tea-leaves or cinnamon. The regular version of the Cabernet is
temptingly composed of blackberry, plum and
a slight herbaceous touch; it is also a supple
wine, with adequate body and good balance.
But in breadth, depth and length this wine is
overshadowed by the Cabernet Sauvignon
Reserve, a creation with lots of ripe fruit
(berries especially), no herbaceous notes and
attractive accents of oak and toast.

A variety of whites

Besides a smooth, grassy, citrusy Sémillon, the
range of white wines include a decent
Sauvignon Blanc and a Fumé Blanc Reserve. In
the Fumé the fruit tends towards peach, and
a touch of vanilla and some toast give this
substantial wine extra depth. Of the two
Chardonnays, the Reserve is clearly the better.
All of it undergoes malolactic fermentation, and
it is notable for juicy fruit – particularly mango
– its toasted oak and creamy texture. Both
Chardonnays generally have about 13.5 per
cent alcohol, which also makes them suitable
for accompanying white meat and poultry.

The llavaría, once home to the keeper of the estate's keys, is now an office and hospitality room.

Wine Labels

TIERRAS ALTAS

Cabernet Sauvignon

1 9 9 6

Coquimbo Region

Limarí Valley

Estate Bottled

Produce of
CHILE   Alc.13% vol.
Francisco de Aguirre Vineyards   750 ml

Francisco de Aguirre

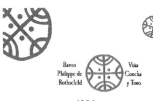

Baron Philippe de Rothschild   Viña Concha y Toro

1996
Almaviva

Alc.13.5% vol.   Produced in Chile by Viña Almaviva S.A. · Puente Alto   75 cl

Almaviva

1996
ANAKENA

Reserva

CABERNET SAUVIGNON
VALLE DEL CACHAPOAL

Produced and bottled by Viña Anakena S.A., Requinoa, Chile.
Product of Chile.75 CL.e 13% VOL.

Anakena

1997

Domaine
PAUL BRUNO
Cabernet Sauvignon

Mis en Bouteille au Domaine

Aquitania

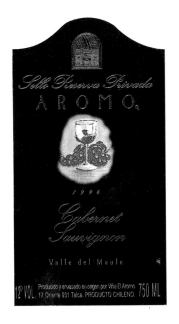

Sello Reserva Privada
A R O M O,

1 9 9 6

Cabernet Sauvignon

Valle del Maule

12° VOL.   Producido y envasado en origen por Viña El Aromo,
17 Oriente 931 Talca. PRODUCTO CHILENO.   750 ML

El Aromo

BALDUZZI

CHARDONNAY

RESERVA 1998
OAK BARREL FERMENTED
Estate Produced & Bottled by Balduzzi
Vineyards in Maule Valley
PRODUCE OF CHILE
12.5 % Vol.   75 cl e

Balduzzi

Bisquertt

Casas del Bosque

J. Bouchon

Caliterra

Canepa

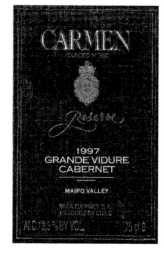

Carmen

Carta Vieja

Casablanca

Concha y Toro

El Condor

Cousiño-Macul

Echeverriá

Cono Sur

Cremaschi Barriga

Córpora

Cooperativa de Curicó

Luis Felipe Edwards

Errázuriz

William Fèvre Chile

Doña Javiera

La Fortuna

Itata

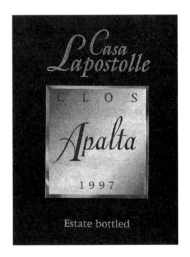

Lapostolle

de Larose

Montes

MontGras

Morandé

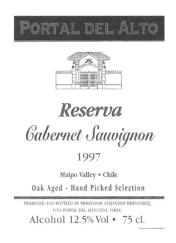

Portal del Alto

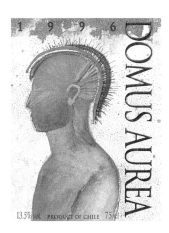

Quebrada de Macul

La Rosa

Rucahue

Salve

San Miguel del Huique

San Pedro

Santa Alicia

Santa Amalia

Santa Carolina

Santa Ema

Santa Emiliana

Santa Ines

Santa Mónica

Santa Rita

Santa Laura

Segú Ollé

Tarapacá Ex Zalava

Seña

Terra Andina

Casa Silva

Tabontinaja

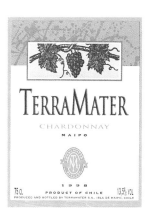

TerraMater

Terranoble

Torreón de Paredes

Miguel Torres

Undurraga

Valdivieso

Los Vascos

Veramonte

Villard

Viu Manent

Index

The main indexes to this book are to be found at the front, where the Contents (pages 4-5) lists every wine producer covered, and the Index of Wine Names (pages 6-7) shows what appears on the labels.

The index below cross-references the people involved, and also other companies that are owners of, or partners in, the wineries.

Page numbers are for the first reference within each chapter.

Picture & design credits

All photographs are by the author apart from the following:
Janet Price pages 92-6, 102-4, 166-8, 182-4, 208-212, 214-6, 221-223
Les Belles Images/Erik Spaans pages 201, 223

The author and the publishers are grateful to the companies and organisations which supplied additional photographs:
Viña Santa Alicia, Terra Andina, Viña Almaviva, Viña Bisquertt, Viña Caliterra, Hacienda El Condor, Viña Cono Sur, Viña Cousiño-Macul, Agrícola y Vitivinícola Itata, Casa Lapostolle, Viña MontGras, Viña la Rosa, Santa Carolina, Santa Ines, Segú Ollé, Viña Terra Andina, Sociedad Vinícola Miguel Torres, Villard Fine Wines.

Maps by *Sue Sharples*

Designed by *Eljay Yildirim, Thunderbolt Partnership*

Bibliography

Nick Caistor, *Chili* (Amsterdam 1997)
Hubrecht Duijker, *Ontdek de Wereld van Wijn* (Wormer 1997)
Hubrecht Duijker, *Wijnnotities uit de Nieuwe Wereld* (Baarn 1995)
Edward Flaherty, *Merlot Seminar* (Panquehue 1998)
Alejandro Hernández, *Introduccíon al Vino de Chile* (Santiago 1998)
Jürgen Mathäss, *Wines from Chile* (Amsterdam 1997)
Jan Read, *The Wines of Chile* (London 1984)
Jancis Robinson, *The Oxford Companion to Wine* (Oxford 1994)
Francisco Sánchez and others, *Guía de Vinos de Chile* (Santiago 1998)
Tom Stevenson, *The New Sotheby's Wine Encyclopedia* (London 1997)
Patricio Tapia, *Descorchados* (Santiago 1998)
Taller Valparaiso, *Chile: a Remote Corner on Earth* (Santiago 1992)

Periodicals:
Alles über Wein (Germany)
Decanter (UK)
Fine Wine Folio (USA)
El Mercurio (Chile)
NCI Nieuwsbrief (Netherlands)
Pers Wijn (Netherlands)
Proefschrift (Netherlands)
Wine (UK)
The Wine Advocate (USA)
The Wine Spectator (USA)
Wine & Spirit (UK)

Created and edited by
Segrave Foulkes Publishers, 8 Kings Road, Kingston upon Thames, KT2 5HR, U.K.